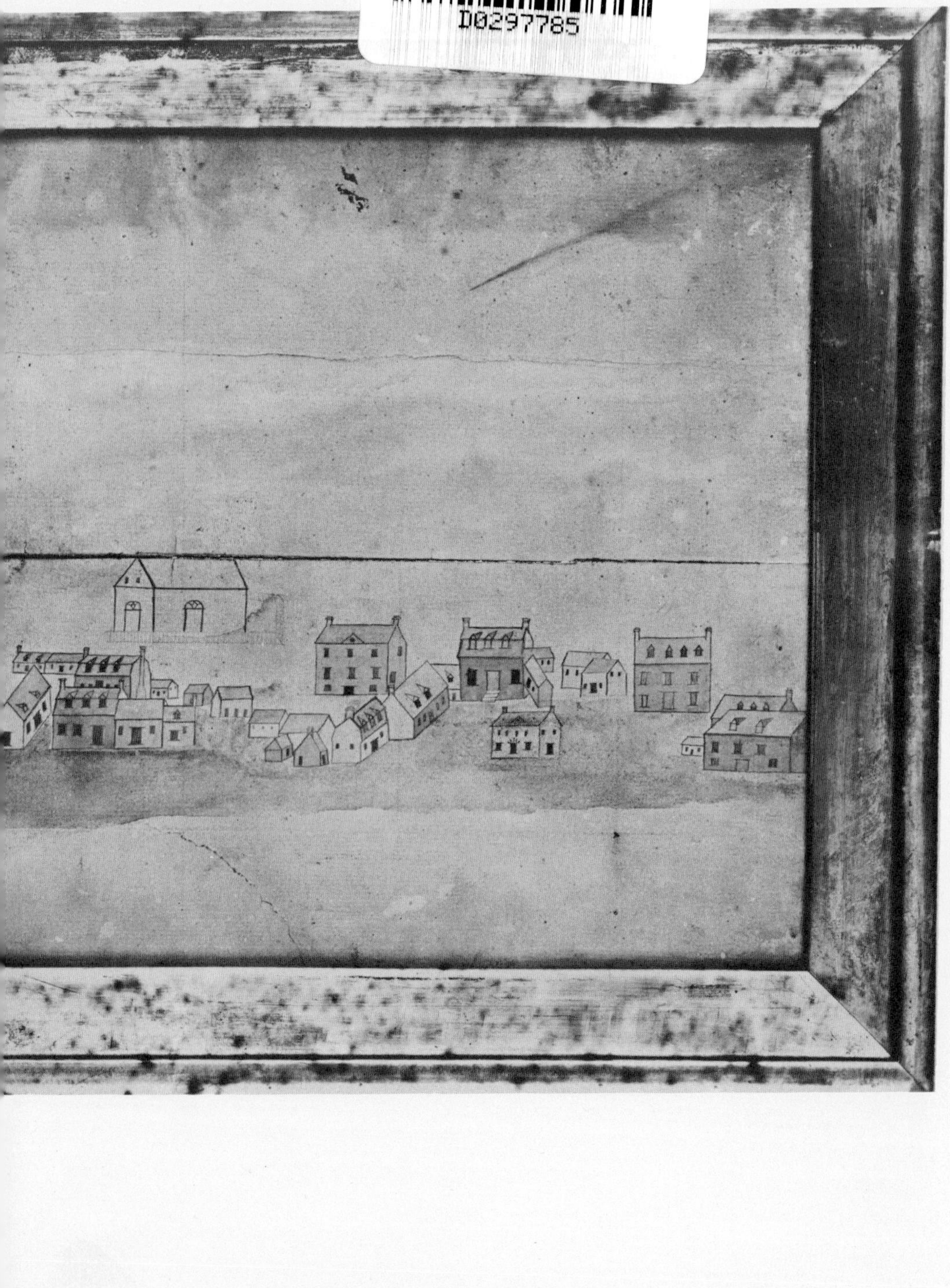

St. Paul's Church   1855

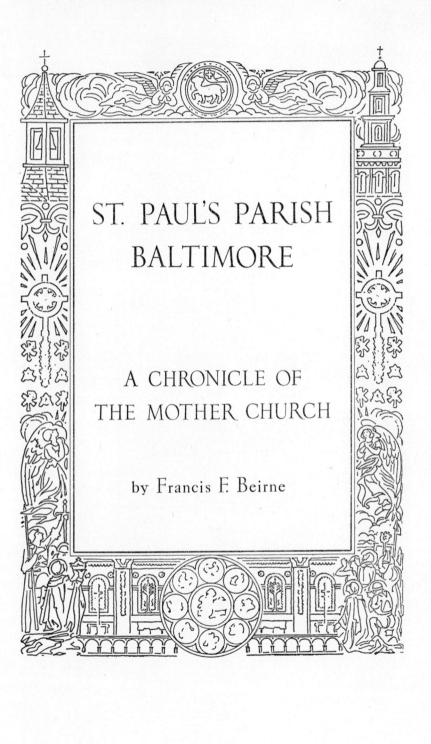

ST. PAUL'S PARISH
BALTIMORE

A CHRONICLE OF
THE MOTHER CHURCH

by Francis F. Beirne

LIBRARY OF CONGRESS
CATALOG CARD No. 67-31296

PRINTED AND BOUND
BY
THE HORN-SHAFER COMPANY
BALTIMORE, MARYLAND

CONTENTS

Contents

ILLUSTRATIONS

CHAPTER I

A PARISH IS BORN

N John Moale's crude boyhood drawing of 1752, which served as the basis for later and more finished pictures of Baltimore Town, a large building sits on a hill in the background overlooking a cluster of smaller houses, like a mother guarding her chicks. The building is St. Paul's Church. Throughout the history of Baltimore a St. Paul's Church has occupied that site. St. Paul's was the first place of public worship in Baltimore Town. From St. Paul's Parish all the other Protestant Episcopal churches in the city trace their lineage. The history of the Parish and the City are inextricably intertwined. So it is that St. Paul's bears the undisputed title of Mother Church of the Episcopalians in Baltimore; and because it is the oldest place of public worship, it may reasonably lay claim to being the Mother Church of the community.

St. Paul's Church in Baltimore Town was already twenty years old when young Moale, eventually to be a vestryman, put his pencil to paper; St. Paul's Parish in Baltimore County was much older than that. Its creation was a local reflection of the religious turmoil in England among Anglicans, Romanists and Dissenters going back to the Reformation and Henry VIII's break with Rome. It was a turmoil attended by the persecution of this or that sect according to the religious tenets and policy of the reigning sovereign. No wonder that when the English colonization of the new world began there was a scramble among the persecuted for homes across the sea where they might worship in peace in accordance with the dictates of their consciences.

George Calvert, first Lord Baltimore, founder of the Maryland Proprietary which had been granted him by Charles I, was a Roman Catholic; and in addition to the incentive of financial gain, he sought to provide a place of refuge for his co-religionists. That object was pursued by his son, Cecilius, second Lord Baltimore, who after the death of his father sent out the first colonists in 1634 in the *Ark* and the *Dove*. There are some who say there were more Anglicans on the expedition than Roman Catholics; the only priests were Jesuits. The Anglicans represented the beginning of a flock that would rapidly increase in numbers, but they were without a shepherd. True, there was a colony of Church of England people on Kent Island as early as 1629; but though this was Maryland territory the colony was rather an outpost of the definitely Anglican colony of Virginia.

What with the outbreak of the Civil War in England in 1642, the execution of Charles I, the period of Cromwellian rule, the Restoration and finally the accession of James II, a Roman Catholic, the Church of England had too many troubles at home to pay great attention to its members in a small colony far across the sea. It was not until 1676 that anybody seems to have looked into the situation in Maryland. In that year the Rev. John Yeo, a clergyman of the Church of England, arrived in the province as a missionary, and was shocked at what he saw. So much so that he reported his findings directly to the Archbishop of Canterbury. "The Lord's Day," said Yeo, "is profaned, religion despised and all notorious vices committed so that it (Maryland) is be-

[2]

come a Sodom of uncleanliness and a pesthouse of impiety."
He estimated the population of the province at 20,000 souls
and stated that there were only three ministers of the Church
of England throughout its length and breadth. He urged
the Archbishop to intercede with Lord Baltimore to remedy
conditions. The Archbishop referred the complaint to the
Bishop of London, who had jurisdiction over foreign missions, and the latter passed it on to Lord Baltimore. Lord
Baltimore's reply was that of the population cited by Yeo,
Quakers and Presbyterians constituted three-fourths. He
maintained that the Church of England ministers in residence enjoyed decent livings and suggested that they were
sufficient to take care of the Anglicans. This reply seems to
have satisfied the hierarchy and all that poor Yeo got for
his pains was a rebuke for speaking out of turn.

Being a godly man Yeo proceeded to do what he could
without official help. He moved into Baltimore County and
for a few years until his death conducted Divine Service
from the Book of Common Prayer in private homes. The
action Yeo hoped for and failed to get came with the English Revolution of 1688. James II, a Catholic, by placing
Romanists in positions of power and moving toward restor-
ing his as the official church, so offended the Protestants and
aroused such opposition among them that he had to flee the
throne rather than wait to be deposed. He was succeeded by
the Protestants, William and Mary, and a violent reaction
against Roman Catholics set in. It had its repercussions in
Maryland where, in a bloodless revolution, the Protestants
overturned Lord Baltimore's government, seized control of
the Assembly and passed a law denying Roman Catholics
the right to hold public office and putting other restrictions
on them. From England came Sir Lionel Copley, a Protestant, as royal governor. It was not until 1715 that the Cal-

verts, who had turned Protestant, had their Proprietary restored to them.

Following up the Protestant victory, the Maryland Assembly, in its June session of 1692, passed a measure entitled "An act for the service of Almighty God, and the establishment of the Protestant religion in this province." Under this law the Church of England became the official church of Maryland. The act provided that every freeholder, or taxable, no matter what his church affiliation, must pay 40 pounds of tobacco annually for the support of the Anglican clergy and the church. The obligation did not sit well with Roman Catholics, Quakers, Puritans, Presbyterians and those of other faiths, but it was a burden they had to bear for a matter of three quarters of a century until the American Revolution and independence brought release.

Next in importance to the enforced assessment was a clause in the act which divided Maryland into thirty parishes and directed the commissioners in each county to appoint six vestrymen for every parish to administer the business of the church and minor matters of local government as well. Three parishes were set up in Baltimore County of which St. Paul's was one, first popularly known as Patapsco Parish. Its boundaries extended from Middle River on the east to the north branch of the Patapsco River on the west, or as far as the present Carroll County line. On the south it spilled over into Anne Arundel County on a line from Bodkin Point to Elkridge, and it stretched as far north as Pennsylvania. At its widest portions it measured some thirty-five miles from east to west and the same distance from north to south.

In that early day Baltimore County was thinly populated. Small settlements clung to the shores of the Patapsco and behind them lay a wilderness of woods through which a few trails had been blazed, and which was pretty well restricted to Indians and wolves. The only road deserving the name was one used by the Susquehanna Indians in their forays against the Piscataways to the south. It passed through what shortly was to become Baltimore Town. When St. Paul's Parish was laid out, in spite of its extensive acreage, it counted a population of only 231 taxables. At forty pounds of tobacco per poll that would give a rector 8240 pounds a year and his clerk 1000 pounds. In addition the Rector was entitled to the return from real property owned by the parish known as "glebe land." As the population of Baltimore County grew, parts of the original area of the parish were separated from it to be added to, or to create, other parishes; so allowance has to be made for these losses in calculating the net increase in taxables.

A painstaking search of the Baltimore County records, made many years ago, reveals the names of the six vestrymen who, pursuant to the Act of 1692, were selected by the county commissioners for St. Paul's, or Patapsco Parish. They were George Ashman, John Terry, Francis Watkins, Nicholas Corban, Richard Sampson and Richard Cromwell. The six were not otherwise distinguished. They played no important roles in the history of Maryland. They may be pictured as sturdy frontiersmen, not outstanding intellectually, chosen by their fellow citizens because they were judged to be able and willing to assume responsibility. They deserve to be remembered because they were the first of an unbroken line of laymen stretching through the centuries and, according to the law and custom of the Episcopal Church, sharing with the clergy the various administrative duties of their parishes, custodians of church property, proud of their position and jealous of their rights.

The first formal action of St. Paul's Vestry was to pick a site for a church and lay plans for building it. What with one thing and another they did not get around to this for a year. September, 1693, they reported to the justices of the

[5]

county court that they had met at the house of Major John Thomas and decided that "at Pettite's old field was the most convenient place to erect a church" and that they had "met again the last Saturday in August at Master Demondedies and confirmed the same." This site was on Patapsco Neck between the waters of the Patapsco and Back River in the general neighborhood of the present Fort Holabird. The first structure erected there is believed to have been a log church and this was followed by one built of brick. There are records of two vestry houses having been built in rapid succession. A vestry house was essential since in those early days the churches were unheated on the questionable assumption that religious fervor would keep the worshipers warm. The vestry house had a fireplace which afforded comfort for the vestrymen while they were performing their official duties. The vestry house, too, served as a school room; since one of the responsibilities of the vestry was providing education for the young. As early as 1765 the shift of population to the west had led to the church's abandonment. It then lay in ruins and the dead in its burying ground had been moved to Baltimore Town.

The Revolution of 1688 having achieved its purpose in excluding Roman Catholics from the English throne, and the Protestants William and Mary being firmly seated on it, attention could at last be directed toward the condition of the Established Church in all the English possessions beyond the seas, including Maryland. There Governor Copley had been succeeded by Sir Francis Nicholson, high tempered and zealous, who set to work with a will building churches and finding clergymen for the new parishes. He and the Assembly petitioned the Bishop of London for help and, in 1700, the latter assigned the Rev. Dr. Thomas Bray to act as his commissary, or missionary representative. This would carry Bray to Maryland; but, before going, he undertook an important project at home, founding the Society for the Promotion of Christian Knowledge. Among other things Dr. Bray raised funds for the purchase of libraries and through his efforts each of the Maryland parishes was supplied with one. Books in those days were a rarity and the Maryland Assembly went to great pains to see that the libraries were properly cared for. The rector of the parish was held personally responsible and subject to heavy fine if books were lost or damaged. Some of the Bray books have survived to this day. St. Paul's has several of them.

Dr. Bray also shared in the recruiting of ministers. To appreciate the Church's handicap in supplying worthy laborers for the vineyard it must be borne in mind, not only that Maryland was remote from the homeland, but also that the rectorship of a parish was regarded first and foremost as a "living," to be disposed of by the authorities, perhaps to take care of a younger son or a friend, or to repay a political obligation. Once a man was installed there was virtually no way to remove him. Parish livings could be bought and sold. In Maryland, following the Revolution of 1688, they were the prerequisites of the Crown; and, after the return to power of the Calverts in 1715, of the Proprietary. Under these conditions parsons often seemed to lack a divine call and were more interested in looking after themselves than after the souls of their parishioners. It is hardly surprising that there were sometimes glaring abuses; rather the surprise is that so many conscientious and godly men were found among the clergy.

Dr. Bray's visitation lasted only two months and a half. He attended the Assembly and is credited with having had a hand in the passage of an act making attendance at Anglican worship compulsory for every member of the Province. In fact he hurried home for the purpose of getting this intolerant measure through Parliament, but in this he failed.

[7]

He could boast of having raised the number of Anglican clergymen to seventeen. His chief claim to fame, however, was that on arriving in England he founded the Society for the Propagation of the Gospel which, as its name implies, was a missionary endeavor. Both the Society for the Promotion of Christian Knowledge and the "S. P. G." survive to this day as instruments of the missionary work of the Church of England.

The defect in the system of recruiting ministers was painfully illustrated by the experience of St. Paul's Parish with its first appointed Rector, the Rev. William Tibbs, who took office in 1702. Nothing is known of his background other than that he was a graduate of Oxford University. He appears to have enjoyed important connections judged by the arrogant manner in which he conducted himself and which led his Vestry to petition the Governor for his removal. They accused him of being a common drunkard whose bad example turned many of his flock to drunkenness and profanation of the Lord's Day. The Governor ruled that this was an ecclesiastical matter and referred it to a body of four ministers, of whom the accused was one. As might have been expected the committee decided in favor of Tibbs, merely admonishing him to mend his ways and reconcile himself to his people. This Tibbs failed to do, for not long after, Jacob Henderson, who succeeded Bray as commissary, reported to the Bishop of London that Tibbs was still "incorrigible."

Nevertheless there were signs of progress. In 1722 the Parish was credited with having twelve vestrymen, twice the customary number, for what reason it is not clear. In that year a new vestry house was authorized, showing that there had been an earlier one. An inventory of the parish library listed forty-one volumes, among them a Hebrew Bible, Great Church Bible, Greek Bible, a geography, an arithmetic, and works bearing such solemn titles as "Cause and Decay of Christian Piety," "Dr. Wake Concerning Swearing" and "Plain Man's Guide to Heaven." By that time the portion of the Parish south of the Patapsco had been transferred to St. Margaret's in Anne Arundel County. Yet the rapid increase in population left St. Paul's with 1000 taxables.

In 1724 Tibbs, perhaps by way of answering the complaints his Vestry had leveled against him, made a report to the Governor which presented a rosy picture of his parish. It stated that he had been resident there from the time of his appointment and had not one month been absent from it. There had, he said, been Divine Service every Sunday and on some holidays, all services being well attended. He had held Communion at least three times a year. He confessed he had converted no Indians to Christianity to gratify the missionary zeal of the church leaders in England, but that was because there were no Indians in the parish. He had offered instruction to Negroes and mulattos but had found them indifferent. The youths in the Parish had been catechized in Lent, and the church now boasted a pewter Communion Service. To meet the educational needs of the young, a schoolmaster had been engaged by the Vestry. A Bible and a Book of Common Prayer, essential to the Anglican service, were on hand. But there was neither surplice for the clergyman, nor pulpit cloth, nor cushions. Mr. Tibbs, who was a bachelor, described himself as occupying a house on the glebe land, and he also mentioned the parish library. On the whole a gratifying account of a growing parish, though quite at variance with the picture presented by the Vestry.

In 1727 allusion was first made to erecting a church on a new site more convenient to the parishioners. At the fall term of Assembly of that year the Vestry obtained the necessary authority to buy one or more acres of land and to raise

[9]

funds to build the church. The following year the Vestry got permission from the county justices for a special assessment of ten pounds of tobacco per poll and land was bought for the purpose on the old York Road. In this same year the controversy between Mr. Tibbs and the Vestry flared again, the Vestry charging the Rector with being uncooperative in the proposed building of the new church. So this plan was abandoned and the Vestry turned its eyes on Fell's Point. Then an event occurred that changed the whole picture. In its August session in 1729 the Assembly passed an act for erecting Baltimore Town on the Patapsco. By that time St. Paul's Parish was already 37 years old.

CHAPTER II

MOVE TO BALTIMORE TOWN

THE urge to erect towns in the Maryland province stemmed from Lord Baltimore's wish to increase his revenues and from the tobacco planters' need for ports from which to ship their crops to markets abroad. The laying out of a town also afforded excellent opportunity for land speculation since a holding increased immeasurably in value when divided into lots. That, of course, was assuming there was a demand for the lots. Several towns bearing the name Baltimore were planned and authorized by the Assembly only to die before Baltimore Town on the Patapsco proved to be a successful venture. The act of 1729 which authorized it stipulated that there should be sixty acres divided into as many acre lots.

The Vestry of St. Paul's, still looking for a site for a new church, was impressed by the Assembly's act for erecting this new town. Of the seven commissioners named to lay it out four were vestrymen; namely, Richard Gist, Dr. George Walker, Dr. George Buchanan, and Col. William Hammond. The upshot was that the Old York Road proposal was abandoned. When the Assembly met in June of the following year these gentlemen brought their influence to bear toward the passage of a supplementary act which empowered the Vestry to "Purchase a lot in Baltimore Town, and to cause a church to be built thereon, which shall be the parish church of the said parish, and to be called St. Paul's Church." Provision also was made for a special levy of tobacco on the taxables to finance the project.

The Vestry lost no time exercising the authority granted it by the Assembly. What was judged to be an ideal site for a church was being offered for sale and it was bought. It was designated on the original plat as "No. 19" and it occupied the highest point on the slope which ran north from the harbor. It proved to be a magnificent long-term investment for the lot has served its purpose from the time of its purchase to the present day, a matter of two centuries and more. The transfer of title was completed a month after passage of the act, and the Vestry proceeded at once with plans for building the church.

Throughout the summer of 1730 contracts were signed with brickmakers, carpenters and joiners. The plans called for a spacious building fifty feet long and twenty-three feet wide, with a height of eighteen feet from floor to ceiling. Already clay suitable for making bricks had been found nearby. Soft pink in color, blending harmoniously with the natural surroundings, they were destined to give Baltimore Town and the city into which it grew a charming aspect until at last, and very recently, progress sentenced it to a cruel death through the practice of covering the brick fronts of houses with concrete veneer. The contract called for 100,000 bricks, half to be delivered in October and half the following May.

Now, too, the building program was expanded to include a vestry house, sixteen feet by twelve feet, and twelve and a half feet high. Furnishings of the church were scant. A retiring Warden delivered to his successor one tablecloth, two napkins, two plates and one tankard which was all the property the church had for administering Communion. Those who imagine that rotation in office is of recent origin will be surprised to learn that an act of the Assembly in 1730 provided that the two oldest members in time of service should go off the Vestry each year and not be eligible again for three years. Another important change in the laws concerning vestries was that persons of other denominations were no longer required to serve on them, the duty being confined to members of the Church of England. Dissenters however were not relieved of their obligation to contribute the forty pounds of tobacco a year for the support of the Established Church.

Meanwhile relations between Parson Tibbs and the Vestry were becoming more strained. Tibbs held St. John's Parish, on the Gunpowder, as well as St. Paul's and the Vestry complained that he was living outside St. Paul's, had taken the parish library along with him and refused to give it up. They appealed again to the Governor and Council, but nothing came of it. Having got nowhere with this appeal they tried going direct to Parson Tibbs. They urged him to visit the Church more often, charged him with neglect of the Communion, dilatoriness in visiting the sick and attending funerals. If, they said, he refused to come in person, would he appoint a curate, or at least a lay reader? To this last appeal Tibbs yielded and sent a curate, but the Vestry protested that his man was a convicted felon. Finally the Vestry complained directly to the Bishop of London. It had some effect for shortly thereafter Commissary Henderson, acting on behalf of the Bishop, engaged two ministers to take over the services, this being done with the consent of Tibbs. The issue, however, was settled effectively and for all time by the death of the Parson who, by virtue of his tenacity, had held tight to the living for thirty years. His death appears to have softened the hearts of the vestrymen, for at his passing they referred to him affectionately as their "old shepherd" and his death as a "matter of sorrowful regret."

Mr. Tibbs's successor was the Rev. Joseph Hooper, an apointee of Governor Samuel Ogle. He served the Parish for six and a half years, a brief space as St. Paul's rectors go, and too brief to make a deep impression on his flock. He remains a shadowy figure who at his death was "generally lamented by his parishioners." He also is described as having been industrious and efficient. That no doubt is based on the continued progress being made in the building of the church. The roof was now on and the joiners were at work on the interior. Pews were being sold for £ 2, a source of revenue that was to continue to be regarded as indispensable for a couple of centuries. By January 1733, the pulpit was being placed in the middle of the north wall and a sounding board erected over it, and the contract had been let for the pews. A refinement of the interior was a gallery supported by columns. An acquisition occurred in 1736 which was deemed worthy of record: Dr. Walker presented the Vestry with a punch bowl. A later church chronicler remarks: "We have a right to suppose, that it was used for the purpose for which the donor intended it, or it would not have been given." Possibly Dr. Walker hit upon this as a practical solution of the problem of non-attendance at Vestry meetings which was as difficult then as it sometimes is today.

At long last, in the first week of May, 1739, work had been sufficiently advanced to warrant the statement that the Church was now finished. Eight years had elapsed since the beginning of construction, and twelve since it had first been planned. Mr. Hooper lived only two months to enjoy it. He died July 12, 1739, and was succeeded a month later by the Rev. Benedict Bourdillon. The new rector had been born in Geneva, Switzerland, of a prominent French Hu-

guenot family. As a young man he went to England where
he was ordained as a minister in the Anglican Church. His
wife, Johanna Gertrud Jennsen, was the niece of a Hollander
who emigrated to England, amassed a fortune, and was made
a Baronet by Queen Anne. The Baronet's two daughters
married respectively Charles, fifth Lord Baltimore, and
Thomas Bladen who was to become Governor of Maryland.
In 1738 Bourdillon and his young wife set sail for America,
and it is obvious that being a first cousin of Lady Baltimore was an important factor in their seeking their fortune
in Maryland. Bourdillon was twenty-nine years old when in
1739 he was appointed by Governor Ogle to the St. Paul's
living. That same year he, his wife and a son who had been
born to them in this country, were naturalized as English
citizens. Two more sons were to follow and be baptized in
St. Paul's Church.

A letter of Benedict written to his brother in England
on October 20, 1742, throws interesting light on the life of
an Anglican parson in Maryland in the middle of the eighteenth century. First of all, he was hard up. He complained
that there was no sale for the tobacco in which he was paid.
His wife was sending a box of clothes to be sold for "money,
china or anything else as well as you can." There also would
be found in the box Seneca snake root, "an excell't one agt
Pleurisies etc; if you think you can sell a quantity, I'll send
you some every Year, as likewise coon Snake Root & bark of
Sassafras." He wanted books, especially books of sermons.

Then he came to the matter of his own clothes: "I have
had but 2 Coats, 2 Hats & 2 wigs made since we came to
Maryland, whereby judge how frugal I have lived, but now I
want some clothes." Among other things he asked for a pair
of black silk stockings, two pairs of worsted and 6 pairs of
shoes. The most extravagant item was "some of the best &
finest Purple broad cloth for a compleat suit and good lin-

[15]

ing." The parson evidently wanted to cut a figure in Baltimore Town and did not propose to confine himself to the
clergyman's conventional black.

To add to his financial problems Benedict had a brother
living with him and the brother was out of a job. He
remarks: "I don't grudge his Boarding, but as for to find
him with Clothes is more than I can do; my own family
increases, my salary is ill paid, & our settlement has overrun
me with debts." He closed by announcing the birth of his
third son whom he proposed to name Thomas in honor of
Thomas Bladen who had succeeded Ogle as Governor.

Mr. Bourdillon's tenure of office was significant for the
establishment of a new parish cut out of St. Paul's. The
wilderness to the north and northwest of Baltimore Town
was beginning to be cleared and settled. To protect the
settlers against possible Indian raids a military post was set
up in Baltimore County about twelve miles from town in
what came to be known as Garrison Forest. A company
under command of Captain John Risteau, based at the fort,
patrolled a frontier extending from Deer Creek, in present
Harford County, to Gwynn's Falls, in the southwest. Under
the best of circumstances people living in that area found
it hard to make the long trip on horseback over the rough
clearing which served as a road, to the church in Baltimore
Town. They wanted a more convenient place to worship
and requested a "chapel of ease," in essence a mission, in
their neighborhood.

The proposal met with the hearty approval of Mr. Bourdillon, the Vestry, wardens and parishioners of St. Paul's who
proposed that the project be financed through voluntary subscriptions to supplement whatever support could be wrung
from the provincial government. Some seventy persons responded to the appeal which brought in a total of 4400
pounds of tobacco and £ 64 10s in currency. Heading the

list was Mr. Bourdillon who out of his modest salary, and in spite of his complaining of poverty, made the munificent gift of 2000 pounds of tobacco, almost half the total.

At its session in the fall of 1742 the Assembly passed an act not only empowering certain persons to receive these contributions but also to assess the less willing parishioners an amount not to exceed £ 132 6s 8d in any one year. With this encouragement a lot was bought in the Forest in 1743 and the building of a chapel begun. Mr. Bourdillon lived just long enough to see the beginning of the project which he had so enthusiastically sponsored and to which he had contributed so generously. In 1745 he died "generally lamented by his parishioners." It had been agreed that on his death the chapel and its congregation should become independent of St. Paul's. This was the origin of St. Thomas's Parish, the oldest and not the least beloved daughter of the Mother Church.

Creation of the new parish was no small sacrifice, for it deprived St. Paul's of all her extensive territory north of the Old Court and Joppa Roads. It also reduced St. Paul's taxables by about one-third, or to 860. It is important to note the distinction between St. Paul's Parish and St. Paul's Church. The Parish today embraces all the territory that remained to it in 1745 after the excision of St. Thomas's Parish, save for a small portion of Baltimore County ceded in 1916 to the new Sparrows Point Parish of St. Matthew's. During the days of the Established Church, which is to say from 1692 to the American Revolution, any congregation of any denomination whatsoever wishing to organize in Baltimore Town or that portion of Baltimore County comprising St. Paul's Parish, had first to obtain the consent of the Vestry of the Parish. So far as Episcopal churches are concerned there has been no abrogation of the law requiring such consent, though in practice St. Paul's Vestry has yielded

[17]

the right to the Diocesan Convention. Today the Vestry still sits in two capacities, namely as the Vestry of St. Paul's Parish and as the Vestry of St. Paul's Church.

In spite of this drastic reduction in its area and its revenue the steady growth of Baltimore Town made the St. Paul's living a desirable one. Within a month of Mr. Bourdillon's death a successor had been found and presented to the Vestry. The Rev. Thomas Chase came of a respectable English family which had given several of its sons to the church. Born in London, he was a graduate of Cambridge University where, after completing his studies in Hebrew and Latin, he turned to medicine. Being of an adventurous spirit he found England too confining and, armed with a degree as a bachelor of physic, he set sail for St. Thomas, in the West Indies, intending there to pursue the profession of medicine. This proved a false start. He shortly gave up the idea of medicine, decided to enter the church, and returned to England for his ordination. He then crossed the ocean once more to take the rectorship of a parish in Somerset County on Maryland's Eastern Shore. There he met and married Matilda Walker, daughter of a prominent countian. His romance was tragically ended when his bride of a year died in childbirth, leaving her bereaved husband with an infant son whom he named Samuel. The loss of his wife no doubt disillusioned him with life on the Eastern Shore. Besides, Baltimore Town on the frontier offered interesting prospects. Thomas had a brother Richard, a clergyman with a parish in Southern Maryland, who was a friend of Lord Baltimore and might be expected to wield some influence toward obtaining an appointment. Thomas was himself known to Governor Bladen for, following Mrs. Chase's death, he had gone as a member of an official mission to Shamokin, an Indian settlement far up the Susquehanna River in Pennsylvania. It was a severe physical test which proved his stam-

[18]

ina. His application to succeed Bourdillon was granted by the Governor and soon thereafter the clergyman with his three-year-old son took up residence in Baltimore.

The widow Bourdillon and her children had been left none too well off; but, according to the custom of the day, her late husband's living represented a cash asset. A price was agreed upon and Chase promised to pay it, presumably with the consent of the Governor and the Attorney-General. These gentlemen, however, had neglected to consult the Lord Proprietary who kept a jealous eye on such benefices, regarding them distinctly as his own. They grew alarmed over what they had done. To complicate matters further Chase defaulted in his payments to the widow Bourdillon. A Chase weakness which his son Samuel inherited was carelessness in money matters. The upshot of it was that the parson was hauled off to debtors' prison, a not uncommon occurrence in those days. There he languished for six months. On the logical argument, however, that he could not serve his Parish from such confined quarters, he was released on the promise to make good the indebtedness.

In spite of this temporary inconvenience St. Paul's continued to prosper. The Assembly gave the Vestry permission to sell the old glebe lands on Patapsco Neck. With the proceeds, and exhibiting sound business sense, the Vestry bought lots adjoining lot No. 19, on which the church stood, expanding the property to take in the area bounded by Charles, Saratoga, St. Paul and Lexington Streets. One Captain Robert North, a parishioner, left a legacy for the purchase of plate for the communion service; and Brian Philpot, a vestryman and large land owner on Fell's Point, was directed to send to England for it. In its early years a wooden fence had been erected around the town, first to protect it against Indians and after that against the more imminent damage caused by stray animals. More destructive than the

[19]

animals, however, were the pioneer Baltimoreans who, during cold winters, tore parts of the fence down and used it for firewood. St. Paul's took a step forward by building a brick wall around its property in place of a fence. The Vestry also toyed with the idea of adding to its facilities a brick vestry house complete with bell and tower. This was authorized in 1750 and erected a few years later.

During this period the Vestry acted in the capacity of a local government, performing such lay duties as taking care of the whipping post and stocks, and inspecting the tobacco which was being shipped out of the port in ever increasing quantities. To provide more room for the growing congregation a new gallery running the length of the church from east to west was installed to supplement the existing gallery running from north to south. Other evidences of progress were the hiring of a schoolmaster and the sending of an order to London for a new Church Bible and Book of Common Prayer. The record showed that in 1753 a church bell had been acquired and an organ installed, the first mention of the music which was destined to play a conspicuous part in the life of St. Paul's. Purchase of horse blocks and horse racks indicate that from the very beginning the church had a parking problem. In 1755 an organist was hired at a salary of £ 20, or $53 a year. In this the Episcopalians were years ahead of their Presbyterian brethren in Baltimore who inherited the Scottish prejudice against the organ as "a kist o'whustles" (chest of whistles). Unfortunately St. Paul's pioneer organ was frequently out of order and couldn't be played. Yet it continued in intermittent use until 1804.

A piquant flavor was added to Parson Chase's early career in Baltimore Town by his feud with James Richards, sheriff of the county. Feeling grew so hard that Richards on meeting Chase on the street knocked him down. The sheriff must have got no little satisfaction out of Chase's confinement in debtors' prison. Nevertheless social relations continued between them and on one occasion this led to Chase's report to the authorities that Richards had cursed and insulted the House of Hanover. Such alleged Jacobite sentiment called for an investigation which revealed that the remark had been made at a convivial gathering where a number of toasts were drunk. Present with Chase was his colleague, the Rev. Thomas Cradock, later spelled Craddock, Rector of St. Thomas's Parish. Richards defended himself on the ground that Cradock had made an equally disloyal remark. When the investigators asked Chase why he had not reported Cradock too, he replied naively: "Surely you can't blame me to favor my poor brother Cradock!" While Chase did not win any battles with the sheriff he may be said to have won the war when Richards was caught with his accounts in arrears and disgraced.

By this time the Church of England no longer enjoyed a monopoly of the town. Friends, Presbyterians, German Lutheran and German Reformed congregations, and Roman Catholics had put in an appearance and some of them had built churches. In 1756 Acadians driven by the British into exile arrived from Canada and settled in Baltimore. They were a pitiful group, had no resident priest and said their masses in private homes. Chase, born when memory of the Protestant Revolution was still vivid, had inherited an unreasonable fear of Catholics. He now demonstrated it by charging that Catholics in Maryland were being educated in private schools contrary to law and by warning against the newly arrived Acadians. From his pulpit in St. Paul's he was reported to have declared that the situation of the Protestants in Maryland was as perilous as that of the Protestants in Ireland on the eve of the Irish massacre. His statements provoked Governor Horatio Sharpe, who had succeeded Bladen, to write Lord Baltimore that Chase's fears were hardly justified, and that if he were asked whether the conduct of the Protestants or the Papists had been most unexceptionable, he would not hesitate to give an answer in favor of the latter.

In 1762 the Presbyterians erected a small place of worship, and two years later followed it with a more ambitious structure on Fayette Street east of Calvert. Their progress and their contribution to the community were enhanced by the leadership of Dr. Patrick Allison, a young man of rare personality, a Princeton graduate, and a finished scholar. Before his long tenure was over he was to engage in valuable intellectual collaboration with fellow ministers of other denominations.

As matters turned out the Established Church had less to fear from the Catholics than it did from a rift in its own ranks brought on by the rise of Methodism. An intimation came in 1760 with the arrival in Maryland of Robert Strawbridge whose inspired teaching won many converts in Frederick and Harford Counties. First to reach Baltimore was John King who also had been licensed by the Methodists to preach the new gospel. King chose a bad time to open his appeal, though he may have done it deliberately so as to strike where Satan was most in evidence. At a militia training day, a public gathering notable for drunkenness and rowdyism, King boldly mounted a table, but had hardly begun his harangue before the crowd upset the table and threw him to the ground. Apparently the incident reached the ears of Chase and his Vestry for, by way of showing their sympathy for King, they invited him to preach in St. Paul's. The experiment in ecumenism was not a success for King's delivery was so noisy that he was said to have made the dust fly from the velvet cushions in the pews. He was not asked to preach there again. This unfavorable reaction could not be blamed entirely on St. Paul's sedateness. King's manner brought a rebuke from John Wesley himself who enjoined him to "scream no more, on peril of your soul," adding: "I often speak loud, often vehemently, but I never scream." A year later Joseph Pilmoor, another Methodist missionary, spoke in St. Paul's at Chase's invitation.

After some twenty years as a widower Mr. Chase took another wife and set out to sire a new family. Sam, only child by the first marriage, was now grown and had moved to Annapolis to study law and lay the groundwork for his distinguished public career. Thus a large gap would separate him from the five half-brothers and sisters who soon began arriving. In fact they would be closer to the ages of Sam's own children.

About this time the clergy of the Established Church were in a ferment over the tobacco tax which was their chief support. It still stood at forty pounds per poll in *uninspected* tobacco and those who paid it would have been less than human if they had not passed off their lower grades on the parsons. The proposed new law provided for the tobacco to be inspected; and, on the ground that it would be of better quality and hence more valuable, the tax per poll was reduced from 40 to 30 pounds, too.

Samuel Chase was now launched on his public career as a member of the Assembly's House of Delegates, representing the city of Annapolis. He was one of the leaders in the fight for the new law in spite of the fact that it would reduce his father's income from the tax. This created a delicate situation in the Chase family, but Thomas came through nobly by deserting the bulk of his fellow clergy and taking his son's side. He announced in the newspaper that, "I am far from being desirous of availing myself of this circumstance to the distress or even inconvenience of my parishioners." It may be assumed that this self denial endeared him to his congregation. It was eloquent testimony to his human touch.

In 1772 Francis Asbury, sent out from England by John Wesley, arrived in Maryland. He was a gifted speaker and an indefatigable traveler who, covering many miles on horseback through the province, rivaled Strawbridge in making converts to Methodism. Chase met Asbury and engaged him in friendly theological discussion. Asbury was unimpressed. Commenting on the incident in his diary with his customary frankness he said of Chase: "But poor man! One more ignorant of the deep things of God, I have scarcely ever met with, of the cloth." However, on closer acquaintance he softened this criticism, went to hear Chase preach and conceded that he delivered "a good discourse on retirement and private devotions, and much of attending on the Lord's day to hear Thomas Chase, but for my part I see but little fruit." Evidently the church was not crowded. Even then attendance was a problem.

The American Revolution was now fast approaching and Chase's son Sam was outstanding among the leaders. In fact he had been loud in his criticism of the British Parliament ever since the Stamp Act controversy in 1765. He served on the committees of correspondence and observation and was chosen as one of the Maryland delegates to the Continental Congress. There he was quickly identified with the group of extremists, among them John and Samuel Adams, who saw independence as the only solution to the problem. The clergy of the Established Church in Maryland, on the other hand, were largely Tory. Most of them had been born in England, they owed their livings to the Proprietary and instinctively they were against change. Thomas Chase fell in this category; but, on the other hand, he was Sam's father. His dilemma reached a climax when the Continental Congress voted for independence. Sam had been a powerful force in bringing a reluctant Maryland into line, and he had signed the Declaration of Independence. He was, moreover, a framer of the first State constitution which, among other things, disestablished the Church of England in Maryland. The church property was left in the hands of the vestries, but the thirty per poll tobacco tax was abolished and such clergy as did not return to England, thus were reduced to depending on whatever voluntary contributions might be made by the church members. The day of decision arrived for Thomas Chase in the face of this bleak outlook.

In the winter of 1777–78 the Continental Congress, driven from Philadelphia, sat for a few months in Baltimore. John Adams, still representing Massachusetts, noted the presence of Thomas Chase in the town with the comment: ". . . who, they say, is not so zealous a Whig as his son." Zealous or not, he threw in his lot with the new nation and took the oath of allegiance to the State of Maryland and to the United States. He had lost his second wife in 1772, and now in the twilight of his life he had to make a new beginning. To keep himself and his children from want, he fell back on his talent as a teacher and opened a school.

St. Paul's was disorganized; there is no record of the Vestry having met from August 1776 to August 1777. Many of the leading members of the Parish were, or had been, busy attending to public affairs. Charles Carroll, Barrister, master of Mount Clare, who had joined the congregation in 1769, had an important hand in framing the State constitution. Captain Charles Ridgely of Hampton, in the period just prior to the war was a member of the local committee of observation, and after the Declaration of Independence a delegate to the State Constitutional Convention.

Brian Philpot held a commission in General Smallwood's command in the Continental Army. Young Nicholas Ruxton Moore, lately moved to Baltimore from Annapolis, cap-

[25]

tain of a troop of light dragoons, had joined Lafayette and marched off to take part in the Yorktown campaign. John Eager Howard, later to become one of the pillars of the church, was earning laurels on the battlefield. John Moale, Zechariah Maccubbin and Andrew Buchanan had served on the local committee of observation. Robert Alexander, a delegate to the Continental Congress in 1776, was among the first men to be elected to the newly created State Senate.

Col. Nicholas Rogers, wealthy owner of Druid Hill, a broad estate to the northwest of the town which would be known to later generations as a public park, was on a mission in Paris at the time of the Declaration. What this mission was is obscure; he occupied accommodations in the hotel where Benjamin Franklin and Silas Dean were lodged. He became aide to the French General Coudray, returned with him to America, fought in the Battle of Brandywine and ended his military service on the staff of Baron de Kalb.

Before the war came to a close, Andrew Buchanan was elevated to the delicate administrative post of commander of the Maryland militia with the rank of General.

Prominent also on Revolutionary committees as well as in St. Paul's Church were three generations of the Lux family—Darby, William and George. Darby was a pioneer merchant who made a fortune in shipping, a rope walk and other ventures. It was for him that Light Street was named. His son William married Agnes, daughter of Dr. George Walker, the commissioner, who built *Chatsworth,* one of the show places of the Town and noted for its hospitality when it was inherited by Agnes from her father. Among the guests entertained there were Washington, John Adams, Lafayette and Rochambeau. All three of the Luxes were vestrymen of St. Paul's. George in turn inherited *Chatsworth* on the death of his father William.

Thomas Chase died in 1779 at the venerable age of 76

years, of which more than thirty-four had been spent as incumbent at St. Paul's. Whatever shortcomings he may have had were forgotten, overshadowed by a sincere appreciation of his worth. One obituary extolled him as "a Gentleman of great learning and urbanity, a divine of orthodox principles, whose precepts and examples reflected the highest honor on his head and heart." Another stated that "he possessed fine natural abilities. In person handsome, noble and dignified in his manner, elegant, courteous and refined." In addition to his pastoral duties he had found time to write an English grammar for girls and to translate an epic Latin poem into English verse. The best reply to Asbury's disparaging remarks about his intellect is that he was responsible for the education of his son Sam and his great nephew Jeremiah Townley Chase; that they both came to be leading lawyers at the Maryland bar; that the former ended his life as an associate justice of the Supreme Court of the United States and the latter rose to be the first Chief Judge of the Maryland Court of Appeals.

During Chase's ministry, the Church of England, from a virtual monopoly at the start, was challenged by the appearance in Baltimore of other sects and by the defection of the Methodists. Yet in spite of all handicaps St. Paul's continued to grow. The church building, completed some forty years before, no longer was large enough to accommodate the congregation. As early as 1771 a proposal was advanced to build a larger church, but the war forced postponement. As monuments to his zeal Chase could call attention to the brick wall, the bell tower and its bell, the installation of an organ and the engagement of a man to play it.

The challenge which St. Paul's Parish now faced was one shared with all the other American parishes of the former Established Church. For nearly a century it had enjoyed the financial support of the State. Denied that, in competition

[27]

with a number of vigorous denominations, and beset with dissension in its ranks there was a grave question whether the church could survive. It was setting sail on an uncharted course in a tempestuous sea, and this called for genius and dedication at the helm. As the Mother Church, in the town which was fast growing into the largest city in Maryland, St. Paul's was destined to play a valuable part in starting the national church on its way.

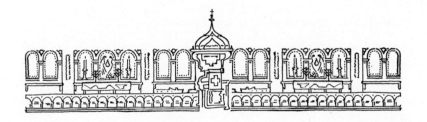

CHAPTER III

STRUGGLE FOR SURVIVAL

WHEN the death of Thomas Chase made it necessary for St. Paul's to go in search of a new rector, Cornwallis's surrender was still two years away and the war still uppermost in most men's minds. In this disordered period the parish was fortunate in attracting the Rev. William West, a man of unblemished character. Anglican clergymen of any sort were hard to find since most of them, being Tories, had returned to England at the outbreak of the war.

Mr. West was a native of Fairfax County, Virginia, a neighbor and friend of George Washington. There is no record of where he got his education but his career showed him definitely to be a man of cultivation. As was the rule before the Revolution, since there was no bishop in this country, candidates for ordination had to go to England. On his return West applied for a parish in Southern Maryland. Colonel Washington agreed to be his sponsor and in a letter to Governor Horatio Sharpe recommended him as a "well behaved young man." West married a lady of means of Anne Arundel County and in the ensuing years served in various parishes on the Western Shore. He was evidently well known to St. Paul's because he had been called in to perform the marriage ceremony for Thomas Chase and his second wife. He was also for a time in Harford County and while there was heard by the Methodist leader Asbury. That gentleman, who had damned Thomas Chase with such faint praise, in West's case was charitable enough to comment in his diary that he preached "a plain useful sermon, which contained much truth."

West had returned to Virginia when the call to Baltimore came. That St. Paul's just then was feeling the effects of having to depend on voluntary contributions is indicated by the Vestry offering Mr. West less than they had given Mr. Chase. On his acceptance, however, six members of the Parish—Thomas Harrison, George Lux, Daniel Bowley, Edward Hanson, William Young and John Edwards—generously made up a purse of $900 to help him move his family to Baltimore. Since at that time there was no clergyman at St. Thomas' Garrison Forest, for two years Mr. West served that Parish as well as St. Paul's.

Inconsistently enough, while the Vestry, presumably for reasons of economy, had cut the Rector's salary, they simultaneously set to work making plans for a new and larger church. Baltimore's population now had grown to 8000 and the prospects were that once peace was restored it would expand even more. A committee to obtain subscriptions was formed. As was the custom of the day construction funds were swelled by a lottery.

The building committee did its work so efficiently and the Vestry was so confident of seeing the project through that the cornerstone to the new church was laid in the spring of 1780. Because of the disruption of the war, however, construction was to take four years. Finally on May 31, 1784, the edifice was formally opened for service. Mr. West took as the text for his sermon: "I was glad when they said to me we will go into the house of the Lord." The new church had 83 pews, an important consideration since their sale or rental was a main source of revenue. This was the second St. Paul's Church to be erected in Baltimore Town. It stood to the south of the old church in the center of the property. The main entrance faced south and a series of terraces, shaded by sycamore trees, ran down to Lexington Street. The land around three sides of the church served as a graveyard. The old church and the bell tower were for the time being allowed to stand, the former being used for a couple of years as a school house before it was torn down.

A conspicuous feature of the church was a large east window covered by a green baize curtain to keep out the sun. There being no vestry room, the clergyman robed behind another curtain, this one red. A gallery supported by pillars provided additional seating and also a place for the organ which was moved from the old church and installed in the west end of the new one.

While the new church was being built the Parish received a bequest, under the will of Agnes Lux, widow of William Lux of *Chatsworth,* of 100 pounds common money and a silver Communion cup and cover. In later years another cup and cover, and a flagon of similar design were donated by other parishioners and all are still in regular use.

The end of the war witnessed the return of the warriors and the arrival of a number of young men from other parts of the world who were newcomers to the town, attracted by opportunities in trade and the professions. Among the latter was Col. Tench Tilghman, aide to General Washington, who had recently made history by carrying the news of the surrender of Cornwallis at Yorktown to the Continental Congress sitting in Philadelphia. In civilian life Colonel Tilghman was a commission merchant who numbered the former commander-in-chief among his customers. His residence in Baltimore was brief since he died in 1786. That he was a member of St. Paul's was made apparent by his burial in

[31]

the Church's graveyard. On the occasion of the visit of the Marquis de Lafayette to Baltimore in 1784, he and Colonel Nicholas Rogers were among the four men who presented an address of welcome.

Foremost among this generation of St. Paul's laymen was Col. John Eager Howard, who had distinguished himself in the Battle of Cowpens. Born in Baltimore County he had inherited property which made him the largest landowner in the town, and he was public spirited and farsighted in planning its growth. His public career would take him to the Governor's chair in Annapolis and to the United States Senate. He did not allow these responsibilities to interfere with his duties as a churchman. For some twenty-eight years he was a Vestryman.

Among the new pew holders were Samuel Chase and Luther Martin. Having left Baltimore as a young man to take up residence in Annapolis, Chase now returned to the place of his birth. He was given the site for a town house by his friend Colonel Howard. One of the four Maryland signers of the Declaration of Independence, he was to represent St. Paul's Parish at several Diocesan Conventions and to take a conspicuous part in rewriting the Vestry Act and seeing it through the Assembly. He would end his days as an Associate Justice of the Supreme Court of the United States. Martin, at this time Attorney-General of Maryland, was recognized as a leader of the bar. He shortly would go as a delegate to the Constitutional Convention in Philadelphia, champion the cause of the small states and be instrumental in obtaining the provision that they should receive equal representation with the large states in the upper chamber of Congress.

Also in this group was Captain Nicholas Ruxton Moore, a vestryman, previously mentioned as taking part in the Battle of Yorktown. He later made his home in Baltimore

[32]

County, entered politics and was elected to Congress. His land abutted the right of way of the Northern Central Railroad. Tradition has it that he was buried near a local station which took his middle name, now extended to cover the expanding community of Ruxton.

The Episcopal Church in America was now in the most critical stage in its history. During the colonial period the church had looked to England for leadership. There had been little or no formal communication between the parishes in the colonies and no sense of unity. There had been no bishop in America, and the nearest thing to central authority were the occasional visits of commissaries representing the Bishop of London. Who then was to take the initiative in charting the American Church's course? Two plans emerged. In Connecticut, the feeling prevailed that the first step was to get an American bishop so that the Apostolic Succession, so important an Episcopal tenet, should be assured in this country. That meant that an American would have to be consecrated, but appeals to the church fathers in England were denied on the ground that before a candidate for bishop could be consecrated, he must first take an oath of allegiance to the King. That obviously was impossible in the case of Americans who had but lately declared their independence. The Episcopal Church of Scotland, however, whose bishops had refused to swear allegiance to the English sovereigns after the Protestant Revolution of 1688, came to the rescue. The non-juring Scots agreed to the laying on of hands in the case of an American candidate. So to Scotland went the Rev. Samuel Seabury, of Connecticut, and at Aberdeen was Consecrated on November 14, 1784.

Meanwhile another group under the leadership of the Rev. William White of Philadelphia, believed that of more immediate importance than making American bishops was planning for unification and the framing of a Church constitution. The Church in Maryland seems to have been more sympathetic with this point of view. Mr. West was in constant communication with Mr. White. He also was active in the Maryland Diocesan Conventions, at one of which the name "Protestant Episcopal Church in the United States" was first proposed. In one of his letters, indicating that his mind was centered on a national church, Mr. West suggested that in line with the political organization which provided a governor for each state there should be a bishop for each state. Mr. White had gone so far as to revise and have printed a Book of Common Prayer for use in the United States and he looked to Mr. West to distribute copies in Maryland. West had to advise White that the new book was not being well received by Marylanders who thought it "too Presbyterian."

As the Episcopalians were groping their way toward unification, the Methodists reached a climax in their organization. John Wesley had not yet severed connection with the Church of England; but having been refused consecration by the English bishops, he boldly assumed the authority to do it himself, or through his representative. Baltimore was the scene of a momentous event in Methodist history when, on December 27, 1784, at the "Christmas Conference" in Lovely Lane Meeting House, the Rev. Francis Asbury was ordained first Methodist bishop in the United States. Performing the ceremony was Dr. Thomas Coke who had been sent by Wesley to the United States as Superintendent.

This dramatic action could hardly be ignored by those Episcopalians who had not been won over by Wesley and continued their traditional form of worship. Something had to be done, but what? Though the odds were against it, there still might be a chance to keep the Methodists in the fold before they declared for separation. At least the attempt was worth a try. But who was to act as spokesman? Seabury, the only Bishop, had been in office but a few months, and he claimed no jurisdiction beyond Connecticut. Mr. West was nearest to the scene which had been enacted at Lovely Lane Meeting House; and nearest to St. Paul's was St. Thomas'. This was no time to weigh nice questions of authority. What ever was done had to be done at once.

West and The Rev. John Andrews, new Rector of St. Thomas', were equal to the occasion. They joined forces and boldly assumed responsibility. It is certain they had the moral support of White in Philadelphia for they were keeping in close touch with him. So, after the ordination ceremonies at Lovely Lane they took the initiative and invited Dr. Coke and Asbury, bishop of three days, to join them at tea in St. Paul's Rectory, then on Charles Street opposite the church on what is now the site of the Fidelity Building. They made no mention of their purpose and they had no idea how the invitation might be received. To their great satisfaction the two Methodist leaders accepted.

The guests arrived at 6 o'clock in the evening and brought with them a gentleman whom Andrews, in a letter to White, describing the meeting, identified at "Mr. Goff." There can be no doubt that the gentleman was in fact Harry Dorsey Gough and his presence there was living evidence of the costly nature of the Methodist defection. For Mr. Gough until very recently had been a Vestryman of St. Paul's Parish. He was one of the wealthiest men in the community with a fortune popularly estimated at $100,000. His presence may also have reminded the Episcopal negotiators that Rebecca Dorsey, the strong willed wife of Captain Charles Ridgely, builder of "Hampton," under the spell of Asbury's eloquence also had joined the Methodists. Who knew but that she might persuade her husband to follow her? The Ridgelys had for years been pillars of St. Paul's.

The Episcopal hosts wisely arranged for the conference

[35]

to take on the nature of a social occasion. While the company drank tea they conversed on a variety of subjects. Dr. Coke was full of vivacity and entertained with a number of little anecdotes. "Not disagreeably" commented Mr. Andrews. When the atmosphere had sufficiently mellowed the Episcopalians got down to business. They said they had read the most recent Methodist writings, including a book entitled "The Sunday Service of the Methodists" and were happy to find that the people called Methodists were to use the same Litany, adhere to the same articles of faith and keep up the same three orders of Bishops, Priests and Deacons, as did the Episcopal Church. These circumstances, they said, had induced them to hope that the breach which had so long subsisted in the Church might at length, in America at least, be happily closed. Developing the same line of argument they remarked that they could not think so unfavorably of the gentlemen who were at the head of the society, as to suppose they would persist in separating, merely for the sake of separating, or cherish in their breasts so unkind a spirit as to create an invidious distinction between two groups where in fact there were no real differences.

Turning to the contemplated organization of the Episcopal Church in America they gave assurance that a bishop here would have no greater power over them than did John Wesley. They even went so far as to suggest that there might be a Methodist bishop as well as an Episcopal bishop in Maryland. With a surprising disregard of the claims of the newly ordained Asbury, they even hinted that Dr. Coke might be so consecrated. At the conclusion of their arguments they made it clear that they were speaking only for themselves.

Having heard the gentlemen out Dr. Coke replied politely that he hardly knew what to answer as the interview had taken him entirely by surprise. He would be glad, however, to pass on to Mr. Wesley any proposition they might see fit to make. He reminded them of the itinerant nature of the Methodist system as opposed to the fixed residences of the Episcopal clergy. He then said that he envisioned the two churches as a couple of earthenware "basons" set afloat in a current of water. So long as they continued to float in parallel lines, both would float securely; but the moment they began to converge they were in danger of destroying each other.

"Mr. Asbury" as he was referred to by Andrews who could not quite get himself up to calling him "Bishop," observed that the difference between the two groups lay not so much in doctrines and forms of worship as in experience and practice. He complained that Methodists had been treated by Episcopalians "with abundance of contempt." He said he had traveled widely over the American continent and but four clergymen of the Episcopal Church had shown him any civilities. He hastened to add that he meant no reflection on the gentlemen present.

On that note the conference ended. Mr. Andrews later followed up the meeting with a call on Dr. Coke at his lodgings. There the latter told him that there had been a time when the Methodists might have been won over by a little condescension but it was now too late. He closed with a recitation of the ill treatment they had received at the hands of the bishops in England. So the confrontation met with failure. But the Rectors of St. Paul's and St. Thomas' could console themselves that they had done all that was possible to prevent it.

Mr. West, along with Dr. Allison and his own parishioners, Luther Martin and Samuel Chase, was showing a lively interest in the founding of Washington College in Chestertown and St. John's College in Annapolis, helping to raise funds from others and contributing generously of his own

[37]

money. In 1785 his support was recognized by the granting of the honorary degree of "D.D." by Washington College and thereafter he was addressed as "Dr. West." Another educational project closer to home was the founding of Baltimore Academy where the young men of the town might obtain a solid grounding in mathematics and the classics. It was sponsored jointly by Dr. West, by Dr. Allison, the Presbyterian; and Bishop John Carroll of the Roman Catholic Church, who also was an accomplished scholar. The idea was that the academy would eventually grow into a university; but, unfortunately it did not long survive. It is interesting chiefly as an early manifestation of ecumenism.

Still another display of Christian fellowship about this time was the aftermath of a flood of Jones Falls which badly damaged the German Reformed Church and led to financial difficulties for its congregation. By way of showing their sympathy Dr. West of St. Paul's, Dr. Allison of First Presbyterian and Dr. Kurtz of the Lutheran Church brought their congregations with them and preached there on successive Sundays. In each instance the proceeds from the collection were turned over to the Reformed Church.

In 1785 St. Paul's Vestry was faced with an important decision. The old Rectory across the street from the Church was considered obsolete and plans were laid for erecting a new one on Lexington Street. At that point Colonel Howard offered as a site a half-acre on a commanding hill, west of the church, which was then outside the town limits. It was up to the Vestry to choose between continuing with the Lexington Street proposal or dropping it and accepting Colonel Howard's offer. After serious consideration the Vestry voted for the latter. That the Rectory erected on the proffered site is still in use and that Lexington Street provided nothing comparable testifies to the wisdom of the decision.

Three years, however, passed before the plan was pursued.

This no doubt was because the nationwide depression which followed the Revolution had set in and St. Paul's found itself in financial trouble. Hard times may have been partly responsible for an apathy on the part of some of the members of the congregation. A number of them were in arrears on their pew rents and protested that these were too high. The situation grew so bad that the Vestry had to write to Dr. West to tell him they had found it necessary to cut his salary. They added by way of apology: "We flatter ourselves that Dr. West will on this occasion believe us to be actuated by what ought to govern every person in a situation similar to that of your most obedient servants." There is a suggestion in this statement that in their effort to balance the budget at Dr. West's expense they took into account that he and Mrs. West were more generously endowed with worldly goods than was the average clergy family.

A Diocesan Convention was scheduled for Baltimore in 1788. Dr. West had acted as secretary at one of these meetings and it was probably at his suggestion that the Vestry of St. Paul's drew up a letter to be circulated among the parishes of the Diocese urging their attendance. In no uncertain terms the letter scolded Episcopalians for their carelessness and inattentiveness as compared with other denominations in Maryland. It lamented that at the Convention at Annapolis in 1786 only two lay delegates attended, and that the attendance at the Convention in Chestertown the following year was not much better. The letter proved so effective that at the Convention in Baltimore seventeen out of forty-six parishes sent representatives and letters of apology were received from nine others. Attendance at the convention of 1789 was even better. The election of Dr. West as president of the Convention which met in Easton the following year, indicated the credit due him for arousing the churchmen to their duties.

Simultaneously progress toward organizing a national church was proving most gratifying. At last the Church of England relented and consented to consecrate American bishops without requiring an oath of allegiance to the crown. Dr. White of Pennsylvania and the Rev. Samuel Provoost of New York made the journey to England and on February 4, 1787, in Lambeth Chapel, were duly Consecrated by the Archbishop of Canterbury, the Bishop of Bath and Wells and the Bishop of Peterborough, thus assuring the Apostolic Succession to the American Church without peradventure of a doubt.

The next issue to be settled was the relationship between the Seabury group and the White group. That was effected by Bishop Seabury's Consecration by the non-juring Scottish bishops being recognized as valid by the White group. A national church was brought into being at the General Convention of 1789, held in Philadelphia, meeting concurrently with the convention which framed the United States Constitution. It adopted the name first proposed some years before at a Maryland convention, "Protestant Episcopal Church in the United States of America."

In 1788 the Vestry authorized a lottery to raise funds for the building of the new Rectory. Because it conflicted with a lottery to finance a public wharf, and because so much of the proceeds from the sale of tickets had to be assigned to prizes the net return was disappointing. By 1790 the roof was on but the funds were exhausted and a subscription had to be opened to finish the construction. Dr. West, under whose rectorship the house had been planned, never lived in it. Early in the summer, just when he was on the point of moving in, he was stricken by a fever which caused his death. Some of those who appreciated his ability said that had he lived he would have been Maryland's first bishop, an honor which fell to the Rev. Thomas John Claggett the following year. Others were of the opinion that he had no such ambition and was quite content to end his days as Rector of St. Paul's. Ever a modest man he left directions for all his sermons to be burned since he did not consider them of lasting importance. In a period when the Roman Catholics and the Presbyterians boasted such heroic figures as Bishop Carroll and Dr. Allison, the Episcopalians were fortunate in being represented in the community by a man of the caliber of Dr. West.

An incident of historic importance occurred in the last year of Dr. West's ministry. At a service on December 6, 1790, "The Book of Common Prayer According to the Use of the Protestant Episcopal Church," which had been adopted by the General Convention of 1789, was used in St. Paul's Church for the first time. The Church in America was on its way.

CHAPTER IV

PRIEST FROM THE COUNTING HOUSE

"WHATEVER facility I possess in discharging any of the duties belonging to me I ascribe, next to the Grace of God . . . to good habits engrafted upon me by a vigilant active teacher, to an even flow of good animal spirits, and to an active principle which stimulates me to be always employed."

Thus in a letter to a fellow clergyman Joseph Grove John Bend disclosed the secret of his ability to perform an incredible number of tasks which was a marvel to those who watched him at his work. As a successor to Dr. West and fifth Rector of St. Paul's Parish he was responsible for the direction of a fast growing congregation, and in addition he took on many exacting extraparochial activities. Another priceless attribute, rare in a man whose calling demanded emphasis on theology and the classics, was a mastery of figures. Born in New York in the middle of the eighteenth century he was taken by his parents to Barbados where he spent his youth. It was there he got from a clergyman a thorough grounding in the classics and at the same time found employment in a counting house where he was trained in book-keeping and other companion mysteries of commerce. There too he developed his habits of regularity and system.

[43]

On returning to this country Mr. Bend felt the call to the Episcopal ministry. He was ordained Deacon by Bishop Samuel Provoost at the first ordination service ever held in the Diocese of New York, along with Richard Channing Moore, afterwards second Bishop of Virginia. He settled in Philadelphia and there was ordained to the Priesthood by Bishop William White. He was a deputy to the General Convention in 1789 at which the Protestant Episcopal Church in the United States was organized. Thereafter he was a delegate from Maryland to every other general convention held during his lifetime. At his very first appearance at a Diocesan Convention after his arrival in Maryland he was elected to the Standing Committee. He attended the Convention of 1792 at which John Thomas Claggett was elected first Bishop of Maryland, and at the Convention of 1793 his talent for organization was recognized by his being made its Secretary. Two years later he was elected Treasurer of the Diocese, and in addition he acted as treasurer of the Corporation for the Relief of Widows and Orphans of the Protestant Episcopal Clergymen in Maryland. He also became a trusted adviser to the Bishop.

When Mr. Bend entered upon his duties at St. Paul's the new "Parsonage on the hill" was ready to receive him and his family, consisting of Mrs. Bend, their sons William and Henry and their daughter Mary. Its distinguishing features were much what they are today, though in the course of years the structure was to undergo various extensions and alterations. The front, which looked down from the hill on what is now Liberty Street, exhibited the characteristic doorway of the Federal period, flanked by pilasters supporting a pediment. Above the doorway was a handsome Palladian window which lighted the upstairs hall, and above that was a bull's-eye. On the ground floor a spacious hallway was broken by a graceful arch; and behind this, set in an octagonal brick

[44]

well, was a circular stairway which wound up to the second floor.

Very likely, as was the custom of the day, there was no architect, the plan coming from a book of designs and being executed by a skillful builder. Nevertheless it is unfortunate that the name of no individual is associated with the construction of this beautiful house. Architects who have studied the parsonage professionally are of the opinion that the original intention was to follow the plan of a symmetrical Palladian country mansion; which is to say, a central main house and dependencies on either side connected by hyphen-like pavilions, such as is found in the Hammond-Harwood House in Annapolis and Homewood House on the Johns Hopkins University campus on North Charles Street. But the subsequent sale of the land on the east prevented such an extension. The property included an orchard and a garden which supplied the family with abundant fruit and vegetables. It was a pleasant place to retire to, though for a man of Bend's energy it could not be said he relaxed there. Among other things he there undertook the education of his children who were never sent to school. It is recorded that, in order to make the best use of his time, he instructed them while he dressed, shaved and performed his other ablutions. A striking feature of the household was a large pot on the kitchen stove always filled with soup ready to be dispensed to any poor hungry soul who passed by and asked for it.

Parson Bend kept a meticulous watch over his flock. He had a book in which was registered the name of every member of the congregation and from which each day he selected in turn those on whom to call until all had been visited. Nor was he unmindful of his duty to the community as a whole. He was active in the work of the Baltimore General Dispensary which served as a medical center for the poor, and he also lent his weight to a society for promoting vaccination. When word reached Baltimore of the pitiful plight of American sailors who had been captured by the Barbary pirates and were languishing in dungeons in Algiers he was designated by the Episcopalians to confer with the clergy of other denominations and the charitable societies which were collecting money for their ransom.

We have noted that the effort of Bishop Carroll, Dr. Allison and Dr. West to found an institution of learning in Baltimore ended in failure. After Dr. West's death, Bend replaced him in this triumvirate of intellectuals who launched another project for the cultural advancement of the community which met with greater success. This was the Library Company, Baltimore's first public library. It filled an immediate need and eventually merged with the Athenaeum which survives to this day as a part of the Maryland Historical Society.

At the turn of the nineteenth century the churches were still keenly aware of their responsibility for the welfare of the unfortunate before the civil authorities took over this function. There was then no such euphemism as "underprivileged;" well-to-do members of society spoke openly of "the poor." It was in this atmosphere and under Mr. Bend's ministry that in 1799 the women of St. Paul's Parish, led by Eleanor Rogers, wife of Nicholas Rogers of "Druid Hill," formed the "Benevolent Society of the City and County of Baltimore." Members of Mrs. Roger's committee were: Mrs. Nancy Hollingsworth, Mrs. Anne Boyd, Mrs. Elizabeth Thompson, Mrs. Sarah Craig, Mrs. Elizabeth Bend, Mrs. Peggy Moore, Miss Mary Grundy and Mrs. Ann McKim. Its purpose was to provide a school for thirty girls between the ages of seven and fourteen years. Preference was to be given to orphans, and the girls were to be taught reading, writing and "cyphering," needlework and "every other kind of work the trustees shall think proper." One requirement was that every scholar should go to church on Sunday; and, as evidence that the organization was intended to serve the entire community, attendance at St. Paul's was not demanded, "but at such place as the parent and guardian shall think fit." The society was authorized to "bind" the girls out to the age of 16 years. The Benevolent Society, incorporated in 1800, was to operate under these conditions for more than a century and a half, until changing times and customs put an end to the demand for such service. The corpus of the Society, however, accumulating over the years, is today being applied to valuable constructive purposes in keeping with present needs.

About the same time, members of St. Paul's Church were actively engaged in another humanitarian enterprise. In fact the movement had begun in the last years of Dr. West's ministry when on September 8, 1789, there was organized "The Maryland Society for Promoting the Abolition of Slavery and the Relief of Free Negroes and Others Unlawfully held in Bondage." This was the fourth anti-slavery society in the United States and the sixth in the world. On the roster of its members were Judge Samuel Chase, Attorney-General Luther Martin and Dr. George Buchanan, all of St. Paul's Church. Dr. Buchanan was a vestryman as his father Andrew and his grandfather George had been before him. Chase and Martin were elected Honorary Counsellors.

On July 4, 1791 Dr. Buchanan used the observance of the Declaration of Independence to deliver an impassioned oration before the Society in which he expressed the then novel theory that there was nothing in the physical makeup of the Negro that prevented him from being as capable of improvement as the white man. To prove his point he cited instances in which Negroes had achieved distinction in science, literature and the arts. That his revolutionary theory was not

[47]

unacceptable to his audience was indicated by the fact that at the conclusion of the address Dr. Buchanan was thanked and congratulated by those present.

While the Episcopal Church was in fierce competition with other faster growing denominations and falling behind them in numerical strength it had at the same time to contend with a division in its own ranks between the so-called "High Church" and "Low Church" parties. The high church group emphasized the Catholic factor in belief and practice. They stressed the Apostolic Succession and attached great importance to the frequency of the administration of the Sacrament accompanying it with relatively elaborate ritual. Their general tendency was to express the corporate side of Christianity and the objective aspect of religion. Central to the way of thinking of the low churchmen was the Protestant factor, relying on the Bible as the source of authority, setting great value on preaching, de-emphasizing the Eucharist, which they called "Holy Communion"; sometimes introducing original prayers in place of those prescribed by the Book of Common Prayer, and leaning toward simplicity in the services. The division has continued throughout the life of the American church. While it has been a constant source of friction, on the other hand it has served to illustrate the tolerance which has enabled the Anglican Church to receive into its communion individuals of widely varied practices.

By association and personal taste Mr. Bend was committed to the high church group and may be said to have established a tradition at St. Paul's which has been sustained from his time to the present day. The Rev. Frederick Ward Kates in his short history of the parish entitled "Bridge Across the Centuries," is careful to point out that this high church attitude is not to be confused with later Anglo-Catholicism. It refers only to a pattern of dignity, beauty and reverence in the services and strict adherence to the canons and rubrics, about which the low churchmen are inclined to be careless or indifferent. Under Mr. Bend's leadership the number of services at St. Paul's was greatly increased. There were two every Sunday, one every Wednesday, a service on the Feast of the Circumcision, every day in Passion Week, on Ascension Day, on two days after Whitsunday, on Thanksgiving Day and Christmas Day. Communion was administered regularly once a month in addition to special observances.

Following the Revolution the growth of Baltimore was so rapid that on December 31, 1796, the Town was incorporated as a City complete with Mayor and Council. St. Paul's Parish had grown along with it so that after little more than a decade, the Church built during Dr. West's ministry and opened in 1784 no longer sufficed for all who wished to attend. So once more thoughts turned to replacing it with a larger building.

Before the plans were far advanced, however, alternatives presented themselves. One was to expand by building a separate church at Fell's Point. Meanwhile the First German Reformed congregation had erected a church edifice at Baltimore and Front Streets, at the east end of the bridge over Jones Falls. They then had run into financial difficulties and offered the building for sale. This appeared to be a way to solve St. Paul's expansion problem, so the Vestry bought the building, gave it the name of Christ Church and provided it with a minister who bore the title of Associate Rector of St. Paul's. It became the custom for the ministers to alternate between the two churches in holding services. Just then the neighborhood of the Falls had become fashionable. It was especially favored by young married people who were starting their own households, and this part of the congregation shifted its affiliations to Christ Church. Both churches were administered by the same Vestry. They con-

stituted one parish. This was in 1796 and the intimate relationship between St. Paul's and Christ Church then cemented
continued for more than thirty years.

Instead of relieving him of some of his many duties the
institution of the office of an Associate Minister added to
Mr. Bend's troubles. The position was regarded as a desirable one and consequently attracted some applicants who
were less so. The first unfortunate incident was provoked
by a gentleman of the cloth named George Ralph. The
Reverend Mr. Ralph was an Irishman whose unseemly be-
havior suggested emotional instability, to say the least. He
entered the picture while a church at Fell's Point was still
under consideration and he wanted it. When this was refused him he put his case before the public in a letter to
the *Maryland Journal and Baltimore Advertiser* in which he
accused the poor unoffending Mr. Bend with having aspersed
his character, so that he could not find employment in the
community. In the columns of the same newspaper Mr.
Bend replied denying the charge and stating that his reason
for not giving the position to Mr. Ralph was because he
preferred the Rev. John Ireland, another candidate. From
July into September of 1792 the controversy raged in the
press to the embarrassment of all concerned except Mr.
Ralph. The Vestry, which included among others John
Eager Howard, supported Mr. Bend. Mr. Ralph then re-
ferred the matter to Luther Martin, Attorney-General of
Maryland and a member of St. Paul's congregation as well.
When Martin presented a learned opinion upholding the
Vestry, Ralph penned one more letter which read: "Poor
Rev. Mr. Bend! 'How are the mighty fallen!' Hapless Rec-
tor of St. Paul's in Baltimore, farewell! farewell! The cause
is consigned to other hands, and much did it stand in need
of an advocate; for thou truly, has made a pitiful defense!"
He closed by chastising Martin, who had ruled against him,

[50]

for degrading the State of Maryland and the office of Attorney-General.

Mr. Bend's victory, alas!, was short lived for Mr. Ireland proved an unfortunate choice. He had not been long installed when rumors spread that he had carried on a questionable correspondence with his sister-in-law. The Vestry demanded the letters and after examining them asked for his resignation. Still Mr. Bend's troubles were not over. Two candidates now presented themselves for the position. One was the Rev. Elijah Rattoone, another Irishman who had a parish on Long Island and before that had been professor of languages at Columbia College, New York. The other was the Rev. George Dashiell, a preacher with a dynamic personality who had a large following in St. Paul's congregation. Dashiell belonged to the evangelical party and for that reason could not have been a congenial associate for Bend. After a bitter discussion in the Vestry the choice went to the scholar Rattoone. Dashiell's defeat split the congregation and his followers withdrew from St. Paul's and founded a church of their own on Sharp Street, in south Baltimore, which they named St. Peter's. Friends of Dashiell soon got their revenge, for his successful rival was charged with the intemperate use of spiritous liquors and was asked to resign. Rattoone claimed that the Vestry was misinformed but the resignation held, even though Bishop Claggett was inclined to take Rattoone's side. He expressed regret that the Vestry had not informed him of the charge before taking action and asked them to show a more lenient attitude. This the Vestry declined to do. Meanwhile Dashiell was having a brilliant success at St. Peter's, attracting crowds to hear his sermons. He was for some time to be a thorn in the flesh of the high church party.

Nor had the last been heard of Rattoone. Against Bend's wishes the next Diocesan Convention gave him permission

[51]

to start a church on Fell's Point which took the name of
Trinity. Those who lamented these unhappy events found
consolation at least in the fact that they resulted in the founding of two new churches—St. Peter's and Trinity. Trinity
unfortunately was short lived.

Further efforts to supply Christ Church with a worthy
rector failed until the Rev. Frederick Beasley was elected.
He was a gentleman and a scholar. Nothing could be said
against him except that, unfortunately, his personality did
not prove congenial with that of Mr. Bend.

Outside his ecclesiastical and community duties, Mr. Bend
was assiduous in the role of a friend in need. He applied his
knowledge of finance in advising his colleagues on invest-
ments. In a letter to the Rev. James Kemp he refers to an
earlier letter which he says was accompanied by "$9,627,
being the balance of the last dividend on your bank stock."
Surely a valuable adviser if the figure is correct. But his
most strenuous endeavor was directed toward solving the
domestic problem of the Rev. William Duke, a not too successful minister who had been left a widower with a small
daughter. In his first letter on the subject Bend expressed
a wish that Mr. Duke might persuade some woman to become his "yoke Fellow." He suggested one with the charm
of Mrs. Kemp, wife of a fellow clergyman of whom much
will be heard later. He added a warning that "Clergymen
of all denominations will hereafter be reduced to the necessity of paying more attention to the main chance in their
matrimonial connections. They must mix a great deal of
prudence with their love; or they will run a risk of laying
up for themselves and families an infinitude of trouble and
sorrow."

On reflection Mr. Bend evidently concluded that his advice
had been too worldly; for in his next letter, after reminding
Duke that each day he was growing older and ought not

to wait too long, he added: "But above all, do not let money be your only, or even your principle inducement in this important step." Pursuing the subject in a third letter he made the encouraging observation that "Your idea of a wife and her personal pecuniary qualifications are so very moderate, that it will be hard indeed if you should not be accommodated to your satisfaction. At present I do not recollect any female who answers the description, who is yet to be disposed of, but whenever I may be so fortunate as to meet with one, I shall not fail to apprise you of the discovery."

Apparently the prospective wives were as prudent as the two scheming gentlemen. Mr. Duke was not much of a "catch." So far as the record shows he never found a second wife. When the death of the first Mrs. Bend placed Mr. Bend in a similar situation he was more fortunate. After a lapse of five years he wrote Duke: ". . . in addition to the usual occupations of my time I have had that of courting . . . Next week I am to be united to Mrs. Claypoole." He invited Duke to the wedding but regretted he could not offer him a bed for the night.

There is today a charming reminder of the second Mrs. Bend's years as mistress of the Rectory. She then owned a silver service and spoons to go with it which she used for afternoon tea. On leaving the Rectory after Dr. Bend's death she took them with her, and for more than a century they were lost sight of. In 1933 Mrs. George B. Stone-Alcock, a great-great granddaughter of Dr. Bend and his first wife, came on them quite accidentally in an antique shop, recognized and bought them. She presented them to St. Paul's for use in the rectory as a memento of the first occupant. The service and spoons, stored in a bank vault for safe keeping, are brought out on special occasions when the present Rectory occupants are entertaining.

An example of a member of St. Paul's Parish participating

in the activities of the community was the election of Thorogood Smith, a vestryman, as second Mayor of Baltimore City in succession to Mayor Calhoun. Mr. Smith, a native of Accomac County, Virginia, came to Baltimore in his youth and was successful in business. He served two terms (1804–1808) and during his incumbency the outmoded system of watchmen was replaced by a professional police patrol composed of constables of the city. His support of law and order was tested when an English journeyman shoemaker was tarred and feathered by some of his fellow workers and driven through the streets in a cart. Mayor Smith followed the procession and had the ring leaders arrested and brought to trial where they were sentenced to fine and imprisonment. A portrait of him, now in the Peale Museum, shows him in spectacles of odd design. They are suspended from a metal band around his forehead. The explanation given is that he was very proud of his nose and did not wish to have it marked by the bridge of standard spectacles.

A mild mannered man in most respects Bend was capable of violent prejudices in matters of religious doctrine and forms, and of politics. The Methodists were in his eyes both an annoyance and a threat. To Duke he wrote in 1800: "The late stir of the Methodists has been general. I am told that the extravaganza wanted very little of the grade which it reached in the year 1790 in Baltimore." He hoped their high water mark had been attained, for he added: "The almost annihilated congregation in Garrison Forest is reviving . . ." His high church predilections for dignity and decorum made it impossible for him to reconcile himself with the manners of the Methodists. "It is much to be lamented," he writes Duke, "that they cannot think it compatible with Christian duty to give up ranting, noise and other follies, which disgrace their profession and to promote the cause of the gospel, in the same rational and dignified way, in which the clergy of almost all other churches proceed. I am not an advocate for lukewarmness or negligence, but I am persuaded that they hurt the cause of Christianity among its enemies by their intemperance more than they benefit it among their friends."

Having about this time received an honorary degree Mr. Bend became "Dr. Bend." The older he grew the more concerned he was over the indifference of the low churchmen to the forms he loved so dearly. He expressed his displeasure over those who "not only cut down our service to something little better than a Methodistical form of worship, but even maintain doctrines, not unworthy of a camp meeting! . . . When people disregard the canon and rubrics, we have no hold of them; and when they find impunity, they go from one extreme to another. I am not in favor of latitudinarians and deists, but surely there is a middle course between Arminianism and Calvinism . . . Such a course I think our church has happily pursued . . . Indeed the more I think of and inquire into the principles of that venerable church, whether they respect doctrines, government or worship, the more I am convinced that she approaches nearer in these respects, to the primitive church, than any other of which I am acquainted."

In Virginia young William Meade was battling bravely against heavy odds to put life into an almost moribund church. His methods shocked Dr. Bend: "What Meade could be at I cannot divine. A gentleman of strict veracity and great intelligence was in his church, about a month ago, and heard him give notice to his congregation, that Mr. Muir, the Presbyterian clergyman would preach there in the afternoon; that, at the same time, the Methodist preacher would officiate in Mr. Muir's church, and that he should preach at night in the Methodist Meetinghouse." Such an ecumenical gesture was totally beyond his comprehension. Dr. Bend could join freely and enthusiastically with Catholic Bishop Carroll and Presbyterian Dr. Allison in starting a public library; he could join other Protestant denominations in distributing Bibles in the community, or work side by side with them ministering to the sick and needy or in collecting funds for the ransom of sailors. But to invite them to join in worship in his Church or to tolerate Episcopalians who treated the canons and rubrics lightly was to his way of thinking desecration.

Dr. Bend's distress reached its peak in concern over what he thought the Jeffersonian Republicans were doing to destroy the infant nation. As an ardent Federalist he shared the sentiments of the most prominent members of his congregation. John Eager Howard was leader of the party in the State and Judge Samuel Chase and Attorney-General Luther Martin were ardent followers. While the Jeffersonians hated Great Britain the Federalists were equally prejudiced against France. France's seizure of our merchant ships on the high seas led to the so-called "Quasi-War" with that country. When President Adams recommended a day of solemn humiliation and prayer Dr. Bend was prompt to comply, composing a special and beautiful form of service to be used by the congregations of St. Paul's and Christ Church. His personal sentiments were expressed in a letter to the Rev. James Kemp in which he referred to some of the Jeffersonians in Kemp's parish: "I am sorry you did not break with hard words, every bone in the body of those scrubs . . . They are, I dare say, filthy democrats, fit only to be citizens of Regenerated France." A year later he exulted that "The disasters which have lately befallen the French, are healthy to the souls of every Federalist." In another letter he assailed Jefferson, who succeeded John Adams as President, and the publicist Tom Paine: "That Mr. Jefferson wrote to the infamous Tom Paine, and offered him a passage to America in the United States Ship *Maryland,* is now no more a vague rumor, but reduced to absolute certainty . . . it most exceeds belief that the President of such a nation as this, a nation once rising fast to the front rank among the empires of the world, a nation growing into esteem for moderation, good sense, magnanimity, and enterprise, should so far forget his station as to decide to correspond with this pitiful creature."

Dr Bend was so emotionally upset that, rightly or wrongly, he imagined his anti-Republican feelings were marking him out for punishment. Not having received an expected letter he suspected "some Jacobin has laid his happy claws upon it, seeing it indorsed with my name; and wickedly curious to know the nature of my correspondence." His concern increased as relations with England in Madison's administration approached the breaking point. "Our government," he wrote, "seems determined on war with Britain; and what is worse we appear on the eve of intestine convulsion . . . May a merciful Providence remember mercy in the midst of judgement, and restrain the torrents of evil which threaten to overwhelm us."

Dr. Bend was not aware that these violent political sentiments were creating an atmosphere in his own household which came near to leading to tragedy. Nowhere in the country more than in Baltimore was feeling so divided over the issue of war with Great Britain. Congress's declaration on June 18, 1812, brought matters to a head. In the city was published the *Federalist Republican,* an organ edited by Alexander C. Hanson, a fiery and outspoken Federalist who in his newspaper declared his violent opposition to the War. Within a matter of hours a pro-war mob formed, marched to the office of the offending publication and demolished its entire printing apparatus.

Editor Hanson was not to be cowed. Action by the mob

forced him to leave town, but at the end of a month he was back again and had rented a house on Charles Street from which he planned to distribute his newspaper. Anticipating trouble he assembled a group of kindred spirits, including Light Horse Harry Lee and General Lingan, another Revolutionary veteran, and fortified the house. When a threatening mob approached, Hanson's party fired on it and killed a boy. Here the town authorities, backed by the militia, stepped in and persuaded Hanson's people to be conducted to the jail on the promise they would be protected; but the promise was broken. When night came the mob stormed the jail and brutally attacked the prisoners. General Lingan was killed, Lee and others terribly mutilated.

Young William Bend, in his late teens, obviously impressed by his father's political sentiments, without the knowledge of his parent, joined Hanson's party and was among those imprisoned in the jail. Dr. Bend got word of it and, according to the popular story, spent the night in St. Paul's graveyard adjacent to the jail, fearful of what might happen to his son. Fortunately, William slipped out of the jail without being identified by the mob and reached home safely. Dr. Bend died shortly thereafter, supposedly from exposure on the night of the riot. Since more than a month, however, elapsed between the riot and his demise, this seems rather a long time for the exposure to have taken effect.

In the winter of 1800 the Vestry had appropriated money to put both St. Paul's and Christ Church in mourning "on account of the much lamented death of General Washington," the mourning not to be removed until Easter. Now, twelve years later, as evidence of the esteem in which Dr. Bend was held by his congregation the Vestry voted to wear crepe for three months, his pulpit and desk were dressed in mourning and a tombstone was ordered, while Mrs. Bend was invited to remain in the Parsonage until a new rector was elected.

In his later years, fraught with political turmoil, Dr. Bend seems to have become more and more a victim of his persecution complex. His fear of retaliation for his anti-Republican sentiments led him to cancel his subscription to a Federalist newspaper. Another evidence of it was his complaint that other denominations were drawing off proselytes by misrepresenting the Episcopal Church's principles, abusing her members and vilifying the characters of her clergy. He charged that malicious and untrue stories were being circulated against himself. Nevertheless St. Paul's doubled its membership during his incumbency. The most impressive tribute to his character and his talents were the many signs of healthy progress in the parish. Silver basins to serve as baptismal fonts had been presented both to St. Paul's and Christ Church, and each had a new organ. The bell tower had been provided with a chime of bells.

Another accomplishment of the Bend ministry was the purchase in 1800 of land for a graveyard to the west of the town and the beginning of the removal of bodies from around three sides of the existing Church on Charles Street. This had been done when a new church was being contemplated before the edifice that became Christ Church was bought from the German Reformed congregation. But even the acquisition of Christ Church was not enough to meet present and future needs, and so in 1810 the proposal to erect a new and larger St. Paul's was revived.

On the other hand the many duties involved in looking after the congregations of St. Paul's and Christ Church inevitably resulted in neglect of that extensive part of the Parish which lay outside the city. Vestrymen ceased to be elected from the country, a chapel at Back River had been allowed to run down and country parishioners either had strayed to other folds or abandoned all religion. But these shortcomings could not be blamed on Dr. Bend whose zeal according to all accounts was phenomenal. Thanks to conscientious, godly men like himself the Episcopal Church, whose very existence was for a time in doubt, was showing signs of healthy progress.

The ministry of Dr. Bend was marked by an event of historical interest in 1808 when the General Convention of the Church was held in Baltimore. St. Paul's was the center of its activities. There the opening sermon was delivered by Bishop White of Pennsylvania, who preached on the "Character, Commission and Message of the Gospel Ministry" and there the House of Deputies held its sessions. The House of Bishops met in an upstairs room in the Rectory which is now marked by a commemorative tablet. No record survives of its proceedings. They must of necessity have been informal for only two members were present—Bishop White, and Bishop Claggett of Maryland.

KEMP-RECTOR AND BISHOP

SIX weeks after the death of Dr. Bend his associate rector, the Rev. Frederick Beasley, addressed a gracious letter to the Rev. Dr. James Kemp, rector of Choptank Parish on the Eastern Shore, to tell him that he was inclined to believe the Vestry of St. Paul's were going to elect Kemp associate. He added: "I need not assure you that this will be very satisfactory to me." The only hitch was that some of the Vestrymen had asked further time for consideration and had postponed the election until November.

Mr. Beasley's prediction was correct. November 26 he wrote again to tell Kemp he had been elected. While Bend and Beasley were administering St. Paul's and Christ Church jointly there had been no question that Beasley was subordinate to Bend. Beasley assured Kemp that if the latter were to accept the call the situation would be different. He told him that he would enjoy full equality with Beasley with respect to salary and administration. Furthermore, Kemp was offered the Parsonage on the hill as his residence. On receipt of this news Kemp was strangely silent and Beasley wrote again to express surprise that his first letter had not been acknowledged.

Dr. Kemp's reticence may have been the result of letters

received from Dr. Bend's widow and from his son William showing concern over Beasley succeeding Bend. Mrs. Bend repeated the prospect of Dr. Kemp getting a call to St. Paul's. She then declared that Dr. Kemp had always been a favorite of her husband, adding: "Oh let me *entreat* you to come if call'd on." She sent her love to Mrs. Kemp and asked her not to stand in the way of Dr. Kemp's coming. She concluded: "Your church requires such a man as you are to be on this spot." Young William was equally insistent: ". . . I will not conceal from you, my dearest Dr., *that no intimacy did, or could subsist between my father and Mr. Beasley* (who is desirous to get this parsonage). For though Mr. Beasley is a very good man, yet there was a great contrast in the tempers and dispositions of the two Rectors: and imbibing perhaps my parent's sentiments, I cannot feel an affection for Mr. Beasley, though I esteem Him." Such critical comments could hardly have failed to prejudice Kemp against Beasley and make him careful how he met Beasley's overtures. Beasley's offer of the parsonage to Kemp refuted young Bend's charge that Beasley wanted it. On the whole the correspondence does more credit to Beasley than it does to Mrs. Bend and William.

At this point in his career Dr. Kemp was proud of his standing in and outside the Maryland diocese. St. Paul's was not the only place vying for his services. There was a concerted movement among his parishioners on the Eastern Shore to keep him there. In fact his ambition rose considerably higher than an associate rectorship at St. Paul's. He already had given indication of his superior talents. A native of Aberdeenshire, Scotland, he was brought up as a Presbyterian. Educated at Marischal College, he won a prize in mathematics, and with laurels fresh on his brow came to Maryland to engage himself as a tutor in a private family in Dorchester County. Shortly thereafter he abandoned Presbyterianism and took orders in the Episcopal Church. He attracted public attention by a sermon preached on the occasion of the death of George Washington in which he defended the late president from his radical detractors. He sent a copy of the sermon to John Adams who praised him for his sentiments, declared that truth would prevail and concluded: "I wish you, Sir, as an able champion for it, all the success you can possibly wish for yourself." In 1802 Columbia College, New York, deemed him worthy of an honorary doctorate.

At the Maryland Diocesan Convention of 1811 Bishop Claggett, who was growing old and not in the best of health, asked for a suffragan. Dr. Kemp was the choice of the clergy, but the lay delegates held back and he was not elected. His chief rival was that champion of the evangelicals, the Rev. Mr. Dashiell. To add to Dr. Kemp's uncertainty as to what his next step should be he had been offered the presidency of the University of Pennsylvania as well as a call to another parish on the Eastern Shore. Fortified by these several evidences of esteem it is small wonder that he put a high value on himself. Nevertheless he accepted the call to St. Paul's though it brought reproaches from admirers on the Eastern Shore. One ardent lady wrote: "Well I suppose by this time the Parsonage has got on its new suit, and you are all now quite in style. I fear you will not be able to exist in one of our shabby Eastern Shore Houses . . . take care you don't among all these fine doings, get your Head turned round . . . your letters all begin My dear Miss Polly, now I don't like it at all, so pray put by your fine Baltimore *airs,* when you write to a plain old fashioned Eastern Shore friend."

To his friend, the Rev. Joseph Jackson, Kemp wrote early in January, 1813, to announce that he was fixed in the Parsonage on the hill. "The manner and circumstance of my call," he exulted, "were such as to leave me hardly any

[63]

option. The congregation, at least the great bulk of them, were so much intent upon having me that they would hardly bear to hear any other person mentioned." He understood that only one member of the Vestry had been against him, and added that his "reception and success have exceeded my most sanguine expectations."

In spite of the failure of the Convention of 1811 to elect him, Dr. Kemp had not given up the idea of being Suffragan Bishop. Even while he was getting settled in Baltimore he dropped a reminder to Bishop Claggett, attacking his rival Dashiell for departing from the canons and doctrines and intimating that Bishop Claggett was not doing all he might to throw his weight behind the Kemp candidacy. "My late friend, Dr. Bend," he said, "declared unequivocally in New York that I ought to be the person. I have been advised by at least two of the Episcopal order, on more occasions than one, to remain in Maryland with this in view." He ended on a note of humility: "I close this statement of my views and sentiments by assuring you that altho shut out from exertions and services, which I have performed, and would have to perform, with delight, I shall with the grace of God continue to be a zealous and industrious parish priest." Having thus prodded the Bishop he remarked to his friend Jackson: "I most sincerely hope that nothing escaped me to wound the good old man's feelings." There the matter of the bishopric rested for more than a year.

All the while the war with England was going on. The summer of 1813 was disturbed by a raid of the British fleet in Chesapeake Bay. Havre de Grace and Frenchtown were assaulted and burned, St. Michael's threatened, Kent and other islands occupied and plundered. Yet in spite of these attacks Kemp commented that "Little alarm exists here, but a great deal of distress. It does seem that we must suffer for our sins. God grant that our punishment may produce refor-

mation." The Rev. Frederick Beasley resigned to accept
the position of Provost of the University of Pennsylvania;
that left a vacancy that needed to be filled. An even more
trying problem was the animosity of Dr. Kemp's low church
adversary. "The most painful thing attending my situation,"
he lamented, "is that I cannot live in free and affectionate
intercourse with Mr. Dashiell which is very unpleasant."

Among the candidates for Associate Rector to replace Mr.
Beasley was a young clergyman from New York, the Rev.
William E. Wyatt, who preached at St. Paul's and made a
favorable impression there. He was sounded out but no
commitment was made. In March, 1814, Wyatt addressed
a letter to Dr. Kemp stating that he almost despaired of
being called to Baltimore. He had thought of accepting a
call to Wilmington, N.C., but that was far away from his
and his wife's family. Besides, he would like to be associated
with Dr. Kemp whose reputation for scholarship he knew
and whom he greatly admired.

The delay in giving the call to Mr. Wyatt may be explained by correspondence then passing between Dr. Kemp
and one Francis Scott Key, a practicing lawyer in Georgetown, District of Columbia, whose name had not yet been
made famous by writing the words for a song. He was an
ardent churchman who in his youth had thought seriously
of entering the Episcopal ministry, and was at the moment
a lay reader in the church at Georgetown. Kemp's letter
to Key has not survived, but Key's letter of April 4 in reply
indicates that Kemp suggested his taking orders and joining
him at St. Paul's. Key expressed doubt that at this late date
he could shift from law to the ministry and called attention
to the domestic problem involved. He reminded him that
he was a low churchman and differed with Kemp in respect
to strict adherence to forms. Two weeks later he followed
with another letter definitely rejecting the idea. Shortly after

the close of this correspondence Mr. Wyatt was called and accepted.

William E. Wyatt came of a New York Loyalist family. His father was an Englishman, his mother a New Englander who traced her ancestry back to the Mayflower company. He himself was born in Nova Scotia to which a group of Loyalists, including his parents, had fled at the time of the Revolution. Following the peace the Wyatts returned to New York. Young Wyatt was graduated from Columbia College, ordained to the priesthood and began his ministry on Staten Island, where he met and married Frances Billopp, granddaughter of Col. Christopher Billopp, another Loyalist. From the outset his tastes directed him toward the high church party in which he eventually became the leader in Maryland. This quality fitted him admirably for association with Dr. Kemp. His career would shortly reveal him also as a theologian.

The next few months were busy ones. May 4, 1814, the cornerstone for the new church was laid. The importance given to music in St. Paul's services and ceremonies was exemplified when the congregation assembled in the old church where an "Elegant anthem appropriate to the occasion was sung with great effect by a large number of the first description of singers." The congregation then proceeded to the site of the new church where an address was delivered by Dr. Kemp, a plate with the names of the rector, vestry, building committee and architect was inclosed in a stone which was deposited in place, and a blessing pronounced upon the undertaking.

In June the Diocesan Convention was held and, at long last, Kemp's ambition was realized; he was elected Suffragan Bishop. The victory, however, was not without tarnish. Dashiell and his clerical and lay supporters drew up an address in which they charged that the election had been achieved by surprise; that there had been no previous notice of it that would have put the low church people on their guard. Dashiell took the opportunity to point out that for the past fifteen years the church in Maryland had been divided, that both clergy and laity were involved and that the Convention "frequently exhibited more the appearance of an infuriated mob, than an harmonious assembly of Christians." A copy of the address was sent to the House of Bishops whose duty it was to pass on the action of the Convention.

Surprisingly, among the signers of this protest against Kemp's election was Francis Scott Key. In a letter to Kemp, Key explained that he had signed, not out of disrespect to his friend, but because he disapproved of the way Kemp had been elected. Bishop Claggett expressed similar sentiments, more strongly. He said little doubt could be entertained of his willingness to receive Kemp as Suffragan, but he opposed the mode of election as "unfair, unprecedented, and dangerously unfair because it was introduced and precipitated through the house at the eve of the convention, without one moment's previous notice to the party opposed, when I was satisfied that a few days, or even a few hours notice would have enabled them to defeat the object of the mover."

In spite of Bishop Claggett's obvious effort to be fair to both sides he failed to appease Dashiell who took the matter to the civil courts, but without success. On hearing of this the Bishop notified him that he had been guilty of contumacy and contempt of the Standing Committee. Dashiell retorted hotly that the Bishop was doing everything in his power to prejudice others against him.

Dashiell's address to the House of Bishops was no more fruitful than his appeal to the courts. So it came to pass that, September 1, Bishops William White of Pennsylvania,

John Henry Hobart of New York, and Richard Channing Moore of Virginia, wrote to Bishop Claggett to inform him that on that day they had consecrated Dr. Kemp as Suffragan Bishop of Maryland, and explaining their reasons for doing so in spite of the objections raised. The sacred ceremony took place in St. Paul's Church. Just as after a violent storm that clears the atmosphere the sun comes out and all is serene, so Dr. Kemp entered upon an exemplary administration that proved his choice to have been fully justified, however questionable the means of achieving it. Though Suffragan he continued as Rector of St. Paul's.

One of the first letters of congratulation to Kemp on his elevation came from Beasley in Philadelphia who wrote: "I consider that now . . . a light has arisen in the Church of Maryland out of the profound darkness which enveloped her affairs so long a time past." Beasley could not resist a facetiousness which may very well have been what prejudiced the serious minded Bend and Kemp against him. He concluded his letter: "Since Dashiel (sic) is down also you had better advise him to go over to his majesty (Napoleon) and offer himself to become his private chaplain to give him spiritual consolation for his misfortunes. (Napoleon was then in exile on the Island of Elba). As he has failed of the mitre, this will be a good post for him and his fallen fortunes."

Meanwhile the war with Great Britain reached a tragic climax when a powerful amphibious enemy force, including ships of the line, frigates, rocket ship and fireships, and transports bearing an army of several thousand men, entered Chesapeake Bay. In August they landed troops at Benedict, on the Patuxent River, marched across country toward Washington, routed an American army at Bladensburg, and completed the nation's shame by putting the government to flight and burning the Capitol, White House and Navy Yard.

Unlike Washington, which was totally unprepared, Baltimore had anticipated an attack even before the debacle there. For weeks working parties had been erecting fortifications on the city's eastern front from which direction the invaders were expected to come. The line of trenches, reinforced at intervals by artillery emplacements, extended along the ridge of Loudenslager's Hill, from the harbor all the way to the York Road. A bastion at the far southwestern end, in what is now Patterson Park, mounted with cannon, served as a link with Fort McHenry across the entrance to the inner basin. The local militia, some of whom had had their baptism of fire at Bladensburg were put on the alert, ready to take their posts at the first warning signal. They were joined by neighbor militiamen from Pennsylvania and Virginia.

The stillness of Sunday, September 11, was broken when the bell in the tower of St. Paul's along with the bells of all the other churches in town rang out to let the people know that the British fleet had been sighted. More than a hundred sail were standing off Bodkin Point at the mouth of the Patapsco. Within minutes the streets were filled with excited citizens, while militiamen in their picturesque uniforms said a hurried goodby to their families and went off to join their commands.

In this agonizing moment members of St. Paul's Parish stood ready to play their part. John Eager Howard, pillar of the Church and leading citizen of the town, had raised his voice in the counsels framing a plan of defense. The aging hero of Cowpens was a Federalist and as such had opposed war with England, but now that the enemy was at the gates his fighting blood was up and he forgot politics. The invading force was known to contain a goodly number of Wellington's veterans of the bloody Spanish Peninsula campaign against Napoleon, and the rout at Bladensburg discouraged the belief that the citizen soldiers of Maryland were any

[69]

match for them. The more timid townspeople therefore proposed offering the enemy a cash ransom to keep them away
from the city.

When Colonel Howard heard about it he was indignant.
"I have as much property at stake as most persons," he
declared. "And I have four sons in the field, but sooner
would I see my sons weltering in their blood and my property reduced to ashes, than so disgrace the country." He
spoke the sentiments of the majority.

In the early morning of Monday, September 12, mounted
videttes on the outposts galloped in to report that troops
under General Robert Ross had been landed at North Point,
on the peninsula between the Patapsco and Back River. From
the main defense line on Loudenslager's Hill the City Brigade, four regiments of infantry and an artillery detachment
marched out to meet them. Its commander was Brig.-General
John Stricker, a rock-ribbed Presbyterian. Presbyterians,
too, were General Samuel Smith, commander of all the forces
in Baltimore, and Col. Joseph Sterett of the 5th Regiment
which formed part of the City Brigade.

But men of St. Paul's were there too. Colonel Howard's
claim to having four sons in the field was no idle boast.
They were John Eager Jr., Benjamin, George and William.
Benjamin was captain of a company of the 5th. Another
member of the parish serving humbly in the ranks was none
other than William Bend, son of the old rector. The young
man who, two years before, had risked his life protesting
against the war, now was risking it in defense of his home
and fireside. Fortune was on his side and again he came
through unscathed.

The major contribution of St. Paul's to the victory on the
12th was that of a vestryman, Major Richard K. Heath.
Heath was second in command to Colonel Sterett of the 5th.
As the City Brigade moved out it fell to his lot to lead an

advanced detachment whose mission was to make contact with the enemy. This group opened the battle and in this first exchange of fire General Ross, the British commander, was killed. His death turned the tide in favor of the Americans. Though in the engagement on North Point Road the British drove the City Brigade back to the fortifications, they were so discouraged by the death of their leader that they did not risk an attack on the American main force in the trenches on the hill.

On September 13 it was the turn of the defenders in Fort McHenry to stand up under the bombardment of the British fleet and they did it so stoutly that the enemy gave up and the fleet sailed away. The land troops simultaneously retreated down the peninsula on the road by which they had come. Commanding the garrison of McHenry was another member of St. Paul's, Lt.-Col. George Armistead. A native of Virginia and a soldier in the regular army, he married a Baltimore girl a few years before the British invasion and thereafter called the city his home. At his death he was buried in St. Paul's graveyard. When a monument to him was proposed the suggestion was first made that it be erected in St. Paul's Church. Instead it was placed at City Spring, the present site of Mercy Hospital. From there it was moved to Federal Hill where it now stands.

Another of the St. Paul's people who showed up nobly under the test was their shepherd. As the British approached the city many civilians fled from it. But not Bishop Kemp. There was no question in his mind where his duty lay. Ten days after the battle he wrote: "I remained with my family in the city trusting to a divine hand that overrules all things. I am truly thankful to the Almighty that amidst the tremendous scene our hearts never fainted. Burying the dead, visiting the wounded and comforting the bereaved, has been my melancholly (sic) business ever since."

[71]

Bishop Kemp found time also to compose a prayer of Thanksgiving for the victory:

"O God, the Almighty Ruler of Nations, in whose hands are all power and dominion, while we note in grateful remembrance, the preservation of our city and people, on this memorable day, give us grace to deserve a continuance of thy protection and of thy favors. Preserve us from the influence of sin and the dangers of impiety—may we ever remember that while righteousness exalteth a nation, iniquity is the ruin and reproach of any people—and while we ascribe our preservation and our happiness to thy overruling power, let us ever worship and adore thee in spirit and in truth. Through Jesus Christ our Lord. Amen."

St. Paul's also figured in an historic sequel to the battle. To Francis Scott Key it brought imperishable fame as author of "The Star Spangled Banner." How Key went down the Bay on a cartel boat to the British fleet seeking the release of his friend Dr. Beanes, who was being held a prisoner; how he himself was detained during the bombardment of Ft. McHenry, and next day by "the dawn's early light" was thrilled to see the flag still flying and wrote his poem, is a familiar story. After Key got his inspiration he returned to the city and repaired to the Indian Queen Tavern where he put the poem down on paper and submitted it to his brother-in-law, Judge Joseph Nicholson. Delighted with it the Judge suggested that it be printed as a handbill under the title "The Defense of Fort McHenry." This was done and it became an instant popular success.

The next step was printing it as music. The tune to which the poem is sung has been identified as that of a drinking song called "To Anacreon in Heaven," Anacreon having been an ancient Greek poet, and an intemperate one. Prior to the American Revolution there sprang up in England Anacreontic Societies which used it as their theme song.

After the Revolution the tune found its way to America where it also achieved popularity and was used for a number of patriotic songs, Key's words fitted the tune so perfectly there is little doubt that "Anacreon" was running through his head when he composed the poem.

At this time Joseph Carr and his son Thomas were organists at Christ Church and St. Paul's. They also had a music store on Baltimore Street. Key not only was a friend of Bishop Kemp but his daughter had married a son of John Eager Howard. In view of these close relationships with the parish, Key took his problem to the Carrs. Thus it came about that in late September, 1814, Key's poem was published as music under its now familiar title: "The Star Spangled Banner." The original sheet music bears the words: "Adapt. and Arrg. by T.C." "T.C." was of course Thomas Carr.

There is an interesting sequel to St. Paul's part in perpetuating Key's work. March 3, 1931, more than a century after Key took his poem to Carr, by act of Congress "The Star Spangled Banner" was officially designated as our National Anthem. Author of the House Resolution which led to the passage of the act was Representative J. Charles Linthicum, of Maryland. At the time, Representative Linthicum was a communicant of St. Paul's Church.

CHAPTER VI

A SCANDAL AND A NEW CHURCH

Y the end of January, 1815, Baltimore was so secure from the enemy that Dr. Beasley, in Philadelphia, could write playfully to Bishop Kemp: "If those dogs, the British, will be acting so uncivilly as to be frightening your women and children . . . I think you clergymen had better take upon yourselves the task of meeting them, and try if your gowns, lawn sleeves and preachings and Dashiell's long visages and wry faces, sanctimonious airs and ex tempore prayers will not prove a defence against their firelocks, muskets and bayonets and ammunition."

Now firmly installed as Suffragan, Dr. Kemp was taking on much of the aging and ailing Claggett's responsibilities. He presided at the Diocesan Convention which met in the spring and reported to his superior: "Never did I attend a more harmonious and more agreeable convention. The order of the clergy was not numerous. The laity were able, respectable and more in number than I had calculated upon. I exhibited my commission and of course presided . . . in consequence of a conversation which took place between Bishop Moore of Virginia and myself on the conduct of Mr. Dashiell, I strongly recommended to my particular friends to manifest a degree of moderation, that might soften his refractory spirit."

[75]

Nevertheless the fiery Dashiell continued to be a disturbing element as Bishop Kemp disclosed in a letter to his friend, the Rev. William Duke: "I have indeed much joy and delight in the prosecution of the duties of my office, but our poor church is still harassed by the artifice and party spirit which still exists. Were Mr. Dashiell and his brother Handy a little more humble and more pacific, all would be harmony and love."

Relief from this torment came in a sudden and quite unexpected way—common report charged Dashiell with immoral conduct! He was summoned before the Standing Committee of the Diocese. Bishop Kemp had surrendered his seat on that body to his assistant minister, Mr. Wyatt, and he had no desire to attend in his official capacity ". . . until I see what turn the present disgusting and horrible business, that has astonished and agitated this city for some days respecting Dr. Dashiell takes . . . Our poor church is bleeding at every pore." Evidently the painful task of sitting in judgment was one he did not relish and he hoped Bishop Claggett would undertake it. He concluded his letter to the Bishop: "God knows I have a heart above anything like joy in the fall of my enemy." The result of the hearing was that Mr. Dashiell resigned and was degraded from the ministry. In justice to him let it be said that he lived for many years more in the community and that nothing further was said in criticism of his morals.

On August 2, 1816, Bishop Claggett died at his home in Prince George's County and Dr. Kemp moved up to the bishopric, being the second to hold that office in the diocese of Maryland. That, however, did not prevent his continuing as Rector of St. Paul's where he had the help of his able assistant Mr. Wyatt. There is only one other instance in the American church of a clergyman serving simultaneously as parish priest and bishop of a diocese, namely that of John

Henry Hobart, Rector of Trinity Church, New York, and Bishop of the Diocese of New York.

Peace once more restored by the signing of the treaty with Great Britain, work on the new church, which had been laid aside for four years, was resumed. Finally on February 11, 1817, it was consecrated by the Bishop who at the Diocesan Convention referred to it as "perhaps the largest and most elegant building of the kind in the United States."

The new edifice stood at the extreme northwest corner of the lot at Charles and Saratoga Streets. It was built of brick trimmed with marble, and was 126 feet long and 84 feet wide. The style was "Grecian Doric." It had a handsome portico facing on Charles Street supported by four coupled fluted columns. Its steeple, reminiscent of Sir Christopher Wren's churches in London, was three stories high and each story was supported by columns: the first being Grecian Doric, the second Corinthian and the third Composite. The whole was surmounted by a cupola, under which was hung a bell, and the height of the steeple was 126 feet. The front of the church was enclosed by a handsome iron railing. Seating in the interior was increased by a gallery, also supported by columns, in the Greek style. This was the third church to occupy the lot which had been bought at the time of the laying out of Baltimore Town.

The edifice was unquestionably the masterpiece of the local architect Robert Cary Long. Simultaneous with this ambitious structure of the Episcopalians was the erection of the beautiful Roman Catholic Cathedral a few blocks north on Cathedral Street, the work of *the* Benjamin Latrobe. Maximilien Godefroy's Unitarian Church at Charles and Franklin Streets, his gothic chapel at St. Mary's Seminary on Paca Street, and his Battle Monument; Robert Mills's Washington Monument and his First Baptist Church, and Latrobe's Exchange, all rising within a few years of each other, represented a golden age of architecture and testified to Baltimore's importance as one of the great cities of the nation.

The new church called for a new bell, leaving the old one in the bell tower to be disposed of; and thereby hangs a tale. Move the clock forward some thirty-one years to September 21, 1848, when the newly built St. Philip's Episcopal Church, in Laurel, Maryland, was consecrated. At 11 o'clock that day, Bishop Whittingham in his robes, preceded by twelve priests in surplices and stoles and one deacon in his surplice, went in procession to the church and commenced the solemn services of the occasion. Says the *Church Times* in reporting the ceremony: "To some who were present the sound of the bell which was ringing in the tower gave an additional interest to the scene, and awakened pleasant associations, as it was the bell which belonged to St. Paul's Church, Baltimore." This must have been the bell that was discarded in 1817. It continues to ring in St. Philip's today. It bears no mint or other identifying mark. Its St. Paul's lineage, however, is supported by the fact that there were close family and social ties between the vestrymen and members of St. Paul's and the Caprons, Snowdens, Heaths and Ellicotts who constituted the Episcopal pioneers in Laurel.

The new church also boasted a new organ comparable to it in size and volume. So, as in the case of the bell, the old organ could be discarded. It will be recalled that two organs were imported from England in 1804, one for St. Paul's and one for Christ Church. January 2, 1817, a month before the consecration of the new church, the *Federal Gazette,* a Baltimore newspaper, advertised for sale an organ made of mahogany with gilt pipes. The name of the builder was given as G. P. England, London, and the date of construction as 1804. Today in St. Joseph's Roman Catholic Church, Taneytown, the organ bears the original nameplate of G. P. England and the date 1804. It exactly fits the description of

[78]

the organ in the advertisement. It has been there since 1875. There can be little doubt that it is the old St. Paul's organ. Its history between 1817 and 1875 and how it got to St. Joseph's has yet to be traced.

Mention has already been made of the "elegant anthem" sung at the laying of the cornerstone of the Long church in 1814. That a choir capable of performing elaborate music was functioning in 1820 is noted in a newspaper clipping of that year: "An Oratorio was lately performed at St. Paul's Church. The music was indeed sweet, but the result was much sweeter, for, after deducting all necessary expenses, it placed the handsome sum of $703.67 in the hands of the ladies directors of the Female Charity School, a well managed and highly interesting institution." The event fitted in with the installation of Christopher Meinecke, as organist and choirmaster, and its success may well be attributed to him. Mr. Meinecke, who had just come to this country from Germany, was a well trained musician. A bachelor, he had a house at Lexington and Liberty Streets. He is recorded as giving numerous piano recitals and having many pupils. His teaching brought him a good income and by wise and careful investing he amassed a sizeable fortune. Mr. Meinecke continued as organist until 1855, and his tenure of 35 years is the longest of any organist and choirmaster in the history of St. Paul's.

With the nation's material growth and prosperity there came worldliness and indifference to traditional moral standards. Deism and agnosticism increased. This circumstance could not have failed to affect the religious life of the Baltimore community in general and St. Paul's Parish in particular. But there still were many devout people among the various denominations who recognized the challenge and fought back. Bishop Kemp was eminently fitted as leader in a church militant. In embracing the Episcopal Church he had not cast off his strict Scottish Presbyterian habits. He had determined opinions of his own and the courage to express them. One might question his judgment, and at times his impetuosity, but nobody could deny his frankness and his courage in following wherever his conscience led him. At St. Paul's he continued the high church tradition and vigorously opposed any departure from a strict observance of the canons and the liturgy. This brought him into conflict with the leaders of the Episcopal Church in Virginia which was dominated by the evangelicals. Since the District of Columbia was then in the Diocese of Maryland Bishop Kemp was painfully aware that part of his domain was particularly vulnerable to Virginia influence. His correspondence reveals that he was in controversy with Virginia churchmen over a period of years. He objected to the proposed publication of a church paper in the District on the assumption that it would support Unitarianism. Nor could he bring himself to approve the establishment of a theological seminary in Virginia. Bishop Moore, who had been one of his consecrators, wrote reproaching him for a long silence, asking in what way he had given offense, assuring him that he had defended him before the Virginia clergy and had tried to keep the church united. The Rev. William H. Wilmer, another member of the Virginia party, felt that Bishop Kemp had accused him unfairly of meddling in Maryland matters.

The Bishop kept a close eye on church newspapers and did not hesitate to voice his protest against articles he deemed injurious. He canceled his subscription to the "Portico" for publishing one which he charged with being "an open and outrageous attack upon Divine Revelation." To the Rev. William Hawley, editor of a paper called "Repertory," he wrote, taking him to task for insinuations in the editorial notes which Kemp thought reflected on him. This Hawley denied though he later charged the Bishop with having exceeded the constitution and canons in criticizing others. Yet these heated arguments over beliefs and forms did not lead in this case to personal animus. When shortly thereafter the Bishop was saddened by the death of Mrs. Kemp, Mr. Hawley was among the first of many to extend his condolences.

When the Bishop felt it his duty to reprove individuals he did not let personal friendship or the important status of the person under censure deter him. An impressive case in point was when the Bishop learned that Francis Scott Key had taken it upon himself to baptize an infant. He sat down at once and, in spite of his past intimacy with Key, addressed a letter to him emphasizing the importance of Baptism as a sacrament, the necessity for the church's sustaining a distinction between the clergy and the laity and for reserving to the clergy the administering of the rite of Baptism.

To this reproof Key replied hotly. He said the mother had brought the child to him at night thinking it was dying and asked him to baptize it. This was while he was lay reader of the church in Georgetown. He suggested that she go instead to the Rector but she said she did not believe the child would live long enough for that. Under those circumstances Key said he felt justified in using his own judgment, and he baptized the child. He intimated that under similar circumstances he would do the same thing again. As others had done in controversies with the Bishop, Key regretted that the latter had discussed the incident with other people before getting the facts from him.

Another instance of the Bishop's interference in a highly personal matter was in threatening to withhold Communion from Hannah Kitty Chase, the elderly widow of Justice Chase who for so long before his death had been active in church affairs. If one may judge by Mrs. Chase's letters to the Bishop her offense had been nothing more than failure to give one of her daughters, Mrs. Barney, the financial help the Bishop thought proper. Justice Chase died without leaving a will, the widow claimed her dower rights, and this resulted in an unpleasant quarrel between Mrs. Chase and her children and stepchildren. On receipt of her first letter of protest the Bishop went directly to see her and, according to her story, dictated what provision she should make for Mrs. Barney. This, she declared, was counter to the advice of other respectable gentlemen of the town. The matter ended with Mrs. Chase's announcement that if denied Communion by the Bishop she would leave St. Paul's and worship elsewhere.

In Great Britain, too, the Church had encountered a godlessness such as the practicing Christians in Maryland bemoaned. There the antidote was the printing of religious tracts to be distributed among the public. The tract movement achieved great popularity, found its way across the ocean and reached Maryland. As early as 1815 there was organized "The Protestant Episcopal Female Society of Baltimore, for the Dissemination of Religious Knowledge." Its declared object was to purchase or publish tracts "to promote practical piety." Every tract so used had first to be submitted to Bishop Kemp and approved by Mr. Wyatt and two-thirds of the board of managers of the society. The Bishop took great interest in the movement and eventually became head of the society. By the time of the annual meeting in May, 1818, it was reported that some 9000 tracts and books had been distributed. To Episcopal congregations there also were sent catechisms and Prayer Books. Tracts were circulated among "the poor," on steamboats, in the almshouse, the jail, the dispensary, the hospitals, and to most of the taverns in Baltimore city.

The tracts themselves were little homilies directed at such evils as profanity and irreligion, and at such conventional sinners as the spendthrift, the drunkard and the Sabbath breaker. As the movement progressed boys were organized into the "Juvenile Male Auxiliary Tract Society," whose members subscribed a penny a week to finance the purchase, publication and distribution of the tracts.

Still another manifestation of the program of educating people in the Christian ideal was the establishment of Sunday Schools. The first step was taken at St. Paul's on August 20, 1817, when the proposal to establish a Sunday School was adopted. A constitution and by-laws were drawn up and on September 14 the school opened with 21 scholars in attendance. All of them were boys. Membership called for no little physical and spiritual fortitude, for the scholars were expected to be present at sessions both in the morning and afternoon and also both at Morning and Evening Prayer. This program was observed on Sundays throughout the entire year. None the less, on the afternoon of the first day, two more scholars were added to the original 21. Membership continued to grow until at the meeting on February 15, 1818, there were no less than 103 scholars on the roll. Here the pace appears to have faltered for only 50 answered to their names while 53 were marked as absent.

Administration of the School was in the hands of a superintendent and a board of managers, and they too were subject to stiff discipline. A manager or a teacher who was late was subject to a fine of 25 cents, while a tardy superintendent had to pay a penalty of a whole dollar. For some unexplained reason, during the first decade of its existence the Sunday School was confined to boys. It was not until February 3, 1827, that the first girls were admitted. It seems that the attitude and conduct of the boys was not left to depend entirely on their godliness. One of them in his old age remarked: "Vividly do I remember the cross old sexton, with his rattan switch. How I dreaded it. He failed not to use it when needed. There were no $5000 damage suits in those good old days."

The revival spirit saw sin lurking in unexpected places and called for the most strait-laced conduct. Thus, for example, one young man of the St. Paul's congregation, writing to a young lady whom he later married, confessed to a lamentable fall from grace. His offence was that he had been so wicked as to attend the theater, having been persuaded to do so by his father who accompanied him! That Bishop Kemp promoted this feeling is indicated by a letter received by him from a man who said the Bishop had implied that the man had gone to the theater on the sly. This the writer denied, adding for good measure that he considered going to the theater no sin. To an Eastern Shore Tilghman, who had dodged attending a diocesan convention on the excuse that it conflicted with his farming, the Bishop wrote a reproachful letter: "It cannot, it must not be so. Are our church concerns to be superceded by seeding wheat!" One wonders if the "seeding" pun was intentional.

The manumission of slaves, which a decade before had received stimulus from Dr. George Buchanan and the anti-slavery society, was creating a problem. The freed men found much difficulty adjusting to their new condition for they had virtually nowhere to go. A possible solution which attracted many people was the proposal to establish a nation for them in Africa. Again some members of St. Paul's took an active interest in the plan. John Eager Howard was vice-president of the Colonization Society which was organized on a national scale with headquarters in Washington. He also was president of a local branch which eventually sponsored one of the provinces of Liberia bearing the name of Maryland. When some years after Bishop Kemp's death the time came to write a code of laws for this province, it was a vestryman of St. Paul's, Hugh Davey Evans, a lawyer, who did the work. Bishop Kemp was keenly interested in spreading the Gospel in Africa and preached a sermon on it which brought a grateful letter from the Rev. Samuel Bacon, a missionary there, who said the sermon introduced ". . . a new era in missions and a bright page in their history. I will insist the mission to Africa has been begun by our church. It was begun by you, Sir, and it will assuredly prosper."

Closer to home was the need for missionary endeavor in western Maryland. While Episcopalians wrangled among themselves over high church and low church, other denominations were making inroads into their membership. The Hagerstown congregation addressed a complaint to the Bishop against their Rector, The Rev. Joseph Jackson, whom they charged with affectation and insincerity. This must have been embarrassing to the Bishop since he and Jackson were close friends. The problem was solved for the time being by Jackson being removed from Hagerstown and sent as a sort of missionary on a tour of the western counties. His journey brought from him a succession of lamentations over the state of the church in that quarter. At Williamsport Jackson said he found a few "nominal professors," but they seemed half inclined to surrender either to the Presbyterians or the Methodists. Jackson laid the blame to ignorance on the part of the laity of what they professed to believe. On the other hand he recognized the risk of combat when the Episcopalians were so weak. ". . . were we to hold up the Church as having exclusive pretensions to a Divine origin, we should provoke war at an impossible moment." Jackson's departure from Hagerstown did not improve the situation there. His successor, the Rev. John Curtis Clay reported strong antagonism between the high and low church parties in his congregation. He complained of the liberal members and was shocked when two of them went so far

[85]

as to take communion in a Presbyterian church. Next to vice, he said, nothing pained him more than "the amalgamative spirit which thinks all sects equal."

Most disturbing too was the activity of another religious group which had staked a claim in Baltimore, calling themselves "Unitarians." They were composed chiefly of New Englanders transplanted in the city who at the time were still affiliated with the Congregational Church. They scoffed at such doctrines as the Trinity and the Apostolic Succession, and also questioned whether there was any scriptural justification for the three orders of the ministry—Bishops, Priests and Deacons. Rather defiantly they had erected that beautiful edifice not a mile to the north of St. Paul's and within the very shadow of the new Roman Catholic Cathedral. This raised a question whether the Episcopalians should defend themselves against this assault on the very foundation of their faith, or proudly ignore it. There was precedent aplenty for the criticism of one sect by another. A Presbyterian divine had but lately from the pulpit criticized the Episcopal Prayer Book to point a moral. A Unitarian minister, the Rev. Jared Sparks, had not hesitated to take issue with a book written by Bishop White of Pennsylvania. And Dr. Sparks had come to Baltimore to serve as minister of the Unitarian congregation. He later was to be President of Harvard College and biographer of George Washington.

It was generally agreed that if an Episcopalian David was to go forth to meet the Unitarian Goliath the person best fitted for the job was the Assistant Minister of St. Paul's, Doctor Wyatt, for he had been honored with a "D.D." degree by the University of Maryland. He was professor of theology at that institution and recognized as a scholar of the first order. The upshot of it was that the Episcopalians decided to do battle. With no little coaching from Bishop White and others of his fellow clergy, Dr. Wyatt from his pulpit delivered a comprehensive address later published under the formidable title: "Sermon Exhibiting Some of the Principle Doctrines of the Protestant Episcopal Church of the United States by which the Church is distinguished from other denominations of Christians." As had been anticipated, Dr. Sparks rose to the challenge and replied in a series of "Letters on the ministry, ritual and doctrines of the Protestant Episcopal Church addressed to the Rev. William E. Wyatt, D.D. etc. in reply to 'a Sermon'." "The controversy aroused lively interest at the time. It is doubtful if either church won any converts by the exchange. Certainly no blow of either champion reached a vital spot, since both churches survive to this day.

Meanwhile Dr. Wyatt found himself engaged in another controversy that threatened to end his ministry in St. Paul's Parish before it had fairly begun. This one was with the Vestry. Soon after his arrival in Baltimore as assistant to Bishop Kemp he evinced keen interest in the prisoners in the Maryland Penitentiary and voluntarily served that institution as its chaplain. Imagine the consternation of some members of the congregation when it was learned that Dr. Wyatt had permitted a convicted murderer to be buried in St. Paul's graveyard, where rested all that was mortal of certain former rectors of the church and leaders of the community, as well as of those other members of the congregation who regarded it as a mark of prestige to be interred there. The Vestry lost no time advising Dr. Wyatt of their displeasure.

Dr. Wyatt was equally prompt to defend his action. True, he said, he had allowed the murderer to be buried there. It was in a section of the graveyard reserved for strangers. The murderer was a young man who, before his execution, had repented his act, professed the Christian religion, and been baptized by Dr. Wyatt. His dying request was that he be buried in St. Paul's graveyard. Dr. Wyatt declared that nobody was more deserving a Christian burial; and, since the Vestry had made no rule against such a burial, he had violated no law.

Then in a letter to Bishop Kemp he stated that he felt entitled to the support of the Vestry and warned: "Should they not afford it, but yield my wishes to the unchristian caprice of a few individuals who are always clamouring about something whether of moment or not, they do not manifest that kind of regard for my services which should induce me to overlook other considerations, prompting me to the choice of another situation." This was nothing short of an ultimatum. He asked that a meeting of the Vestry be called at once to settle the matter. They apparently had adopted a resolution to which he objected; probably a proposal for disinterment. A few weeks later Dr. Wyatt reported to the Bishop that he was not yet satisfied, but he had calmed down. He concluded that the "clamour and discontent" was confined to a very few. He was mollified also by expressions of astonishment and disapprobation over the proposal to disinter the body and by offers of two gentlemen to receive it into their own lots if the Vestry persisted. He was generous enough to add that he was convinced the Vestry was doing what it thought was right. There the record of the incident ends. Dr. Wyatt stayed on.

About this time Dr. Wyatt's health became a matter of concern to his friends, some of whom expressed the fear his days were numbered. The nature of his ailment was not disclosed. In the hope of getting relief he made a long trip to the South and followed it with a visit to England where he underwent an operation by the well known English surgeon, Sir Ashley Cooper. He returned home considerably restored. One member of the clergy who informed Bishop Kemp that he was offering up "sincere prayers for the restoration of

Dr. Wyatt's health" was the Rev. John Johns. In view of their later relationship his interest is significant. A son of the Chief Justice of Delaware he recently had accepted a call to the Maryland diocese. The clergyman who introduced him to the Bishop stated that Johns was a graduate of Princeton College and its Theological Seminary where he was highly esteemed, and that he might be considered a valuable acquisition to the church. His examination for orders had afforded the highest satisfaction to those who were present at it.

It was as well that Dr. Wyatt's health had improved for very soon he was called on to assume greater responsibilities. In the autumn of 1827 Bishop Kemp went to Philadelphia to take part in the consecration of the Rev. Henry W. Onderdonk. On the way home he traveled in a stagecoach whose driver was drunk. Trying to pass another coach on a narrow road the driver lost control, the coach went off the road and landed upside down in a rocky gully. The Bishop was thrown against a pile of rocks and severely injured. He was brought home alive but died the next day. He was then in his sixty-second year. News of his death was received with sorrow throughout the Diocese. Resolutions expressing their admiration for his services were adopted by the clergy and many letters of condolence were received by members of his family, by the assistant minister and the Vestry and congregation of St. Paul's. Mrs. Kemp had died a few years before; surviving were a son and a daughter. At a meeting of the Vestry it was resolved that all members wear crepe on the left arm for three months and that the clergy wear crepe scarfs for six months while officiating.

At the time of his death, in addition to being the Bishop of the Diocese of Maryland and Rector of St. Paul's, Dr. Kemp was Provost of the University of Maryland, president of the Bible Society and an active member of all the general benevolent societies of the city. During his incumbency Baltimore's population had grown from 50,000 in 1813 to 75,000 in 1827, making it close to the largest city in the nation. St. Paul's and Christ Church had grown along with it, their communicants combined having increased from 170 to 350. This, in spite of the fact that two new Episcopal churches had been erected, raising the number within the territorial limits of St. Paul's Parish to six. Communicants in the city had increased from 327 in 1817 to 900 in 1827.

This favorable picture in the city was offset by a continued lagging in the country portions of the parish; and also by the distressing fact that little or no progress had been made in relieving the animosity between the high church and the low church parties. Though many of the reports of parishes in other parts of the Diocese revealed churches that were languishing and losing members to more alert denominations, nevertheless some progress had been made. At the time of Bishop Kemp's consecration there had been but 30 clergy in the entire Diocese; at his death there were 52.

Dr. Kemp was recognized by his contemporaries as a fine scholar and theologian. He was said to have had an extreme aversion against any display of learning and to have cultivated simplicity in style and manner. In relations with his fellow men he was determined in his opinions and little inclined to compromise with those of others. In his earlier career when he was aspiring to be Suffragan his correspondence indicated neither reticence nor false modesty. This was not conceit but his downright honesty in believing he was the best man for the job. Events proved that his judgment was correct. So too when he felt a member of the church needed correction, as has been noted, he allowed no personal considerations to soften the rebuke. Even those who experienced the sting recognized the value of his discipline. Perhaps his manner is best expressed by Bishop Hobart who, in a letter to him remarked: "I shared some of my happiest hours in your company; even when you are engaged in scolding me you do it kindly."

There was no question that Dr. Wyatt would succeed Dr. Kemp as rector of St. Paul's Parish where he had already served for thirteen years. Who would succeed him as Bishop of Maryland was another matter.

CHAPTER VII

WYATT TAKES OVER

IT was altogether appropriate that Dr. Wyatt deliver the address at the funeral of the Bishop, which was later published along with excerpts from Dr. Kemp's sermons and a biographical sketch under the title "The Monument." Dr. Wyatt was president of the Standing Committee and, as such, presiding officer of the Diocese until a new bishop should be chosen. He was now 39 years old, his family was large and still growing. There were six children—four boys and two girls, the oldest of whom was William, aged eleven. Two children had died in infancy, and two boys and a girl would be born in the Parsonage to which the family now moved.

Family tradition has it that Dr. Wyatt's mother and father came to live with him. Mrs. Wyatt, too, had a widowed mother, a sister and a brother who made periodic visits so that the household was a prodigious one. In fact it was more than the existing parsonage could accommodate, and it was at this time that it was enlarged. Within its walls was staged the beginning of the Wyatt clan which eventually spread broadly over the local area and put out branches far and wide. Two sons, William and Thomas, were to follow their father's calling while the third and youngest, Charles

Hanfield, was to be a stalwart layman, serving St. Paul's as a vestryman for 34 years. A descendent known to all television audiences throughout the nation today is Jane Wyatt.

In the nineteenth century it was quite the vogue for English travelers to come to the United States, take notes, and return home to write books about their impressions, usually of a critical and supercilious nature. Americans appear to have been pleased at any attention paid them, no matter how uncomplimentary the authors. So the books found ready sale. Baltimore, interestingly enough, came off better than most cities of the country.

One such traveler was Mrs. Basil Hall who unblushingly entitled her book *The Aristocratic Journey* and in the subtitle described it as "outspoken letters." That she was an aristocrat and that she was privileged to speak out was based on the slender qualification of being the granddaughter-in-law of an English nobleman. In December 1827, she visited Baltimore, a few weeks after Dr. Wyatt had succeeded Bishop Kemp as Rector of St. Paul's where Mrs. Hall attended a service. We can be grateful to her for this first-hand account of her experience: "We went in the morning (December 24) to St. Paul's Church where we were much gratified both by the reading and preaching of Dr. Wyatt, the clergyman who (sic) we met at Saratoga, though we had no idea then who he was, or even his name. He is infinitely the best reader and the best preacher that we have heard in this country." Two days later Dr. Wyatt escorted the visitor to the jail and penitentiary, in which he was especially interested and which at that time were generally included in Baltimore's sightseeing tours. Mrs. Hall was less complimentary of these than she had been of Dr. Wyatt's reading and preaching.

It must have been about this time, or perhaps a little earlier, that a fellow clergyman described Dr. Wyatt as being "a gentleman of the old school who went to church in small clothes, silk stockings and silver-buckled shoes, and always wore a silk gown in the streets. He wore gloves in the pulpit with one finger cut for convenience in turning the leaves of his manuscript."

On his visit to England Dr. Wyatt enjoyed an intimacy with John Henry Newman, John Keble and Edward Pusey, leaders of the Oxford Movement, an experience which accentuated his high church leanings. He brought back with him a Eucharistic vestment which he used in services at St. Paul's, the first to be worn in this country. He is credited also with having initiated in the American church the practice of "reserving the Holy Sacrament," which is to say, reverently putting away for future use the elements which have not been consumed in the service.

By now Christ Church felt strong enough to stand on its own feet and St. Paul's was quite willing to surrender the responsibility which was inevitable while the two congregations were administered jointly. Consequently in the spring after Bishop Kemp's death, by mutual agreement, Christ Church became a separate congregation. It was inevitable that there should be some dispute over the terms but this was not serious. Another factor entering into the separation was that Christ Church became the Baltimore headquarters of the low church party.

Its first act as an independent body was to call the Rev. John Johns as Rector. He was the promising young clergyman who had come to the Diocese of Maryland from Delaware by way of the Princeton Theological Seminary. Simultaneously Thomas Farmer Billopp, Dr. Wyatt's brother-in-law, was installed at St. Paul's as Assistant.

When in 1829 the first Diocesan Convention met after the death of Bishop Kemp to elect his successor, the two leading candidates were Dr. Wyatt, representing the high church faction, and Dr. Johns the low. Sentiment was so equally

divided between the groups, and the feeling being too intense for compromise, neither candidate received the requi-
site number of votes. Another Convention was called and
a second attempt made to elect, but again failed.

On June 22, a letter was sent out addressed to "the lay
members of the Protestant Episcopal Church of Maryland"
purporting to have been signed in behalf of "a majority of
the lay members of the convention." It pointed out that
under the Constitution of the Diocese until two-thirds of the
clergymen had concurred in recommending a candidate, the
voice of the laity could not be expressed. They wanted the
Constitution changed. While Dr. Wyatt had the majority of
lay delegates behind him, Dr. Johns had the support of a
majority of the clergy. The latter had been heavily infil-
trated by graduates of the Virginia Theological Seminary
which was strongly evangelical. Bishop Kemp's fears when
he refused to give his support to the founding of that institution appeared to have been justified.

Nevertheless the stalemate continued. At this point Francis Scott Key entered the fray. Another convention was
scheduled for the spring of 1830. In a letter to a friend Key
stated that he planned to attend as a lay delegate and that
he had a proposal for putting an end to the troubled and
divided state of the church. This was ". . . to lay aside
both Wyatt and Johns and take a new man from another
diocese . . . let both sides give up something and meet in
a spirit of conciliation." He confessed that he was a low
churchman, adding, "I never could believe (though I tried
hard) in the '*jus divinum*' or draw any of the conclusions
that are usually deduced from such a position by those who
hold it." Whether or not Key alone was responsible, Dr.
Wyatt and Dr. Johns withdrew and an election resulted,
though the new Bishop did not come from another diocese.
He was the Rev. William Murray Stone who had a parish

on the Eastern Shore and traced his ancestry to William Stone, a provincial governor of Maryland.

If Dr. Wyatt was disappointed over his failure to be elected, he gave no indication of it. He had little time for self pity and little reason for it since he was virtually bishop in everything but name. As president of the Standing Committee, an office he was to hold for the rest of his life, he had to attend to many of the administrative duties of the Diocese, including such unpleasant ones as hearing charges against members of the clergy. Bishop Stone was not in the best of health and at least on one occasion took a prolonged trip during which Dr. Wyatt assumed all of his responsibilities.

Nor were Dr. Wyatt's executive talents overlooked by the national church. Beginning with the General Convention of 1817 he appeared regularly as a clerical delegate representing the Maryland diocese; in 1829 he was elected president of the House of Deputies, and was re-elected seven times. He might have continued in that office even longer had he not in 1853 declined re-election. In addition to all this he found time not only to prepare scholarly sermons but also to write a number of tracts which won popular appeal. "The Christian Altar," "Christian Office for the Use of Families and Individuals," and "Morning Visits to the Rector's Study" were among the titles. "The Parting Spirit's Address to His Mother" had the greatest success. It was read not only in Maryland but throughout the country, and went through many editions, one of them appearing nearly fifteen years after the author's death.

Dr. Wyatt possessed a dignity and reserve that at times was mistaken for indifference or arrogance. He once offended one of his best friends, a fellow clergyman, by failing to answer a letter reporting the death of the writer's child. It brought the rebuke: "Your ardour and tenderness are not

often equalled. But you are, if you will allow me to express
my opinion, too much inclined to doubt the warmth and
sincerity of those who call themselves your friends." Dr.
Wyatt promptly made amends for what obviously was an
oversight. Bishop Jackson Kemper, of Wisconsin, once accused him "of selfconceited and arrogant views which com-
pel him to insult any bishop who may come in contact with
him upon his own ground (the precincts of his own parish).
If I am wrong I shall be particularly gratified to be set
right." This came with ill grace from the Bishop of Wisconsin, Dr. Wyatt having given financial aid to a church in
Bishop Kemper's struggling frontier diocese. These occasional reproaches were more than offset by admirers who
considered the very ground he walked on sacred. St. Paul's
was now getting many appeals from the mission field. One
came from its namesake, St. Paul's, in Monrovia, capital of
Liberia. They were to increase with the years and with the
growing reputation of St. Paul's as a prosperous congregation.
They seldom went unanswered.

It is inevitable that in a Church as old as St. Paul's legends
arise which on close examination are found to have little
basis in fact. For example, an aged parishioner included in
his reminiscences the statement that he had been present in
the Church when the Marquis de Lafayette attended service
there during his visit to Baltimore in 1824. Yet, though
contemporary newspaper accounts carried a detailed report
of his movements, they nowhere mention the incident. On
the contrary they state that he and his party went to Mass
at the Catholic Cathedral, which seems plausible since he
was a member of that faith.

Still another incident which had it occurred would have
been during Dr. Wyatt's ministry, was the rumored secret
marriage at St. Paul's of Edgar Allan Poe to his first cousin,
Virginia Clemm. The poet then was 26 years old and Vir-

ginia was but thirteen. One biographer states that he took great pains to examine the report and found it correct. This was based on a marriage license taken out by Poe on September 22, 1835, and on the reported statement of Maria Clemm, Virginia's mother. But there is no record of the marriage on the Parish Register. A more detailed account says that the ceremony was performed by the Rev. John Johns. Dr. Johns was never a rector of St. Paul's; but he was of Christ Church which separated from St. Paul's before 1835. Thus St. Paul's is denied the claim to this romantic incident even if such a secret marriage occurred in Baltimore before the well authenticated later marriage in Richmond. The Christ Church Register has no record of such a marriage, either.

There is one picturesque episode that merits brief mention. In the 1830's a familiar figure on the streets was a Negro centenarian known as "Old Hagar," who inspired terror among the superstitious. Gowned and capped in white, hooded and veiled in black, supported by a long staff in one hand and an umbrella in the other, and bearing a black bag and book, she hobbled about mumbling to herself. Some said she had the evil eye; others identified her staff as a wizard's wand, imagined that her bag held the making of charms and spells, and that the book was a treatise on the black arts. She was said to sleep in her coffin and her end fitted neatly with the legend; for one night while she slept her bed caught fire and she was burned to death. An examination of her magic bag, however, revealed nothing more than remedies for her "misery." As for the "book of black arts" it proved to be a Psalter from St. Paul's Church to which she turned regularly for charity.

A public spirited member of the congregation in the early days of the Wyatt ministry was Isaac McKim. Associated with his father in the shipping firm of John McKim and

Son he amassed a fortune, and their merchantmen were known in all ports of the world. When the British attack on Baltimore was imminent the firm advanced $50,000 for the city's defenses, and, during the invasion, Isaac acted as aide to General Sam Smith. In 1821 he and his brother established a free school for boys and girls in memory of their parent who was known as "Quaker John," and a few years later built and endowed a second school. In these institutions 200 pupils were educated every year. The austere temple style building with its Doric pillars which housed one of them is still a landmark in East Baltimore.

Most famous of the McKim ships was the clipper *Ann McKim,* named for Isaac's wife. Built in 1832 she was for years the largest and fastest merchant ship afloat. She had a copper bottom, rails and hatches were of mahogany and the cannon she carried were of the finest brass. McKim also served on the Library Board and the Board of the Society to Protect Free Negroes. The year the first school was opened he was elected to the State Senate and after that sat for two terms in the United States House of Representatives. He died in Washington in April 1838, and his funeral service was held in the capitol, after which his body was brought to Baltimore for burial. On the arrival of the funeral train at the B. & O. Depot, thousands were present to pay their respects, and they lined the streets through which the procession passed to St. Paul's graveyard. It was led by the Mayor and City Council and among the mourners were the leading citizens and clergymen, and members of Congress who included the Speaker of the House, Leonidas Polk, John Quincy Adams, Daniel Webster and Thomas H. Benton. All the ships in the harbor had their flags at half-mast and all the church bells in the city tolled. Said *The Sun* editorial: ". . . few men in Baltimore enjoy such perfect respect and attachment from their fellow citizens as Isaac McKim—the rich admire him and poor love him." Without doubt his was the greatest public tribute ever paid a member of St. Paul's.

Bishop Stone, whose health had been poor throughout his administration, died in the spring of 1838. So again the Diocese faced the difficult task of electing a new bishop. Again Dr. Wyatt and Dr. Johns were the leading candidates. In spite of the intense partisanship of their respective followers, there is no hint of the least ill feeling or jealousy between the two men. Both were more than willing to have their names withdrawn, and they joined forces in looking for a successor other than themselves. For two years the seat was vacant. At last the convention of 1840 solved the problem by electing the Rev. William R. Whittingham, of New York. To indicate that all animosities had been buried a testimonial was prepared by the delegates declaring that in every way Dr. Whittingham was fitted for the post. Heading the list of signers were Dr. Wyatt and Dr. Johns. Impressed by such a generous invitation Dr. Whittingham accepted. At the time he held a chair on the faculty of the General Theological Seminary in New York City. He was a high churchman with very positive views as to the authority a bishop should enjoy. Events were to show that neither considerations of expediency or personal popularity would induce him to alter his course once he had made up his mind where his duty lay. Dr. Whittingham's intellectual interests led him to make an extensive collection of rare books primarily having to do with church history. By the time of his death this library called for a special building to hold it.

As president of the standing committee the arrangements for Dr. Whittingham's consecration fell upon Dr. Wyatt. This took place on September 17 in St. Paul's Church in the presence of Bishops Doane, Griswold, Moore and Onder-

donk. The service of Morning Prayer was read by Dr. Wyatt
and the sermon was preached by Bishop Griswold. Dr.
Whittingham was the fourth Bishop of Maryland and the
second to be consecrated in St. Paul's. As he had done during the administration of Bishop Stone, Dr. Wyatt served
as Whittingham's right-hand man. Thomas Wyatt, son of
the Rector, having arrived at the age of twenty-one years and
been ordained a priest, joined his father as Assistant Minister. He replaced the Rev. Thomas Billopp who had resigned
some years before to go as Rector of St. Barnabas Church,
Prince George's County.

Any disappointment Dr. Johns may have suffered through
failure of election in Maryland was relieved when shortly
thereafter he was elected Coadjutor to Bishop Moore in Virginia. In the Old Dominion he found himself in the congenial company of low churchmen. In due course he succeeded Bishop Moore and has gone down in Virginia church
history as one of the great bishops of that State.

An outstanding event in Dr. Wyatt's ministry and one in
which he took a lively part was the founding of St. Paul's
Boys' School. The combined school and home for girls had
been a success ever since the incorporation of the Benevolent
Society in 1800. With that example before them it was
natural that members of the parish should consider doing
something of a similar nature for the boys of the community.
A meeting of subscribers was called for February 9, 1849.
Dr. Wyatt presided and the outcome was the appointment
of a board with the Rector as chairman. The members were
Thomas Swann, S. Owings Hoffman, Robert A. Taylor,
J. Hanson Thomas, Samuel W. Smith, G. Somerville Norris,
Reverdy Johnson, Jr., Gustav W. Lurman, William Wyatt,
Jr., John M. Gordon, C. C. Jamison and Thomas H. Morris.
The school began as a parish day school and so continued
for several years.

On March 28, 1853, the school was incorporated as "The Boys' School of St. Paul's Parish." The incorporators, who included some of the original board were Dr. Wyatt, Mr. Swann, Mr. Johnson, William B. Duvall, William R. Travers, Frederick W. Brune, Jr., William B. Perine, Edward W. Wyatt, B. M. Hodges, Jr., E. W. Blanchard and G. S. Morris. The object of the school stated in the charter was "to establish an institution for the maintenance and education of poor boys." In its early years classes were held in the Sunday School room for whose use the trustees paid the Vestry $150 a year. It so continued throughout the ministry of Dr. Wyatt.

The forties and fifties were a great period in Baltimore and its environs for the erection of new churches to keep pace with the rapid growth of the population. By 1855 there were 40 Episcopal churches within the limits of St. Paul's Parish as it existed in 1692. Among those not already mentioned were St. James' (1824), St. Andrew's (1837), Ascension (1839); St. Timothy's, Catonsville, and St. John's, Huntington (1843), St. Luke's (1848), Grace (1850) and Emmanuel (1852). As for St. Paul's itself the *Baltimore Church Times* in 1847 gave a glowing account of its condition. It was described as being the largest and most spacious edifice in the city, capable of seating 1700 people. Yet at that the number of pews was inadequate; there was not a single vacant one to be had. What provision was there, asked the *Times,* for the children of the present congregation as they married and formed new families? By 1853 the church could boast that it had paid off the debt incurred with the erection of Robert Cary Long's edifice, amounting to some $30,000.

Then fate rudely stepped in to spoil the picture. The evening of Friday, April 28, 1854, was rainy and cold in spite of the lateness of the season. Fires had been built in the Rector's study and in the room near the choir gallery in anticipation of a rehearsal which for some reason did not take place. Persons living in the neighborhood later recalled that around bedtime they smelled something burning. But it was not until 2 A.M. that one Penington, a night watchman of the city, on making his rounds saw flames issuing from the building. He gave the alarm and within a few minutes half a dozen fire companies were on the scene. By then the fire had gained great headway, sweeping across the whole body of the church and threatening the parochial school building which stood on the south side. In three hours destruction was complete except for the side walls and the steeple, though the base of the latter was so weakened that the bell, which weighed 3000 pounds and was rated as one of the finest in the country, crashed to the ground, making a mournful parting clang as it landed.

Dr. Colbourn, secretary of the Diocesan Convention, who lived across the street, arrived ahead of the firemen. With the help of volunteers he managed to rescue cushions, prayerbooks and hymnals from the pews and the "Bishop's Chair" with its gilded mitre which had been given in 1815 by a vestryman—George Grundy of Bolton—for the use of Bishop Kemp. Also saved were the marble baptismal font; and, most miraculously, the stained-glass window now over the main entrance of the church. Perhaps the greatest achievement of the salvagers was the removal of a heavy iron safe containing the records of the diocese. This suggests that Bishop Whittingham used St. Paul's as his headquarters.

Loss of the beautiful church was as greatly lamented by the people of other denominations as by the Episcopalians and they generously offered their facilities to the St. Paul's congregation. The offers of Christ Church and Grace Church were accepted, the former for Morning Prayer and the latter for Evensong.

The day after the fire Dr. Wyatt preached a sermon at

Grace Church using as his text St. Paul shaking the serpent from his hand at Malta after his shipwreck and making the brave assertion that "the momentary interruption to our privileges, may be followed—sensibly, visibly, by many happy results. Through the good Providence of God, you have the power at once to rise above calamity." And rise the congregation did, setting to work at once on plans for the erection of a new church on what remained of the walls and foundation of the old. Richard Upjohn, of New York, a leading architect of his day was engaged to draw the plans. Insurance to the amount of $20,000 served as basis of a building fund. Thomas Swann, a vestryman later to be elected Mayor of Baltimore and after that Governor of Maryland, was particularly active in promoting the project. It was still customary to buy pews outright as well as to rent them. It is said that those proposed for the new church brought as much as $1000 a piece. Architectural fashions had now moved away from the Wren pattern. Upjohn favored instead the ancient basilica style which came long before the Gothic age. Its chief features were a nave under a flat roof supported by interior arches and flanked by side aisles. Years later the eminent architect Bertram Goodhue was to call the new St. Paul's the best example of a basilica in this country. Upjohn's plan called also for a lofty tower at the northwest corner of the church rising to a height of 150 feet. The funds were insufficient to cover this at the outset and, as a result, it has never been built. Upjohn's church is the one we know today.

In spite of the ill health which had pursued him throughout his ministry Dr. Wyatt managed to accomplish a prodigious amount of work. From the time he succeeded Dr. Kemp as rector he had had an assistant. In 1852 either he or the Vestry concluded the time had come to call in an associate who would assume the major responsibilities of administration. Correspondence between them suggests that when the time came to work out the details the Doctor was loath to surrender his authority. It was proposed that the coadjutor should assume the title of "Vice Rector." Dr. Wyatt, however, would continue as "nominal rector" with right to preach, administer Holy Communion and perform whatever ministerial offices he might think proper. He, too, was to preside at meetings of the Vestry. He was to be allowed to pick the candidate whose name actually appeared in the agreement. All of this was put in writing so that there might be no misunderstanding. But nobody of that name is found in the church records. No doubt the candidate was unwilling to accept a position in which so much authority was left with Dr. Wyatt. From 1855 to 1857 the Rev. Dr. James D. McCabe held the title of "Associate Rector" but thereafter until Dr. Wyatt's death there was a return to that of "Assistant Rector." The phenomenon of two suns in the same firmament has never been a happy one.

As though the indisposition of his right hand man were not enough Bishop Whittingham too began to ail. The cure prescribed was a trip to Europe. He included Italy in his itinerary and this was seized upon by the low churchmen as proof that in the ecclesiastical sense he was "moving toward Rome." The Bishop felt called upon to deny the rumor in a letter to the "Southern Churchman" protesting that he was neither a Tractarian nor a Puseyite, but believed only in following the Book of Common Prayer as he had done since childhood. During his absence he turned all diocesan authority over to Dr. Wyatt as president of the Standing Committee who, regardless of his own health, performed the task courageously and even urged the Bishop to prolong his stay abroad.

About this time need was felt for an institution to provide a place of temporary shelter for the destitute, disabled and

sick members of the church. While the project was not confined to St. Paul's, the Mother Church showed great interest
in it. The Church Home Society of Baltimore City was
granted a charter by the State Legislature in 1855. Dr. Wyatt
was chairman of the first Board of Trustees and so continued
for a number of years. Shortly after the incorporation the
name of Frederick W. Brune, Jr. long a vestryman and active
member of St. Paul's, was included on the board. A vivid
symbol of St. Paul's interest was that the cross from the
steeple of the church destroyed by fire, recovered from the
rubble and placed atop the cupola of the Church Home on
North Broadway, has remained there to this day. In 1857
another Episcopal institution, St. Andrew's Infirmary, was
merged with the Home under the joint name of Church
Home and Infirmary. They continue to serve the community as the Church Home and Hospital. Through the years
St. Paul's people have maintained their interest with cash
contributions and the endowing of rooms, while other St.
Paul's rectors since Dr. Wyatt have served as presidents of
the board.

The disastrous fire behind them, settled comfortably in
their handsome new church, enjoying the prosperity that
came with Baltimore's growing importance as a center of
industry and trade, particularly associated with the South,
the congregation had every reason to be happy. That is,
had it not been for the ominous cloud on the horizon that
warned of mounting tension over the issue of States Rights
and slavery. Did they but know it, they were on the eve of
the most tragic period in the city's history.

CHAPTER VIII

ST. PAUL'S IN THE CIVIL WAR

URING the later years of Dr. Wyatt's incumbency, St. Paul's included among its members a group of men of exceptional ability. Thomas Swann already has been mentioned as a founder of the Boys' School and a leader in rebuilding the church after the fire in 1854. Born in Alexandria, Virginia, he came to Baltimore early in life, the better part of which was spent in public office. He was Mayor of Baltimore, Governor of the State, and a member of Congress. During his term as Mayor, Druid Hill Park was opened to the public, the fire department was reorganized and put on a professional basis and a modern waterworks system was installed to provide the city with running water in place of springs and pumps.

In sorry contrast to Mayor Swann's achievements was the outrageous conduct of those who supported him in the elections. His greatest strength was derived from the so-called "Know-Nothing Party," which in the name of patriotism persecuted newly arrived immigrants and fostered religious prejudice. The election of 1858 was attended by riot and disorder in which a number of persons were killed and wounded. This resulted in demands for reform; and, interestingly enough, a leader of the Reform Party was George

William Brown, also a communicant of St. Paul's. In the election of 1859 the reformers succeeded in taking control of the police away from the Mayor, and in the following year Brown was elected to that office. There is no record of how these political adversaries conducted themselves when they met, as they must have, on the common ground of the Parish.

After attending Dartmouth and Rutgers, Mr. Brown studied law in the office of a Baltimore lawyer; and, on being admitted to the bar, joined his brother-in-law Frederick W. Brune, Jr. in the firm of Brown and Brune. Mr. Brune was for years on the St. Paul's Vestry and a delegate to the Diocesan Conventions. From 1868 to the time of his death ten years later he represented the Maryland Diocese at the General Conventions of the Church.

Still another lawyer and statesman who served his term on the Vestry was Reverdy Johnson. During his long public career he was a member of the State Senate, and of the United States Senate; United States Minister to the Court of St. James', and Attorney General in the Cabinet of President Zachary Taylor. Contemporary with these men was George Washington Dobbin, also a lawyer and a vestryman. Mr. Brown was to end his career as Chief Judge of the Supreme Court of Baltimore City, and Mr. Dobbin as an associate judge of the same court. Both were to serve as trustees of the Peabody Institute and of Johns Hopkins University and Johns Hopkins Hospital. All the wisdom and talent that these men combined would be needed in steering St. Paul's through the trying years that lay ahead.

In the spring of 1861 the political storm which had been threatening for a decade and more broke. Events followed thick and fast. April 12 the bombardment of Fort Sumter began. April 15 President Lincoln issued a call for 75,000 volunteers to defend the capital and on April 17 Virginia

seceded from the Union. As Baltimoreans followed this pre-
lude to the Civil War their emotions rose to fever pitch.
Maryland was a border state. In Baltimore feeling was divided; a rough estimate placed Southern sympathizers in
the majority. By blood ties and trade the city was closely
allied with the South. Even among Union sympathizers
there was an element of State pride which resented outside
interference of any kind. To magnify the crisis, the shortest
route from the North to the capital, which the President
had called the troops to defend, lay through Baltimore.

Friday, April 19 was a black day in the annals of the city.
Early in the morning the 6th Massachusetts Infantry Regiment arrived at President Street Station which was situated
east of Jones Falls. In those days all trains from the North
came into that station, and from there horses hauled the
coaches over tracks on Pratt Street to the Baltimore and
Ohio's Camden Station. There had been warnings that passage of Union troops would be resisted and the authorities
had taken precautions against it. George P. Kane, a compe-
tent man who had been put in office by the reformers, was
Marshal of Police. It was anticipated that if there was any
trouble it would be at Camden Station, and there Kane
massed his men. The Mayor issued a proclamation urging
the citizens to keep the peace. Brown was at his law office
ready to act when word came to him of a clash between the
military and a mob. He at once set out for Camden Station
according to a previously arranged plan, but when he reached
there he learned that the scene of the conflict was not there
but at Charles and Pratt Streets. What had happened was
that the troops, loaded in the coaches, were being hauled
across town, when they were halted by obstructions on the
tracks. The mob had taken anchors from the docks nearby
and used them to block the way. The troops were ordered
by their officers to leave the coaches and make the rest of

the journey on foot; and as they did so cobble stones began to fly. Many times before, these stones with which Baltimore streets were paved had made good and handy ammunition.

Finding that he was in the wrong place the Mayor jumped into the buggy which had brought him from his office to Camden Station and was driven posthaste to the scene of the disorder. Having arrived there, he introduced himself to the officer commanding the 6th Regiment and told him he had come to help. The two placed themselves at the head of the column and the march was resumed. The Mayor hoped that his presence would restrain the mob. Armed only with an umbrella, he looked anything but formidable, yet for a moment his dignity and quiet courage acted as a restraint. But it was only for a moment, then violence broke out again. Hit by a shower of stones the troops retaliated by firing into the mob and were fired on in turn. In the exchange of shots both soldiers and citizens were killed and some were wounded. It was only then that the Mayor, realizing he could do no more good, left his position. By now Marshal Kane had appeared at the head of his police who formed a cordon, drove the mob back and restored order.

Shocked by what had happened the Baltimoreans, whatever their political opinions, were agreed that no more Federal troops should be sent through Baltimore on their way to Washington. In the hope of preventing it Mayor Brown dispatched posthaste to the capital a committee of three prominent citizens to wait on President Lincoln, impress him with the seriousness of the local situation and urge him to use some other route. Of these three gentlemen one was Mr. Dobbin of St. Paul's.

Next day they were joined by Mayor Brown and were received by Mr. Lincoln and General Winfield Scott, Chief of Staff. The President and the General were sympathetic but refused to give more than a conditional promise that no more troops would be sent through Baltimore if another route could be arranged without interfering with military plans. Without waiting, however, to hear the result of the interview, the Maryland militia was called out to oppose with arms any attempted passage; and, as an additional measure of defense, the railroad bridges to the north of the city were burned. This direct action did not help to ease the situation. News of the attack on the troops quickly spread through the North and there was a public outcry for redress.

Resistance ended when on the night of May 13, General Benjamin Butler with another force of Massachusetts troops, entered by stealth, occupied Federal Hill and trained his guns on the town. From then until the end of the war Baltimore was to all intents and purposes a captive city. To soothe northern tempers scapegoats were needed and a number of prominent Baltimore citizens regarded as Southern sympathizers were clapped into prison. Among them were Mayor Brown and Marshal Kane. It did no good for the commander of the 6th Massachusetts to protest that the Mayor had done everything in his power to restrain the mob and protect the troops. On orders of the military Brown was arrested and sent to Fort Warren, Delaware, and there held prisoner for nearly a year.

During this distressing period the lot of the Episcopalians was made no easier by their Bishop. Though he had been resident in Maryland for a quarter of a century, he had no other close ties with the South, and he seemed incapable of comprehending the confusion of loyalties that the war produced. He was a man of stern conscience who demanded a strict adherence to the canons and saw himself as the agent of enforcement. He also was a Union man and he was convinced that in this national crisis the Church should not stand idly by. Several months before the bloody encounter of April 19 he had made his position clear. Immediately after the New Year when people in Maryland were seriously discussing secession, Governor Thomas H. Hicks addressed a proclamation to them which in essence was an argument against it. It met with hearty approval in the Northern states and also that of Bishop Whittingham who wrote a letter to the Governor commending him for his stand and assuring him that, "My humble efforts, therefore, shall not be wanting in my sphere, to back your noble persistence in keeping Maryland in her only true, right and safe attitude of dignified and quiet expectation of legitimate redress of past wrong, and provision against contingent dangers in the regular working of the Constitutional Government of the United States." When the Governor replied, thanking him for his moral support the Bishop offered no objection to his letter being made public. As might have been anticipated the Bishop's stand was assailed by Southern sympathizers and rumors were published in the newspapers that at the next diocesan convention his resignation would be requested. The Bishop even went so far as to approve the proposal that the Maryland clergy be made to take an oath of allegiance.

A hotbed of Southern sympathy was in that part of the Diocese which lay in the District of Columbia. At least one Episcopal church there was seized by the Federal Government and put to use as a hospital. Congregations in Baltimore grew alarmed that similar retaliation would be applied to them. In that instance Bishop Whittingham appealed against it directly to President Lincoln. The President, no doubt informed of the Bishop's loyalty, sent word through his secretary, John Hay, that this would not be done, while the Surgeon General wrote to assure the Bishop that the existing hospital facilities in Baltimore were essential for all the Government's needs.

That the Standing Committee, of which Dr. Wyatt was

president, did not favor as extreme an attitude as that of Bishop Whittingham was indicated as early as December, 1861, when the latter requested the calling of a court to consider charges of disloyalty against three clergymen of the Diocese. The Committee turned down the request on the ground that "ecclesiastical trials in the present temper of the community cannot be expected to conduce either to deification or to peace."

When in 1862 the Bishop issued an order for the reading of a prayer of thanksgiving interpreted as being one for Northern victories, the Committee decided it was time to take a firm stand. They addressed a letter to him in which they pointed to the agitation into which the Church had been thrown through "the calamitous state of the country and the morbidly excited condition of the public mind." Recognizing their duty as a council of advice they asked leave to approach him with a frank communication of their views with regard to the Churches present exigencies. They referred specifically to the displeasure raised by the combined thanksgiving and prayer set forth to be used in the District of Columbia. They thought this dissatisfaction had been augmented by the previous actions of the Bishop such as the public commendation of Governor Hicks's proclamation. Coming from various parts of the Diocese, members of the Committee considered they were in a better position than the Bishop to judge the feelings of the laity.

The Committee insisted that no political bias existed among its members and that while they differed in opinion some of them held the same principles as did Bishop Whittingham. They said it was their conclusion that ". . . our obligations to you, to the Church, and to our consciences require us most respectfully and affectionately to apprise you of the critical and alarming condition in which you, with the diocese, are placed." They had heard that in more than one church there was a concerted plan for the congregation, when the obnoxious prayer was commenced, to rise in a mass and leave the church.

". . . a material portion of each congregation," they said, "instead of being grateful for the results of recent battles, only reflect upon them as the occasions of the slaughter of their friends and relatives; and that to *ask them, for this,* to kneel before God with Thanksgiving in his temple is to invite them to an act of equal hypocrisy and profanity." They were confident that if the General Convention foresaw that the introduction of a proposed act of worship into a religious assembly, would disorganize that assembly, drive some away, agitate others, and leave only discord and schism behind it, "we are well assured, it would be far from their decision that such an act was 'expedient,' or that duty to God, the Church or our own souls demanded its performance."

The Committee suggested that perhaps the question might be asked whether the Church had not already provided sufficiently, among her occasional prayers for "periods of war and tumult" and for "the restoration of peace and deliverance from enemies." This argument might have been expected to bear special weight with a high churchman who attached great importance to exact adherence to the liturgy and looked with disfavor on original prayers. Heading the list of signers of the address was Dr. Wyatt, and six other members of the Committee put their names to the document.

To this address Bishop Whittingham replied: "In recognition of the kindness and of the wisdom of the ultimate intention of my brethren, I think it best to take no further notice of the character and contents of the document on which I should otherwise have much to remark." In short, he respected their courtesy but he was unmoved by their advice. During the summer the Bishop's morale was sustained by letters from fellow bishops and other churchmen in the North commending his loyalty to the Union. Throughout the rest of the war the controversy over the prayer of thanksgiving continued. When the Bishop ordered it after the battle of Gettysburg, the Rev. Joseph Richey, Rector of Mount Calvary and a Southern sympathizer, refused to use it. The Bishop justified it as thanks "for deliverance of the State from an invasion by armed rebels and thieves." And again in August, 1864, the Bishop sent out a letter to the clergy giving an Order of Prayer to be used in response to the President's call for a day of humilition and prayer.

Meanwhile, as evidence of the approbation of his conduct by his old colleagues of the General Theological Seminary he was invited to return to the chair on the faculty he had left on coming to Maryland. The invitation greatly alarmed the extreme Union sympathizers in Baltimore who begged him not to desert them. Whether moved by this appeal or fearful that departure might be interpreted as a weakening of the conscience which had sustained him in his fight for what he deemed to be his duty to his high office in the Church and to the nation, Bishop Whittingham declined the call and stayed on.

Unfortunately from the standpoint of history, the minutes of St. Paul's Vestry covering the Civil War period have disappeared. However there is enough existing evidence from which to make reasonable deductions. Most important was the position of the Rector, an aging man whose days were numbered and who therefore was concerned more with the life beyond than that on a troubled earth. Like Bishop Whittingham Dr. Wyatt was a native New Yorker; but, unlike the Bishop, he had close family ties with the South. Three of the sons of his brother-in-law, Thomas Farmer Billopp, had gone from Prince George's County to join the Confederate Army. Another nephew-in-law and his family, who held Dr. Wyatt in the highest affection and who were affectionately regarded by him, were living in Richmond. Dr. Wyatt would have been less than human had he not seen right and wrong on both sides and looked upon the war as a tragic circumstance in which individuals were caught up with no way of extricating themselves.

On the other hand Dr. Wyatt had for a quarter of a century been the Bishop's right hand man. Their mutual interests as scholars and churchmen had brought them close together. The address which Dr. Wyatt as president of the Standing Committee had signed emphasized that it was submitted "respectfully and affectionately." It definitely was not an ultimatum nor a warning that the Bishop's orders would be disobeyed. There is no record that St. Paul's declined to use the prayer of thanksgiving. Had the prayer been used and had the congregation walked out surely such an incident would not have been forgotten.

Like Dr. Wyatt the leading members of his congregation had conflicting ties which would have favored a policy of moderation. Thomas Swann was a native Virginian, Reverdy Johnson was an Annapolitan who was criticized by the extremists for defending certain Southerners charged with disloyalty. Frederick W. Brune, the most active churchman of the lot, could not have failed to be influenced by the fact that his wife was a Virginian with relatives in the Confederate Army. A son of George W. Dobbin, too, was in that army. On the other hand Swann and Johnson were outspoken in their loyalty to the Union. So, too, was George William Brown who later said that he had always regarded secession of the Southern states as a rope of sand. It might be presumed that his law partner and brother-in-law Mr. Brune, held similar views.

So it was that St. Paul's came through the ordeal scarred no doubt, but with no wounds which could not be healed, and prepared to face the post-war period with courage and confidence. This it had to do under a new rector, for in the last year of conflict Dr. Wyatt passed quietly away. He had served faithfully and effectually as Associate Rector, Assistant Minister and Rector for half a century, the longest tenure of any clergyman of St. Paul's.

CHAPTER IX

PERIOD OF RECONCILIATION

HEN Dr. Wyatt died in June, 1864, Appomattox was still some nine months in the future. With a congregation divided in its sympathies wisdom dictated that his successor should not be a violent partisan of either side. The Vestry evidently had this foremost in mind when they called the Rev. Dr. Milo Mahan. Dr. Mahan was born in Suffolk, Virginia, in 1818, the son of an Irish father and a Virginia mother. Early in his life the family moved to Flushing, Long Island, where he attended St. Paul's College, stood at the top of his class and excelled in the classics. His intellectual attainments were such that at the age of 17 years he qualified as a teacher of Greek at the Episcopal High School, in Alexandria; and there he remained for seven years. After that he returned to Long Island to join the faculty of his own school.

It was then that he decided to study for Holy Orders. He was ordained a priest in 1846 and served as Assistant at St. Mark's, Philadelphia, until 1851 when he obtained a professorship at the General Theological Seminary in New York. This gave him the opportunity to develop his scholarship and to turn his hand to theological writing. He was co-editor of *The Church Journal,* a national publication of the Episcopal Church; and when in 1871 the first Vatican Coun-

[121]

cil proclaimed the infallibility of the Pope and the Assumption of the Blessed Virgin, he publicly took issue with its findings. Intellectually he was compared favorably with Bishop Whittingham.

Through his friendship with Bishop George Washington Doane, of New Jersey, Dr. Mahan was induced to leave the seminary to become a Priest of that diocese, and was elected a deputy to the General Conventions of 1856, 1859 and 1862. After coming to St. Paul's he served as a deputy from Maryland at the General Convention of 1865. At the Conventions of 1862 and 1865 sectional spirit ran high. On the outbreak of the Civil War the southern dioceses organized themselves into a union embracing the Confederate States and revised the Book of Common Prayer to conform to the political changes.

In retaliation an extreme group of Unionists at the Convention of 1862 undertook to get a resolution through the House of Deputies strongly condemning the rebellious South. However there were more temperate members of that body who foresaw the eventual defeat of the Confederacy and believed that the Convention should take no action that would encourage a division of the Church at the end of the war. The debate in the House was carried on largely by the lay delegates; one of the few members of the clergy taking part was Dr. Mahan. He spoke eloquently against the resolution and with such effect that the condemnatory version was defeated. The measure proposed in its place and passed was a milder one which merely affirmed the loyalty of the Episcopal Church to the Union, expressed the belief that great evil would result from secession, and studiously avoided employing toward the seceders any term of condemnation or reproach. It concluded however, with the hope that the Union would triumph. Action of the House served to counter a belligerent pastoral letter issued by the House of Bishops.

Dr. Mahan was again a delegate at the General Convention of 1865 and again his policy was one of moderation. Thanks to his conciliatory attitude he has been credited with playing an important role in keeping the Episcopal Church united. His statesmanlike vision and his ability to rise above the bitterness and strife of the time are sufficient reasons for his having been chosen by the Vestry of St. Paul's to lead the congregation during the trying postwar years. Dr. Mahan gave every promise of fulfilling a long and fruitful ministry in keeping with that of Dr. Wyatt and other predecessors, but he had hardly begun when a cruel fate stepped in. He died after having served only six years.

One incident of note during Dr. Mahan's ministry was the attendance of Robert E. Lee at a service at St. Paul's. In the spring of 1869 the General came to Baltimore in the hope of raising funds for the Virginia Valley Railroad Company whose line was to run from Lexington north through the Shenandoah Valley. Sunday, April 25, he accompanied his friend Samuel Tagart, a communicant of St. Paul's, to Morning Prayer. News quickly spread that he was there and when he left the Church at the conclusion of the service, a large crowd had assembled outside. All hats were off as Lee walked between two long lines of silent people come to pay him the respect and veneration his presence invariably inspired. In the 1850s Lee, as a colonel of engineers, had been resident in Baltimore while supervising the construction of Fort Carroll. He then was a member of Mount Calvary Church. His visit to St. Paul's on April 25, 1869, is the only one of which there is record.

A St. Paul's organization formed in Dr. Mahan's ministry was the Men's Guild. It was started in 1868 with nineteen members. Its purpose was to assist the clergy in parochial, missionary and church work in general, such as visiting the sick and the poor, conducting Sunday schools in Canton and Highlandtown, raising money for parish activities, reporting to the Rector persons ready for Baptism and Confirmation, distributing books and tracts, and providing ushers at the services. Members also were expected to improve public worship by making hearty responses and taking the lead in congregational singing. The Guild, too, furnished a reading room which was used as well for social functions. The organization performed these services for a number of years until most of them were taken over by a newly created Guild Association.

Under Dr. Mahan a radical change was made in the character of the Boys' School. A few years after its incorporation the trustees began to worry over the fact that the charter called not only for "education" of the boys but also for "maintenance." The latter they took to mean a school where boys might live. Consequently in 1858 a committee was appointed to inquire into the establishment of an "asylum," an unpleasant word today but one which then connoted nothing more sinister than board, lodging and supervision. The proposal continued to be discussed during the years which saw the death of Dr. Wyatt and the succession of Dr. Mahan. Finally action was taken in 1866 when the trustees voted to purchase a building on Saratoga Street, near Pearl, then occupied by the Maryland Asylum for the Blind. There the school began to provide both education and maintenance which has not since been interrupted, save for one brief period.

The session of October, 1868, opened with nine boarders and a few day scholars. In a statement drawn up by Dr. Mahan as an appeal for financial support, the purposes of the institution were set forth in considerable detail. It was stated specifically that the school was designed for boys of

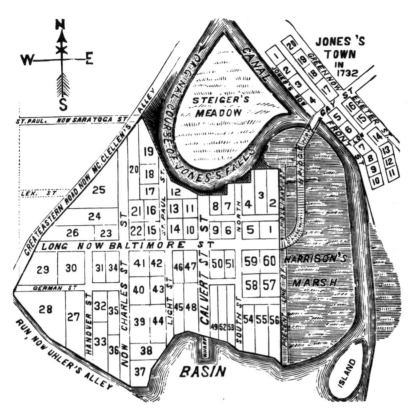

Plat of Baltimore Town and Jones' Town

Old St. Paul's Church 1731

St. Paul's Church   1817

The Rectory

Altar and Chancel of St. Paul's Church

"a higher grade and better capabilities" rather than for "the most wretched class of boys." It was to offer a Christian home, stressing education in Scriptures, and in religious knowledge and habits generally. Pains would be taken to maintain a high moral and religious character among the pupils and no persistently bad boy would be allowed to remain. In view of an important function the school was to perform for the rest of its life, one provision was especially worthy of note: "Constant practice in church music will not be forgotten."

For those pupils showing the capacity for it there was to be groundwork in Greek, Latin and mathematics so as to fit the boys for teaching, the ministry, or any walk of life. In short, selectivity was to stand high among the School's objectives.

Dr. Mahan died in September, 1870, and before the year was out he was succeeded by the Rev. Dr. John Sebastian Bach Hodges. Dr. Hodges was born in 1830 in Bristol, England, where his father was organist in the cathedral and a Doctor of Music of Cambridge University. Edward, the father, migrated to the United States in 1838 to become organist and choirmaster at Trinity Church, New York. His family followed soon after. John was one of a number of children, all of whom bore names of famous composers or Biblical characters. Among his brothers and sisters were George Frederick Handel, Jubal, Asaph, Miriam and Deborah. Contrary to a fairly widespread belief, the Hodges family was not connected by blood with the composer Bach.

Young John attended Columbia College and was graduated with both a Bachelor of Arts and a Master's degree. He had inherited a love of church music from his father and he had displayed exceptional talent as a composer of church music. He also had a pleasing voice and in his college years was tenor soloist at Trinity Church. On graduation from

Columbia he felt a call to the ministry and entered General Theological Seminary, New York, from which he was graduated in 1854. After his ordination he held parishes in Chicago and New Jersey before being called to St. Paul's. Meanwhile he had married Lucy Shaler, daughter of a Pittsburgh judge, and when they took up residence in the Rectory on Saratoga Street they brought with them four sons, ranging in age from two to eight years. Two children had died in infancy and two, a son and an only daughter, would be born in the Rectory. Mrs. Hodges was a woman of great dignity, a devoted parent and grandparent. While she made many friends in the community and shared heartily in its social life, she considered her first duty to be that of mistress of the rectory household. Parochial duties she entrusted wholly to her husband.

Through his father, Dr. Hodges was steeped in the English cathedral tradition and he immediately saw an opportunity for introducing it in the services at St. Paul's. At that time, as in most American churches, the choir was composed of men and women who appeared in their street clothes, the varieties and contrasts of their dress being somewhat tempered by screening the choir from the congregation. Dr. Hodges had in mind eliminating the women, introducing boys in their places and vesting both men and boys. Considering the average congregation's aversion to change, the Rector obviously had set himself a formidable task. He was shrewd enough to estimate the number of toes he was about to tread on. In fact he ran the risk of setting off a new conflict as violent as that which so recently had been closed at Appomattox. He had one great advantage in that St. Paul's prided itself on the beauty of its services; and that a vested choir was calculated to enhance. Another advantage was the Boy's School, one of whose purposes, as already mentioned, was instruction in religious music. Here ready at hand was a means for recruiting boys for the choir. There were twenty pupils in the first years of Dr. Hodges's ministry, and up to 1874 he and his assistant took full charge of the administration of the School, thus laying the groundwork for the musical program he had in mind.

Dr. Hodges set Easter, 1873, for the inauguration of the new choir, and he took the precaution of preparing the congregation for the shock by preaching a sermon explaining his purpose. He asked especially for their unprejudiced consideration and forebearance. He called attention to the difficulty of keeping up the old choir of men and women which, he said, was of fluctuating quality, sometimes good and sometimes bad. He concluded with the assurance that the innovation he proposed ". . . will in time, and after a fair trial, impart to the public services of this church, a dignity and a grandeur befitting this noble building; and of all places most becoming and suitable in this the mother Church of the city." Years later when surpliced choirs of men and boys had become common he was to recall the state of mind of the congregation which required such a sermon.

As Dr. Hodges had anticipated, the change was not accomplished without opposition. At least one couple withdrew to another parish. They were Mr. and Mrs. Harry Elliott Johnston. Mr. Johnston was a banker; Mrs. Johnston, the former Harriet Lane, was the favorite niece of President James Buchanan. Since Buchanan was a bachelor, she acted with great charm as his hostess at the White House and enjoyed the admiration of the public. The song hit of the day "Listen to the Mocking Bird" was dedicated to her and report had it that her beauty had made quite an impression on Prince Edward, later King Edward VII of England, when he was a guest of the President on his tour of the United States in the 1850s.

The Johnstons soon became dissatisfied with their change
of parishes and returned to St. Paul's. A great tragedy befell
them in the deaths at early ages of their two sons. They
were by then so reconciled to a choir of men and boys that
they expressed regret that their own sons had not lived to
sing in it. Furthermore, after the death of her husband,
Mrs. Johnston gave a handsome endowment to St. Alban's
School, Washington, the Cathedral choir school. Another
generous bequest in Baltimore made possible the Harriet
Lane Home for Invalid Children, of Johns Hopkins Hospital.

A memorial window in St. Paul's bears silent witness to
the Johnstons' great loss. The inscription reads: "To the
Glory of God and in blessed memory of James Buchanan
Johnston, whom God took unto Himself, Annunciation Day
1881, in the 15th year of his age, and of Henry Elliott Johnston, whom God also took unto Himself October 30, 1882,
in the 13th year of his age. They were lovely and pleasant
in their lives and in death they were not divided. Their
souls pleased the Lord, therefore hasted he to take them
away. A memorial from their loving parents. We asked life
of Thee and Thou gavest them a long life even for ever and
ever."

St. Paul's congregation soon grew accustomed to the change
and Dr. Hodges was so confident of his strength that he set
to work on another project that even today seems astonishing in its boldness. Just when St. Paul's was making its
radical experiment the Peabody Conservatory of Music was
achieving national distinction in the musical world under
the direction of a dynamic Dane, Asger Hamerik. Hamerik
had organized a symphony orchestra which toured the East
and won high praise from the critics. He and Dr. Hodges
met and immediately recognized that they were kindred
spirits. Between them they worked out a plan for a Choral
Communion, the sacred rite to be accompanied by the com-

bined music of the vested choir and the Peabody orchestra, to take place on Christmas Day, 1873.

One of the flutists in the orchestra was no less a person than the poet Sidney Lanier, then a lecturer at Johns Hopkins University, who was developing his theory on the relationship between poetry and music. Immediately on returning from the service at St. Paul's, Lanier wrote to his wife giving her an account of it. "We were," he said, "a first violin, viola, 'cello, double bass, clarionet, French horn, bassoon, two flutes (Wysham and I) and great organ with a choir of about forty boys and men, and some female voices.

"The service was nearly three hours long, and music, music all the time. We opened with the overture to Mozart's 'Magic Flute' (which was, I am free to say, a most abominable outré affair for a church service) and then played with the choir throughout the service. This is a wonderfully ritualistic church. A shrine is in front-centre, flanked by two enormous lighted candles, and arched over by a number of smaller ones. Three clergymen and a number of acolytes, boys, etc. assisted in the service. The rector marched in stately fashion down from the dais, the other clergymen, the acolytes, and the choir, filed two and two behind him; all marched down into the body of the church, singing a fine chant, then filed to the left, and so went in procession across to a side door, giving into a room in the rear of the church, through which all passed, still singing. The chant was kept up long after they had disappeared, and the door was shut, and as the voices receded and receded, until nothing but the clear treble of the boys could be heard, 'twas dramatically very beautiful.

"Some of the pieces were magnificent, and the crash of the voices and organ and instruments rolled gloriously among the great arches. All of them would have been fine, but some of the music . . . was not properly phrased, though

containing good ideas. Next to me sat Mr. G–, first clarionet.
Presently the communion service came on; Mr. G– watched
with great curiosity. It was the first one he had ever seen!
When he saw the priest blessing the bread, he leaned over
to Wysham (who is a devout member of the Church) and
asked with great interest: 'Does he eat all that?' Afterwards
when the bread was distributed to the kneeling people, I
observed him make gestures of disgust at the smallness of the
portion given to each, and finally he informed Wysham that
that would not begin to be enough for him!

"Ah, these heathenish Germans! Double Bass was a big
fellow, with a black moustache, to whom life was all a joke,
which he expressed by a comical scowl, and Viola was a young
Hercules, so full of beer that he dreamed himself in heaven,
and Oboe was a young sprig, just out from Munich, with a
complexion of milk and roses, like a girl's and miraculously
bright spectacles on his pale blue eyes, and there they sat—
Oboe and Viola and Double Bass—and ogled each other and
raised their brows, and snickered behind the columns without a suspicion of interest either in the music or the service.

"Dash these fellows. They are utterly given over to hea-
thenism, prejudice and beer—they ought to be annihilated;
if they *do* get control of the age, life will be a mere barbaric
grab of the senses at whatever there is of sensual good in the
world . . . In the church sometimes, when looking out of
my dream for a moment, I could find . . . only the small
choir-boy, who in default of a music stand, held up my music
for me." So ended Lanier's account. So far as the records
show this was the only occasion until very recently on which
a full orchestra has taken part in a service in St. Paul's.

The success of the vested choir of men and boys obviously
depended on the success of the School, and there were many
times when one wondered if it would survive. The regular
tuition fee for boarders was $200; some of the pupils, how-

ever, were received at lower rates and some paid nothing at all. The number varied from year to year and so did the ratio between day scholars and boarders. There were 20 boarders in 1871, of whom 17 were free. In 1875 the enrollment increased to 43, of whom 18 were free and 25 paying, and including 18 day scholars. No doubt the success of the vested choir was responsible for the increase.

Meanwhile the cost too was growing; in 1875 a budget of $7000 was barely met and in 1878 there was a deficit of $2000. In 1874 the Board took over the actual running of the institution. This was done by three committees—one for admission and discharge, one for instruction and one for the care of the household. Each of the twelve trustees had charge of the household for a month, obviously an unbusinesslike arrangement. Under it, the situation became so discouraging that a proposal was made to close the School.

One man who refused to acknowledge defeat was Dr. Hodges. He was convinced that the School had a future and he expressed a willingness to reassume the administration he had relinquished to the trustees four years before. On January 1, 1879, the new system was put into effect. Dr. Hodges was entrusted with the authority to engage a faculty and matron, to handle admissions and dismissals, and to be responsible for all miscellaneous operations. The trustees were to confine themselves to taking care of the invested funds, the income of which would be turned over to the Rector. There was only one condition, but it was a big one; namely, that the School did not come to the end of any year with a deficit. Looking back in later years Dr. Hodges pointed with pride to the fact that he had always met that condition.

Nevertheless the days immediately ahead were grim ones. In the first year of the agreement the property on Saratoga Street was sold and the School moved to 95 St. Paul Street.

The number of boys had been reduced to twelve. The following year the School reached its lowest ebb; there were but nine boys, and while they were boarded they were sent to public school for their education. From St. Paul Street it moved again, this time to East Monument Street. What Dr. Hodges had banked upon was help from parishioners who had captured some of his enthusiasm. Now at a crucial moment his hopes were realized. In 1884 Miss Frances Donaldson, a member of the congregation, came to the rescue with a generous gift which, with the proceeds from the sale of the Saratoga Street property several years before, made possible the purchase and furnishing of the house at No. 8 East Franklin Street which for the next thirty-eight years, later combined with No. 10 next door, was to be the home of the School. From now on its future was reasonably sure and Dr. Hodges could proceed with confidence in developing the choir. By 1887 the number of free scholars had been raised to 40.

There were many other matters which required the Rector's attention. St. Paul's since Dr. Wyatt's time had become even more widely known as a wealthy congregation and consequently was the object of a variety of appeals. Some "Notes from the Rector's Mail" tell the story: " 'Will you send $35 to Père Vilatte for a scholarship for an Old Catholic theological student in Wisconsin?' Promised to do so. 'Will you pay a month's board for a lady in the Women's Hospital?' Paid it, $32. 'Will you give a patient a bed in Church Home?' Could not, as all our beds are filled. 'Will you give us 50 hymnals for Sparrow's Point mission?' Sent them. 'Can you set up a poor man by giving him a little stock of material to peddle?' Set him up and started him out. 'Can you send out some altar linen to a mission church in Nebraska?' Referred to Embroidery Society. 'Can you send me

$50 for church building at Mt. Airey?' Must do this if I can. Etc., etc., etc."

January 27, 1878, Dr. Hodges preached a sermon which showed astonishing foresight and also served as a guide to policy. He reminded that the history of St. Paul's Parish went back close to two centuries, more than one-tenth of the time since Christ sent his disciples to preach the Gospel. Here in St. Paul's had ministered, in succession, every Bishop of Maryland, from Bishop Claggett to the present venerable Diocesan, Bishop Whittingham. One of them, Bishop Kemp, had been Rector of the Parish as well. He estimated the number of churches and missions within the Parish's ancient bounds to be 43. He drew attention to the fact that St. Paul's already had become a downtown church, that the residences of very few of the parishioners were near it, that many of them passed by more than one church on the way to their own. He had noted that the weather greatly affected the size of the congregation.

What then, he asked, was to be done? He presented several possibilities. They could pull down the church and move to a better position. He quickly remarked: "This would virtually and at once amount to the actual abandonment of this large and populous section of the city, so far as the church is concerned." They could do as Christ Church had already done, build an entirely new church and give it the name of St. Paul's and leave the old edifice where it was as a "free church." He concluded, however, that they were not reduced to any such necessity. Then he made the following bold proposal:

"I believe that, as this church has an honorable past, so there lies before it a no less glorious future. Here is the place for this church, to stand from generation to generation. Here should she lift up her completed tower higher than any surrounding object, directing heavenward the eye of the passing Christian. From it should sound forth the solemn call to prayer and praise and worship. Here should the rich and poor alike feel that they can come to the Father's House and be fed continually with the meat which endureth into everlasting life, which the Son of Man will give unto them."

This was Baltimore's golden age of benefices associated with the names of Hopkins, Peabody, Pratt and Walters. In his enthusiasm Dr. Hodges envisioned St. Paul's Parish as also being a worthy object. "This should be the Common Church of the whole diocese. This should be the Bishop's church and here he should have his episcopal chair or throne." Money had been given for a university, hospital and library. Was it possible that "there shall not be found one . . . to do something to enable this church to go on? . . . Or if not this surely it cannot be that all her children combined together will not see to it that her work shall go forward in the future."

Time would tell that St. Paul's future was not to be precisely what Dr. Hodges pictured it in his memorable sermon on that winter day in January, 1878. No one then dreamed of "skyscrapers" that shortly were to make their appearance, let alone the even loftier "high rise" buildings of our own day, that would dwarf the highest of church towers or steeples. The St. Paul's tower was not to rise. Fate was to ordain that St. Paul's would not be the episcopal seat of the Maryland Diocese. Nor was there to be an Episcopalian Hopkins, Pratt, Peabody or Walters to endow the church. It took the Rector ten years to realize it and to return to the alternative of a future depending upon "all her children combined together." At his suggestion, on January 1, 1888, an endowment fund was begun whose goal was set at $100,000 before any income from it was to be used for current expenses. In those days $100,000 was a handsome sum of money. The start was anything but auspicious. During the first year total contributions amounted to exactly $343.40. The second year was not much better. In appealing again to the congregation the Rector figured that at the rate the fund was going it would take 200 years to reach that $100,000 goal!

CHAPTER X

GOLDEN AGE OF THE CHOIR

HE "Gay Nineties," as the era has been called, was hardly an appropriate description of the atmosphere which then prevailed at St. Paul's. Rather it was a period of feverish church activity. No member could excuse himself on the ground that there was no contribution he could make. There was no talent which could not be used by one or more of its many organizations. An active Sunday School called for teachers. The Men's Guild continued for a few years more to fulfill its manifold functions in helping the clergy with their labors. A new undertaking was the arrangement of a program of Sunday evening sermons by visiting clergymen, a popular feature which crowded the church. It would eventually evolve into the mid-day Lenten sermons which have attracted outstanding speakers from all parts of the country, and continue to this day. The Men's Guild itself was to give way to the Guild House Association.

In addition to the Boys' School, the Girls' School which had started with the Benevolent Society in 1800 still flourished. Another instructional project now introduced was the Industrial School where from 90 to 100 girls were taught to sew and received religious training. There was the Altar Society, composed of a small band of devout women, skilled

[137]

in preparing the altar for the many and varied services. A companion organization was the Vestment Society whose function was to look after the vestments of clergy and choir; and there was as well an Embroidery Society, not only keeping St. Paul's supplied with finely embroidered linens, but on request volunteering to do the same for distant missions.

Outstanding among the women of St. Paul's dedicated to the care of the altar and the ecclesiastical vestments was Mary Glenn, daughter of Judge and Mrs. John Glenn. Miss Glenn founded the Altar Society in 1869. In her youth she journeyed to England and became an associate of the Society of St. Margaret, East Grinstead. There she was instructed in the teachings of the leaders of the Oxford Movement. On her return to this country and to St. Paul's she impressed on her fellow workers the significance of Catholic doctrine and the Sacraments. At St. Margaret's she had learned also the exquisite art of ecclesiastical embroidery. Her gifts of altar cloths and furnishings are among the richest and most beautiful in the church's possession—still in use. Her activities during the first decade of Dr. Hodges's ministry were especially appropriate to the innovations which he had introduced, and she established a tradition that has been passed down to later generations of St. Paul's women.

In 1886 St. Paul's House, the now familiar building on Cathedral Street adjoining the Rectory, was completed and opened. Its principal use then and for many years to come was to provide a protected and inexpensive home near the business section for the young women who were the pioneers in the field of female employment. The downstairs rooms could be used as well for parish meetings.

Then there were the Provident Society whose chosen field was the "worthy poor"; the Mothers' Meeting which helped to find employment for poor women; and the Choir Library which had charge of the growing collection of choir books.

Considering the wide range of these activities it was not surprising that a central organization was needed to direct and coordinate them. The Women's Guild of St. Paul's Parish was created in 1891 to do just that.

Christmas and Easter were occasions when the whole of St. Paul's congregation and the people of its missions joined together for celebration and fellowship. A gathering in St. Paul's House on December 28, 1889, was typical. Attending were 100 children of the Industrial School and 53 from St. Paul's Sunday School. The downstairs room was crowded to capacity. A Christmas tree, beautifully dressed, occupied one corner. In those days there were no electric lights; instead unprotected candles were used to the peril of the assembled company. During the holiday season the newspapers were filled with grim reports of disasters caused by trees catching fire. Fortunately on this and all other such occasions St. Paul's passed through the hazard unscathed.

Before the candles on the tree were lit, the boys and girls were entertained with a magic lantern show in which colored slides were projected on a sheet fastened to the wall. That was the nearest thing to the modern movie that contemporary invention provided. Following the lantern show Christmas carols were sung and then Dr. Hodges delivered an appropriate talk. Parishioners who knew him recall that he had a keen sense of humor and an instinctive love of children. There is no record of a Santa Claus having attended, though Dr. Hodges, with his long white beard, would have made a perfect one. The high point of the entertainment came with the distribution of presents. Each child got a "cornucopia," a horn-shaped container fashioned of paper and filled with candy. The thoughtful ladies who planned the affair saw to it that the children of the Industrial School, besides being entertained, should receive a practical gift, so each was presented with a knitted jacket. Every girl also

[139]

received a book and every boy had the choice of a book or a knife. As might have been expected most of the boys chose knives. When it was all over, the recorder of the event reported: "It was a joyous and happy occasion for teachers and scholars and all hearts were made glad in the happiness of each other."

Nor were the grown people forgotten. Each of the fifty women who had attended the Mothers' Meeting regularly was rewarded for her faithfulness with the gift of a basket containing a chicken, a ham, coffee, sugar, apples, oranges, etc.

Lent at St. Paul's in the early nineties measured up to the most exacting specifications of the church fathers as a period of penitence and prayer. Services were held three times a day, respectively at 7:30 A.M., 11:00 A.M. and 5:00 P.M. Communion was offered each day either at 7:30 A.M. or 11:00 A.M., and each day a lecture followed Evening Prayer. All of this was in preparation for Easter, the observance of which, as at Christmas, culminated in a joint festival for the children of the Mother Church and the missions.

This took place in the church in the afternoon. Children of the Industrial School, of the mission in Highlandtown, and of St. Paul's Sunday School marched in procession, each class with its distinctive silken banner. Easter carols were sung after which the children presented their mite boxes. On one occasion the contents reached the impressive total of $37.14!

What Dr. Hodges had in mind and what he accomplished during his ministry was a schedule of services through the day, such as was customary in the English cathedrals, embellished with the music he so dearly loved. This made tremendous demands upon the boys of the school as the Rector took pains to bring to the attention of the congregation.

"How many persons," he asked, "think how hard choir

boys have to work? They are school boys and have first to do all their school work, and then they have to take out of the hours when other boys are playing, all the time for practicing and rehearsals—sometimes in the morning, sometimes in the afternoon, sometimes in the evening till 10 and after 10 o'clock. This soon ceases to be fun for boys who have to work so constantly, having to give up even part of their Saturdays as well.

"All through Lent a service every day in the church and twice or three times on Sunday; and all the work of practicing and getting ready for Easter to be done in addition, for all which they receive on an average *less than a dollar a month.* Surely we owe our thanks, if nothing else, to our choir boys."

On one Christmas Eve (at least) a member of the congregation, his heart warmed by Dr. Hodges's report, made his way to the choir room and handed a roll of dollar bills to Mr. W. H. Whittingham, then the organist and choirmaster, and asked him to distribute them, one to each of the twenty boys. Dr. Hodges commented: "Had the generous donor been present there he must undoubtedly have felt more than repaid by the delight shown as each juvenile found his little Christmas stock thus unexpectedly added to." No wonder, since at the time each choir boy was receiving an average of 25 cents a week!

In the spring of 1890 an ominous warning was given the congregation by Dr. Hodges; it had to do with the condition of the graveyard. For almost a century now it had been located at Fremont Avenue and Lombard Street, in southwest Baltimore. The bodies were moved from the graves which surrounded the second Baltimore church to make room for the erection of the Robert Cary Long church in 1817. Dr. Hodges commented: "We all share the feeling that our burial ground is not kept in the condition we should like it to be kept in." That was the first intimation of a frustrating problem which has worsened through the years; and all efforts at solution might be best described as always "too little and too late." Greenmount now had become the fashionable cemetery and St. Paul's no longer derived revenue from the sale of lots. The Rector pointed out that the sources were an annual offering made at Easter and the interest on $2000 which had been subscribed some years before. The total available for upkeep came to $150 a year. Shortly thereafter Dr. Hodges reported that not more than 20 or 25 lots were cared for, while from 500 to 600 went untended. He called it a "deplorable condition." "Three dollars a year," he said, "would keep a lot in condition while $100 would secure perpetual care." The appeal met with no appreciable response.

The more immediate interest of the congregation was centered on the installation of a new organ which was played for the first time on Tuesday, November 22, 1892, at a Choral Service in which the organist was Mr. Whittingham. A large congregation filled the church and after the regular service there followed a recital in which three organists took part. The especial significance of the event was that one of the three was a young man named Miles Farrow, and this is the first time he was mentioned in connection with St. Paul's. Two years later Mr. Farrow became organist and choirmaster. Born in South Carolina, he early in life showed such musical ability that he was the organist of a cathedral at the age of 18 years. In 1890 he came to Baltimore as organist of First Presbyterian Church where he remained only six months. From there he moved to Mount Calvary for a term of a year and a half before coming to St. Paul's. Then began a remarkable partnership. It has been said that probably nowhere else in America had there been brought together a rector of such musical gifts and liturgical insight as Dr. Hodges and an organist and choirmaster of such singular skill and success as Mr. Farrow. To complete the essentials there was the Boys' School to provide the voices; the boys under Dr. Hodges's insistence upon perfection already disciplined to produce whatever was demanded of them.

The School at this time was closely patterned after the English choir schools and for the next decade and more a familiar sight on Charles Street every evening during the week, and twice or more on Sunday was the boys of the School in academic caps and gowns, shepherded by Mr. Farrow, marching to services at St. Paul's. Not satisfied with the training he already had received in this country, Mr. Farrow made five trips abroad to study church music in England, thus keeping abreast of what was being done in a country distinguished for its cathedral choirs. He was to continue in his position for fifteen years and for a time add to his other duties that of Headmaster of the school.

It would be impossible at this late date to assemble the names of all the boys of exceptional ability who qualified as soloists. One, however, stands out in the history of the school. He was Harry Percy Veazie, a youth who came to St. Paul's from New Jersey. During the early 1900s his fame spread from Baltimore throughout the East. He had the rare distinction of having his voice recorded by Columbia, leading producer of phonograph records, an honor usually reserved for grand opera singers. When in due course his voice changed he stayed on at the School as a master. Soon thereafter he had the opportunity to complete his education in England and on his return became organist and choirmaster of a church in Washington. Following that he entered the church and was ordained a Priest in St. Paul's. At the time of his death not many years ago he was rector of a church in California.

A community project sponsored by St. Paul's which gained momentum under Dr. Hodges was St. Paul's Chapel and

Guild House. The Guild House traced its origin to the middle of the nineteenth century when a rented building on North Calvert Street, operated by St. Paul's, provided rooms and board for young men and boys working in the city. Fostered by the Men's and Women's Guilds of the Mother Church, it moved to a larger building on Lombard Street and expanded its activities to include a kindergarten and a unit of the Boys' Brigade. This last was a uniformed, semi-religious body which enjoyed quite a vogue in Baltimore at the time, and whose ideals resembled those of the Boy Scouts of today. In 1895 the Guild House moved again to 539 Columbia Avenue (now Washington Boulevard) and enlisted the help of an exceptional group of workers. A Guild House Association was formed, composed of all members of the Parish who contributed to the project. Mr. Jeffrey Brackett was elected its first president. He was ably assisted by Mr. and Mrs. John Glenn, who soon were to move to New York where Mr. Glenn became secretary and director of the Russell Sage Foundation. The Guild House program was a Baltimore counterpart of the Settlement House Movement which was being carried out at Toynbee House in London's East End, at Hull House in Chicago, and at University Settlement in New York City. It represented the most up-to-date and approved method of rendering religious, educational, recreational and medical service to the industrial workers of the community.

A big step forward in the Guild House program was taken when in 1902 the Rev. Frank Hay Staples was called to become Vicar or Priest in Charge, a position he was destined to hold for more than a quarter of a century. Already things had begun to move, for when he arrived there were 179 communicants and the Sunday School numbered 200. The building, however, which they occupied was inadequate and it had not yet been paid for.

Among the ardent church workers and benefactors at this time were Elizabeth Dwight Woolsey Gilman, Frances Donaldson and Susan Asenath Harwood. Mrs. Gilman was the wife of the great first president of Johns Hopkins University, Daniel Coit Gilman. When the Women's Guild was introduced to co-ordinate the various parochial activities, she was elected as its head. For twenty years she was president of the Mothers' Club, and she was also interested in the Guild House where her daughter, Elizabeth Gilman, was deeply involved, along with Margaretta Poe and Gabrielle Clements, the latter an artist well known for her altar pieces and etchings of Baltimore. In her will Mrs. Gilman left a bequest sufficient to wipe out the mortgage on the Guild House as well as a generous contribution to the endowment fund.

Miss Donaldson was one of the original members of the Altar Society. Dr. Hodges said of her: "Her gifts for the altar and its adornment, and for everything conducing to the beauty and enrichment of the service of the Church and the glory of God, were never failing." Her contribution was not confined to the Altar Society but extended to every department of the work of the church. She was closely associated with the Boys' School and St. Paul's House. Her annual contributions to the School were the largest in the parish in her day. For over twenty-five years she paid the entire coal bill, and she also provided funds for the purchase of the house on East Franklin Street. In several financial crises it was Miss Donaldson's support which kept the School alive.

Miss Donaldson was the prime mover in the program to provide living quarters and board for young working women at St. Paul's House. It was estimated that during its first twenty years it provided homes for 350 permanent boarders and gave temporary shelter to nearly 2000 transients.

The turn of the century saw extensive alterations to the interior of the Mother Church, the most conspicuous being the new altar window and the reredos. The reredos was the gift of Miss Harwood and was erected as a memorial to her brother-in-law, Gilmor Meredith, long a vestryman. It is fashioned of white Caen stone, of chaste design, and reaches across the entire sanctuary and up to the foot of the altar window. It replaced the original walnut paneling which was dismantled and installed at the west end of the church. Miss Harwood, the daughter of Judge James Harwood of the Orphans' Court, was Baptized and Confirmed in St. Paul's during the ministry of Dr. Wyatt. The reredos was only one of her many generous gifts. She also was the donor of a costly chalice set with jewels and a paten of gold, a memorial to her sister, Sarah E. Hindman Meredith. Like Miss Donaldson she was keenly interested in the Boys' School, frequently gave it financial support during her life and, at her death in 1911, left provisions in her will which made her the largest benefactor of the School and of the parish throughout its entire history.

The beautiful great east window actually was completed and dedicated in 1902, some two years before the dedication of the reredos. It was given by Miss Anna M. Glenn and John M. Glenn in memory of their mother. The idea was first conceived by Miss Glenn, and after her death her brother carried it out according to her wishes. The window was designed by Maitland Armstrong, of New York, a well-known artist of his day, and executed by his company. As described by Mr. Armstrong himself, it illustrates the verse of the *Benedicite, omnia opera Domini:* "O ye Spirits and Souls of the Righteous, bless ye the Lord; praise him and magnify him forever." The subject is portrayed by sixteen figures in different attitudes of adoration representing spirits and souls of various sorts and conditions of men who, in Paradise, offer in praise the symbols of their different lives. Among them are a scholar, a kneeling king, a knight in armor holding aloft his sword and a banner on which is a cross; a martyr with a palm, mothers dedicating their children, a rustic, a bishop in mitre and gorgeous vestments, a prophet, and a crusader. Through the center flows the River of Life and beyond it is a landscape with distant mountains and an open sky flecked with clouds. At the extreme top are two adoring angels looking up toward the bright light above, which shines down through the center of the picture."

The altar window had been in place less than a year and the reredos had not yet been dedicated when both of them, along with the entire church, narrowly escaped destruction. Sexagesima Sunday, February 7, 1904 was another tragic day in the history of the City. It was the day of the GREAT FIRE. The weather was raw and blustery. Shortly before noon a fire broke out in a warehouse on Hopkins Place, three blocks south of the Rectory. Driven by a high wind it was soon out of control and swept eastward. Throughout the afternoon the fire raged, increasing in intensity as it leaped from block to block on its way along Baltimore Street and Fayette Street and farther south through the wholesale market district toward the ships tied up at the Light Street docks in the basin. From the Rectory looking down Liberty Street one could almost see the point at which the fire had started. As it progressed gusts of wind turned it northward and eastward and it looked as though in an hour or two it would reach the church.

Improbable as it seems, contemporary accounts say that inside the church the regular schedule of Sunday services continued, and that until 5 P.M. worshippers were there. If so, their minds could hardly have been on the service, what with the fire coming closer and closer. At this critical point a group of parishioners joined Dr. Hodges and members of his family in a mission of rescue. Mentioned among them were Dr. Robert W. Johnson, a vestryman who lived nearby; Mr. Leigh Bonsal, the treasurer; Miss Harwood and Mrs. Duncan C. Clark. Through their combined efforts valuable altar cloths, Communion services and other furnishings were transferred to the Rectory which by now was judged to be out of danger. Historic parish records which were in the office of Mr. Conway S. Hodges, clerk to the registrar, fortunately were rescued before the fire reached the Law Building where Mr. Hodges had his office.

Throughout Sunday night the fire raged, presenting an awe-inspiring spectacle as one after another of the presumably fireproof skyscrapers in the business district went up like flaming torches. It was not until Monday morning that the wind which had fanned the flames died down. By then everything had been leveled to the water's edge at the basin and the fire had halted at Jones Falls. All the area for many blocks south of Fayette Street and from Hopkins Place to the water had been reduced to smoldering rubble. Then the people of Baltimore, and among them the members of St. Paul's Church, recovering from the first shock, began to take stock of their losses. Few were the men whose offices and other places of business had not been destroyed. Most of the banks with their records had gone up in flames, while safety deposit boxes lay in the ruins, their owners not knowing whether bonds, stock certificates and other evidences of ownership had survived the terrific heat to which they had been subjected. Anxious days lay ahead; eventually the courage of the people triumphed over the losses and a new and better city arose out of the ashes of the old. Members of St. Paul's could at least be thankful that the church and the rectory had been spared.

Men of St. Paul's Church played a conspicuous part in the program of recovery. Mayor McLane's first move was to appoint an emergency committee of prominent citizens. Members connected with St. Paul's were Blanchard Randall,

John P. Poe, Sherlock Swann, J. B. Noel Wyatt and Douglas H. Thomas. On the advice of this committee, a Burnt District Commission to administer the reconstruction program was appointed, and of this body Mr. Swann was named chairman. He was without doubt in the most responsible position in the organization, and the thoroughness and expedition with which the work was done spoke highly for his judgment and drive. Mr. Swann was a grandson of Thomas Swann, Mayor and Governor, and a founder of the Boys' School; and his father was a St. Paul's communicant in his day. Like many other members of Old St. Paul's families, Sherlock Swann later found it convenient to move to another church farther from the center of the city. He maintained a sentimental interest in the Mother Church, was married in it and at his death buried from it.

In May, 1904, local bookstores advertised the sale of a book of hymn tunes composed by Dr. Hodges. It was described as a new and revised edition. Perhaps the best known of these is the beautiful Communion hymn numbered 196 in the Hymnal today and frequently used: "Bread of the world, in mercy broken, Wine of the soul, in mercy shed." The book is only one of many evidences of Dr. Hodges's gift as a composer.

The following year Dr. Hodges reached the age of seventy-five. He had served St. Paul's faithfully for 35 years. In spite of the growing competition from parishes more conveniently located, St. Paul's under his guidance continued to flourish. Thanks to his efforts, combined with those of Mr. Farrow, the choir had attained a high degree of excellence. Not only had he solved the immediate problems of a downtown church, but he could claim credit for laying sound plans for the future. The endowment fund which he had initiated was growing gradually, but at a much faster pace than in its early years. Through its schools, missions, Chapel and Guild

[149]

House, Mothers' Club, St. Paul's House and other activities, it had demonstrated its awareness of its responsibility to the community. This load was a heavy one for a man of Dr. Hodges's advanced years to carry. There always are persons in a congregation who toward the close of a long ministry are impatient for change. Dr. Hodges came to the conclusion that he was not receiving the unanimous support of his Vestry which he deemed essential to his work. So, at a Vestry meeting on October 9, 1905, he tendered his resignation, to take effect at the end of the year. At a meeting a month later the Vestry accepted the resignation and at the same time elected him Rector Emeritus with the request that he continue to serve as Rector until the following Easter. As Rector Emeritus he was destined to continue to take part in the services of the church for many years more. No man could have completed an active career in the ministry with a better claim to the tribute, "well done."

CHAPTER XI

THE KINSOLVINGS ARRIVE

"I HAVE been in touch during my life here with all sorts and conditions of men, and I can truly say that I never paid an irksome visit in my life. My growing conviction is that whatever may be the fashion of the day, there are very rich rewards accruing to personal ministry. A minister must care most for lives and souls."

The foregoing is from Dr. Kinsolving's sermon preached on the twenty-fifth anniversary of his coming to St. Paul's as Rector. It sums up neatly the nature of the man and discloses the force which lay behind his ministry. As soon as Dr. Hodges's resignation had been accepted the search began for a successor. It ended with a call to Dr. Kinsolving to take over in October, 1906.

Arthur Barksdale Kinsolving was a native Virginian whose family was identified with Albemarle County. His grandfather was a neighbor and personal friend of Thomas Jefferson; his father an Episcopal clergyman. Arthur, the older son, was born February 20, 1861, at Middleburg, in adjoining Loudon County. His mother died the following year giving birth to his brother, Lucien Lee. Soon thereafter the elder Kinsolving married Lucy Lee Rogers, a descendant of the Lees of Virginia, and the two boys were brought up by their stepmother. The second Mrs. Kinsolving was an accomplished musician; young Arthur was devoted to music and enjoyed singing while his stepmother accompanied him on the piano. As a student at the Episcopal High School, Alexandria, Va., he was well grounded in the Bible, Shakespeare and the classics before entering the University of Virginia. He elected to follow in his father's footsteps and was graduated from the Virginia Theological Seminary in 1886. A brother and a step-brother made the same choice and both ended their careers as bishops.

After a brief ministry in a country parish in Virginia, young Kinsolving accepted a call to Christ Church, Brooklyn, in 1889; and while there he married Sally Bruce, a daughter of the prominent Virginia family of that name. While there he also received a Doctor of Divinity Degree from Washington and Lee University. When the Kinsolvings arrived in Baltimore in October, 1906, to take up residence in the old Parsonage, the family, in addition to the parents, consisted of three daughters (Bruce, Eleanor and Anne) and a son (Arthur). Two more daughters (Sally and Lucinda Lee) and a second son (Herbert) were to be born in Baltimore. Dr. Kinsolving was six feet tall. He had a ruddy complexion, black hair in youth which in later life turned to iron gray. Temperate in meat and drink, he was extremely active physically and throughout his life he gave the impression of slenderness. Pince-nez suggested the scholar that he was. His voice was rich and cultivated and seemed naturally attuned to the King James' version of the Bible. In later years a split retina caused the loss of sight in one eye, but it did not discourage his reading or even the driving of his automobile.

As a girl in Richmond Sally Bruce was acclaimed a beauty in an age when that title was highly prized and not carelessly bestowed; and in the passing years no one ever grew old more gracefully. She was also to achieve a reputation as a poet.

On assuming leadership of the St. Paul's congregation the Kinsolvings needed all the charm, wisdom and discretion they could muster. As there always are people impatient to try a new pastor, so there always are people who find it difficult to shift their allegiance from the clergyman who is going out to the one who is coming in. Some parishioners undertook to show their loyalty to Dr. Hodges by being deliberately rude to the new Rector. Some of these in later years became his best friends.

The choice of Dr. Kinsolving to succeed Dr. Hodges marked a drastic departure from the St. Paul's tradition. For more than a century, with the exception of Dr. Mahan, whose ministry was short, all the rectors had been recruited from the North and, with respect to ritual if not tenet, had been classed as high churchmen. Would Dr. Kinsolving undertake to introduce the customs of the low church in which he had grown up in Virginia? Such fears proved to be unfounded. Dr. Kinsolving could not claim to be the musician that Dr. Hodges was; but he had a keen appreciation of what Dr. Hodges and Mr. Farrow had been doing. One of his first acts was to pledge a continuance of the high standard of excellence they had attained in the religious services. Dr. Hodges would continue to live in Baltimore and it was agreed that as Rector Emeritus he would take some of the services, especially Holy Communion on Thursdays and on certain feast days. In facing this delicate situation Dr. Kinsolving was greatly helped by his admiration for his older colleague which he constantly expressed in his formal communications with the congregation.

One of the first persons to call on Dr. Kinsolving after his arrival in Baltimore was Cardinal Gibbons, then the universally beloved leader of the Roman Catholic Church in the

United States, and this was the beginning of a lasting friendship. Dr. Kinsolving was totally free from religious prejudices and applied to ministers as well as laymen of other denominations the principle he once expressed in a Lenten sermon: "If you want a man to serve you, get him to love you." His secretary, Miss Sara Banks, was a Baptist. Her pastor was a fellow member with Dr. Kinsolving in the Eclectic Club; and once Dr. Kinsolving complained to him that though he had for over 23 years dictated his sermons to Miss Banks, he had never made a dent in her theology. To which the Baptist minister replied: "Has she ever made a dent in yours?"

Dr. Kinsolving was never more at home than in the company of men and he had a remarkable gift for breaking down the barrier of reserve that so often separates laymen from those of the cloth. His camaraderie might be explained by a remark he was once heard to make in a convivial gathering: "Not a drop of Puritan blood in my veins!" His humor was infectious and sometimes it was mixed with mischief. A story is told of one occasion on which he volunteered to drive a visiting bishop from Baltimore to Washington to attend a conference. The offer was accepted, and accompanying them on the trip was the Rev. (later Bishop) Noble C. Powell. Dr. Kinsolving drove with the carefree abandon characteristic of his handling of an automobile, and to the terror of his companions. By the time the party had reached Washington the bishop had had quite enough of it and he implored Dr. Powell to drive them back to Baltimore. Dr. Powell approached Dr. Kinsolving tactfully, suggested to him that he must be tired and that he would be delighted to spell him at the wheel. Dr. Kinsolving brushed off the suggestion, protesting that he had never felt fresher; and so on the way home the passengers were subjected again to the ordeal they had endured on the way over. The Doctor appeared to be totally unconscious of his effect on them. They arrived safely and miraculously, however, in Baltimore. After the visiting prelate was put aboard a train for the North, the Doctor turned to Dr. Powell and with an exultant smile remarked: "Wasn't it fun scaring the bishop?"

Dr. Kinsolving was a devoted alumnus of the Episcopal High School of Virginia, which had impressed him with the value of church schools and what a church school should be. From the moment of his coming to Baltimore his interest was focussed on the Boys' School of St. Paul's Parish, and it was not long before he envisioned it as being something more than a mere adjunct to the choir. The transition was, however, still many years in the future. Meanwhile, the choir under Mr. Farrow continued its reputation as a Baltimore institution. It was not a large choir, invariably consisting of twelve boys and six men. One of the boys who served under Mr. Farrow recalls that "his educational background and musical training were limited and that, compared to the many virtuosos of today he was not a great organist; but he had a character that was fascinating to boys of choir age and they would do anything for him. And his conception of the church service was individual, extraordinarily religious and rare, and he certainly was one of the greatest *service* players of our time . . . . Year after year he produced boy-choirs of incomparable beauty."

Two or three times a year, as in the days of Dr. Hodges, special musical programs were presented. Admission was by ticket and these were distributed among the members of the congregation. Fifteen minutes before the beginning of the program, if there were vacancies, the general public was admitted. Such vacancies were rare since the church invariably was packed and many were turned away. The boys continued to pursue their Spartan existence though there were occasional breaks. One interested member of the church provided ice cream and cake as a treat on the first Sunday in each month. Another supplied each boy with an umbrella. The boys must have presented quite a spectacle as they paddled along in the rain on their way to the church in gowns and mortar-boards, each holding an umbrella. The entertainment best remembered was that provided after the special musical programs by Mrs. Caroline Rennert, widow of Robert Rennert, whose hotel stood less than a block from the church. There the boys were shown to a table laden with the food for which the Rennert was famous and invited to eat their fill.

Exercise was something of a problem. Since in that horse-and-buggy age traffic on East Franklin Street was not heavy, the boys could play "one-eyed cat" on the cobblestones without much danger of being run over. East Franklin Street then ran straight down the hill to Calvert and provided a wonderful place for coasting when snow was on the ground, that is, if the coasters stopped short of the Calvert Street car line at the foot of the hill. Another solution of the exercise problem was gymnastics for which use of the Marston's School gymnasium on Cathedral Street was arranged; later this shifted to the Y.M.C.A. when its building was opened a block from the School. Hard as it is to believe, there was a time when the boys used Druid Hill Park for baseball, football and lacrosse, walking the several miles there and back. Some years after that a lot was rented in Roland Park to serve as an athletic field for soccer.

Then there were phenomena, natural and man made. One boy recalls Halley's Comet about which he wrote a composition. The first airplane flight in Baltimore with Hubert Latham at the controls, passed directly over the School in November, 1910. Almost as great a thing of wonder was Dr. Llewellys Barker's red automobile standing in front of his office at 6 East Franklin. One warm night the boys

were awakened by a pattering like rain which turned out
to be a drove of pigs being herded across the city, a common practice in Baltimore and carried out at an unearthly
hour to avoid conflict with daytime traffic. The stench the
pigs left behind, says the recaller, was "terrific."

Another choirboy reminiscing of those days concludes that
the boys had enough to eat and the school and choir work
was not too enslaving "though we thought so." The academic standards were not high, but comparison with other
contemporary schools may not have been too unfavorable.
There seems to have been great difficulty in finding a capable headmaster who would stay and changes were frequent.
As has been mentioned, Mr. Farrow, the Choirmaster, had
to take over at one point. Among the trustees who were
particularly helpful when the School was on Franklin Street
were J. B. Noel Wyatt, J. Marshall Thomas, Herbert M.
Brune, Leigh Bonsal, Bernard Carter, John E. Semmes, Walter de Curzon Poultney, G. Herbert Boehm, and J. Harry
Lee. Mr. Wyatt, a leading architect of the city and a grandson of the former Rector of St. Paul's, over a period of years
took boys into his home and helped them with their education after they had graduated from the School. Miss Donaldson and Miss Harwood have been mentioned as benefactors, and Miss Elizabeth Gilman made it possible for no
fewer than thirteen boys to get training and education far
beyond the requirements of the choir.

Nor in these days had the distaff side of the church's educational endeavors been neglected. The Girls' School, now
over a hundred years old, had moved to commodious quarters in a large house in the center of an equally large lot
on North Charles Street, between 24th Street and 25th
Street. There were usually in the neighborhood of forty
pupils in attendance. A branch of the Girls' Friendly Society, organized by Dr. Hodges in 1882, but long dormant,

was revived. Weekly meetings were held preceded by a supper, after which the members engaged in such feminine pursuits as crocheting, weaving, and fine sewing, and in this the girls of the School participated. Dr. Kinsolving was as keenly interested in the Girls' School, as in the Boys' School, and when any of the girls became seriously involved in love affairs, he showed as much concern as though they were his own daughters.

Another ambitious program was that being carried out by the Chapel and Guild House under the inspired leadership of Mr. Staples, the Vicar. Eight blocks below the Chapel on Columbia Avenue was Henshaw Memorial Church, an Episcopal mission. Its Vestry approached that of St. Paul's with an offer to hand over the building in fee simple provided St. Paul's would promise to take care of the spiritual needs of the community. The St. Paul's Vestry accepted the offer and in July, 1907, the transfer was consummated. Some $6000 was spent on the building, much of the money being contributed by the people of the neighborhood. The Vestry then bought a lot adjoining and on it erected a finely equipped guild house. The total cost came to $65,000, a good part of which was covered by a mortgage. With these splendid new quarters the Chapel and Guild House entered upon the most active period of its history. More than thirty organizations of one sort or another held meetings there. In a few years the Sunday School boasted an enrollment of 525 pupils, the largest in Maryland. Just short of 100 children attended the kindergarten and the Mothers' Club flourished. A medical clinic with nurse in attendance looked after the health needs. A particularly popular feature was the gymnasium class conducted under the auspices of the Public Athletic League in a gymnasium that was part of the Guild House facilities. A great loss was sustained when Mr. Glenn, a pioneer volunteer, left Baltimore to join the Russell Sage Foundation.

In those early years of his ministry Dr. Kinsolving had another great loss when in the spring of 1909 Miles Farrow resigned to accept an offer to become organist and choirmaster of the Cathedral of St. John the Divine in New York. The boys of the St. Paul's choir had received no warning. The day the resignation was announced happened to be one on which a friend had given them a welcome treat by taking them to the circus. As they were returning to school by streetcar they read the news in the evening newspaper. One of them recalls that they broke down and wept.

Two years before Mr. Farrow's resignation, a youngster from Virginia had entered the School and almost immediately displayed a keen interest and talent in music. He was Channing Lefebvre. Recognizing the boy's ability, Mr. Farrow taught him to play the organ, and Channing also became the choir soloist. Upon leaving school Lefebvre went as organist at the Church of the Incarnation in Washington where Harry Percy Veazie was choirmaster. The following year he was invited by Mr. Farrow to join him as assistant organist at the Cathedral of St. John the Divine. His next step was to Trinity Church, New York, as organist and choirmaster, and from there he went to St. Paul's School, New Hampshire, to head its music department. His last assignment took him to the Philippines to map out a musical program for the new Episcopal cathedral in Manila. He returned to the United States in the Spring of 1967; and just as one of his compositions was being played at St. Paul's as part of the celebration of the Parish's 275th Anniversary, Baltimore received the sad news of his sudden death as the result of a heart attack in New York.

The departure of Mr. Farrow was a loss to the choir which was not immediately remedied. It was four years before the

[159]

position was satisfactorily filled by Alfred Willard. Before coming to St. Paul's Mr. Willard had served capably as organist and choirmaster at St. Mary's, Burlington, N.J., seven years at Pomfret School, Connecticut, and at St. John's, Troy, N. Y. Soon after Mr. Willard took over, Dr. Kinsolving was able to report that under him the choir had greatly improved and again was meeting the high standard that had been set by Mr. Farrow. Mr. Willard held the position until 1921 when he resigned to enter business. From his time to the present day St. Paul's has been exceedingly fortunate with its organist and choirmasters.

While Dr. Kinsolving was a loving parent he also could be stern when occasion demanded; and for this his children in later life thanked him, realizing how it prepared them to face the hard knocks of the world. There were times, too, when his patience was sorely tried. One such occasion was a Christmas holiday which brought to the rectory the two young sons of Bishop Lucien Kinsolving of Brazil, for whom Dr. Kinsolving acted as guardian while the boys were attending the Episcopal High School. The elder was the Doctor's namesake. The prize gifts of the Doctor's son Arthur that year were a desk and a saw. During part of the busy day when the Doctor was at the church the boys were left to their own devices. Arthur, the nephew, thought it would be a good idea to use the saw on the desk. The legs had just been neatly sawed off when the Parson came in, saw the damage, and with a roar went after the future Bishop of Arizona who fled the avuncular wrath so precipitately that he left a dent on the stairs that could be seen for twenty years.

Having grown up on a farm, Dr. Kinsolving felt that his son, a city boy, should know something about country life. So he tried raising chickens in the back yard of the Rectory. The experiment was anything but a success. Young Arthur was disgusted with the chickens because they were dirty and attracted rats. The experiment ended by making him more prejudiced than ever in favor of life in the city.

The children could not fail to be conscious of the struggle the Doctor had to make to support his large family in spite of his efforts to conceal it. He economized on his clothes, stoked the Rectory furnace himself and used soft coal because it was cheaper. The Kinsolvings welcomed gifts of clothes, particularly the girls. One Easter morning when Mrs. Kinsolving emerged from the Rectory with all five clad in hand-me-downs, Anne, the wit of the family, remarked: "Ma, more suspicious elegance comes out of this Rectory than ever came out of the Ritz."

One of Dr. Kinsolving's first concerns was the endowment fund which in the spring of 1907 had reached $83,000. A campaign was set in motion to bring it up to the total of $100,000 proposed by Dr. Hodges in 1888. Both a men's committee and a women's committee were organized to make the appeal. The former was headed by Douglas H. Thomas, a banker, and included some thirty men, all active in the business and professional life of the city. Mrs. Gilman headed the women's committee and working with her were Mrs. George William Brown, Miss Ann C. Perine, Mrs. J. Hall Pleasants, Mrs. Josias Pennington, Miss Sophie C. Milligan, Mrs. George S. Jackson, Mrs. Leigh Bonsal, Mrs. Charles M. Franklin, Miss Frances C. Semmes, Mrs. Edward H. McKeon, and Miss Katharine B. Johnson (later Mrs. Robert Garrett). Thanks to their combined efforts the Easter offering came close to $10,000, but it was not until the following Easter that the goal was reached. The barrier broken, the fund started to grow rapidly.

St. Paul's took pride in the election in 1908 of the Rev. Alfred Harding as second Bishop of Washington (D.C.). Dr. Harding was pleasantly remembered as Assistant to Dr.

Hodges from 1883 to 1887. He was the sixth to be thus elevated, the first having been Bishop Kemp. Others consecrated were Charles C. Grafton (Fond du Lac), Isaac L. Nicholson, Jr. (Milwaukee), Charles R. Hale (Cairo) and John L. Jackson (Louisiana).

That same year the church was once again put in jeopardy when the Masonic Temple next door was seriously damaged by fire. Fortunately the fire department quickly got the fire under control and prevented the flames from spreading to the church. In 1909 St. Paul's lost a devout member through the death of John Prentiss Poe, a former vestryman and one of the leaders of the Maryland bar. While Mr. Poe was distinguished in his own right through his legal talent, he was perhaps better known to the sporting world as father of the six Poe brothers who made football history at Princeton in the nineties, two of them, (Edgar Allan and John P., Jr.) winning places on Walter Camp's All American Team. Edgar Allan also became a St. Paul's vestryman.

At the General Convention of the Church in New York in 1913 a great honor was paid Dr. Hodges, then at the venerable age of 83 years. The meetings took place at the Cathedral of St. John the Divine and Mr. Farrow was in charge of the musical program. At his request a seat was arranged for Dr. Hodges in one of the choir stalls and the reunion of those two kindred spirits who had made musical history together must have been a touching one.

Meanwhile the peace of the world was broken when on August 1, 1914, war was declared between the allied nations of Great Britain, France and Russia on the one hand and Germany and Austria on the other. Though at that time the United States seemed remote from the conflict the women of Baltimore felt called upon to do what they could to alleviate the suffering that is the inevitable accompaniment of war. In December a Red Cross Committee was organized to make hospital supplies for wounded soldiers in Russian Poland where the need was reported to be greatest. The women of St. Paul's took part in this work under the leadership of Mrs. Julian S. Carter as chairman and Mrs. W. Graham Bowdoin, Jr. as treasurer. Great sympathy also was felt for Belgium after it had been invaded and occupied by the Germans. In December, 1915, St. Paul's choir, under the direction of Mr. Willard, gave a concert at the Lyric for Belgian Relief at which $1000 was raised.

In May of that year Dr. Hodges passed away. Active to the last, he celebrated Communion a few days before his death. His funeral was held in St. Paul's Church. The Rt. Rev. John Gardner Murray, Bishop of Maryland, read the burial service, and Holy Communion was celebrated by Bishop Harding of Washington, his former Assistant. Twenty clergymen in their vestments occupied stalls in the choir, and the Vestry of St. Paul's also was present. Providing the music were the boys and men's choir which he had done so much to perfect. After the funeral the body was taken to Pittsburgh to be buried beside that of Mrs. Hodges who had died some years before.

In the same month the sinking of the Lusitania by a German submarine in which a number of Americans lost their lives, and the consequent deterioration of relations between the United States and Germany warned of the danger that lay ahead; yet the crisis was averted for two years. Meanwhile, the St. Paul's women who had been making hospital supplies for Poland, affiliated with the National Surgical Dressings Committee and turned their attention to France. Their chairman was Alice Rich Dubarry. War with Germany was now imminent and the Committee reported that it was prepared to transfer its services to American needs at a moment's notice. That came with our declaration of war on April 3, 1917. St. Paul's House became a center of activity.

There the Red Cross offered its class in the making of surgi-cal dressings, and this was attended by about 100 women from other churches as well as from St. Paul's. By New Year, 1918, they had supplied 10,000 dressings. The Girls' School contributed handsomely to this effort. St. Paul's House was soon to figure prominently in another way.

Throughout the spring and summer young men were being called into the service and the khaki-clad soldier "Rookie" was getting to be a common sight on the streets. Late in October a meeting was called to organize the St. Paul's women more fully for war relief. A chapter of the Navy League was formed to help look after the needs of the sailors and a Hospitality Committee to extend a welcome to all service men who might be in the vicinity. With the training of an army division of close to 30,000 men at Camp Meade there soon were plenty of service men around. At St. Paul's House the women set up a club that was very popular on weekend leaves. Light snacks were provided, and a man might find paper and a pen if he wanted to write a letter home. There was singing around the piano, and a class in French for men who expected soon to be overseas. Between September, 1917, and March, 1918, the register showed that at least 5,500 soldiers and sailors had been entertained. They came from every state of the Union and from Great Britain and Australia as well.

St. Paul's young men were joining up with all the rest. As 1917 drew to a close there were fifty stars on the service flag that hung over the door of the Mother Church, while 46 men had by then gone from the Chapel and Guild House. There were to be many more before the war ended. One of the earliest casualties was Johnny Poe, the former All Ameri-can football player. He had not waited for the United States to enter the war but enlisted in the Black Watch of the British Army and died in battle.

A dramatic occasion at the peak of the war was the visit to Baltimore of the Most. Rev. Cosmo Gordon Lang, D.D., Archbishop of York, later to become Archbishop of Canterbury. He was present at a service held at noon on April 3, 1918, in St. Paul's. The church was packed; including those standing, probably 1200 people were there. Taking part in the procession were eighty members of the clergy, three crucifers and two flag bearers (one flag American, one British). Assisting Dr. Kinsolving in the reception of Archbishop Lang was Maryland's Bishop Murray. The service was symbolical of the solidarity of the two branches of the Anglican Church. It was a reminder as well that the Parish in which it was held began under the British flag.

At last, after the bloody fighting in the autumn of 1918, came Armistice Day, November 11, which marked the surrender of Germany and the end of the war. Sunday, November 17, two services were held at the church in thanksgiving for victory. The first, in the morning, was primarily for the congregation. After the singing of a verse of "The Star Spangled Banner," Tertius Noble's "Festival Te Deum" was rendered by the choir and after that Dr. Hodges's "Jubilate." The service closed with the congregational singing of "God of Our Fathers" and "My Country 'Tis of Thee."

The afternoon service was in the nature of a community celebration at which the British Consul and the Belgian Consul were present. On this occasion the music was Sullivan's "Thanksgiving Te Deum." In a brief talk Dr. Kinsolving reported that 170 men and 8 women of the Parish had been in the United States' service, of whom 82 men were from the Mother Church and 88 from the Chapel and Guild House. Three from the Church and four from the Chapel had given their lives. The indefatigable "Miss Lizzie" Gilman had gone to Paris in January, 1918, to do Y.M.C.A. work in Paris; and in December following the Armistice

[165]

Mrs. James Mauran Rhodes, a very active member of the congregation, set sail for Europe to engage in work among the soldiers of the army of occupation.

Of all the St. Paul's women who volunteered their services as war workers quite the most remarkable was Clara Maria Brune Brown. She was a daughter of the first Frederick Brune who came to Baltimore from Bremen, Germany, and was largely instrumental in establishing the mercantile relationship which was so valuable to both cities. Clara Maria was born in 1817 and was one of the first children to be baptized in the old marble font. She vividly recalled Lafayette on his visit to Baltimore in 1824. She was the widow of Mayor Brown who played such a courageous part during the mob's attack on the Massachusetts troops in June, 1861. Though she was more than 100 years old by the time the first men of the American Expeditionary Force landed in France she was still in full possession of her faculties and proud that she had the strength and the enthusiasm to work two hours a day for "the boys over there."

The Nation's ordeal was not yet ended, however. In the fall of the year an epidemic of influenza broke out and was at its peak as the Armistice was being signed. The disease struck especially hard at the Chapel and Guild House where Mr. Staples buried 33 persons. During the same period Dr. Kinsolving had twelve funerals, one of them being that of the youngest daughter of the sexton. The Rector raised his voice to lament that "this terrible visitation has left unspeakable sadness in its wake and God grant that it may now have passed. Undoubtedly between 20,000 and 25,000 soldiers and sailors on this side of the Atlantic have died."

In the spring of 1919 as demobilization was in progress, St. Paul's House continued to open its doors to service men, though the peak load had long since passed. It was estimated that during the previous 20 months it had welcomed more than 32,000 service men. On the whole as the Rector, Vestry and congregation reflected on all that had happened since the first war committee made its supplies for wounded soldiers in Poland, they could be sure that, to use the popular term of the day, they had "done their bit."

CHAPTER XII

PEACE, PROSPERITY, DEPRESSION, WAR

WHILE Baltimore and St. Paul's Parish were closest to his heart Dr. Kinsolving was thoroughly acquainted with the world outside. Every summer, from June 1911 to September 1935, he went with his family to Fisher's Island where he served as Rector of St. John's Church. Five times he made trips to Europe and there was introduced to the leaders of the Anglican Communion. His first trip was as Rector of Christ Church, Brooklyn, when he was the house guest of the Archbishop of Armagh, in Ireland. In 1901, accompanied by Mrs. Kinsolving, he toured England, Scotland and the continent as far south as Italy. In 1908 he was a delegate to the Pan-Anglican Conference in London, on which occasion he and Mrs. Kinsolving were entertained by Bishop Talbot of Southwark, later Bishop of Winchester. A fellow guest was Bishop William Temple who was to end his ministry as Archbishop of Canterbury. The Kinsolvings in turn entertained the Talbots in the Rectory in Baltimore. The Kinsolving children were quite a shock to Lady Talbot who was heard to remark: "They positively roar like lions." Other trips were made in the summers of 1929 and 1931.

One of the results of these contacts was an increased awareness of the close relationship of St. Paul's with the Church of England. Before Dr. Kinsolving's ministry St. Paul's had held a commemorative service on the death of Queen Victoria and another on the death of Edward VII. During his ministry a service of prayer and thanksgiving was held in 1935 to commemorate the twenty-five year reign of King George V. The custom established, in days to come there would be special services on the death of Archbishop Temple, on the death of King George VI, on the coronation of Elizabeth II and on the death of Winston Churchill.

Recognition of a slightly different nature was the memorial service held, on January 1, 1920, for Sir William Osler to synchronize with one being held the same day in Oxford, England. Dr. Osler was one of the four "Great Doctors" of Johns Hopkins Medical School and Hospital in its infant years. From the Hopkins he had gone to Oxford University to become the Regius Professor of Medicine. During his time in Baltimore he had been a pew holder and frequent attendant at St. Paul's.

The following year the choir lost the services of Mr. Willard. Fortunately this was immediately remedied by the happy choice of Edmund Sereno Ender as his successor. Mr. Ender had been a pupil of Horatio Parker, Professor of Music at Yale, and studied under him for eight years. He continued his training in Europe, and while there made a tour of the cathedral choirs in England as Mr. Farrow had done. He came to Baltimore from Minnesota in October, 1921. Mr. Ender represented the fortunate combination of skillful voice teacher and facile organist. He was an accomplished improviser and service player, exhibiting a refinement of taste and reserve in his performance. His understanding of vocal production gave the choirs he trained an exceptional choral sound. He was a frequent recitalist, playing a large repertoire, and he inaugurated the weekly midday recitals that through the years have been such a popular feature of St. Paul's downtown program.

It was in 1921, too, that an Assistant to the Rector was appointed in the person of the Rev. Smith Hilton Orrick. These two additions to the staff were to serve for many years and in their separate ways make outstanding contributions to the life of the Parish.

Dr. Kinsolving's hope of expanding the Boys' School was encouraged when in October, 1922, announcement was made that it would move from its cramped and quite inadequate quarters on Franklin Street to a new site in the suburbs on Rogers Avenue, Mount Washington. A tract of 9½ acres had been purchased by the trustees for $26,000. It included a large house capable of being converted into use as the main school building. Estimates for renovating the house, laying out the grounds for school use and other expenses connected with the move brought the total cost to $66,000. The Franklin Street property was sold for $55,000. Thus the additional money needed to finance the project was in the neighborhood of $11,000, surely a modest sum for the advantages that were to be gained. The first session at Mount Washington opened in the fall of 1923 with an enrollment of 41 boys.

In October, 1926, Dr. Kinsolving completed his twentieth year as Rector. The congregation took this opportunity to present him with a cash gift and a handsome silver bowl. On Sunday, October 10, he preached a sermon in which he reviewed his ministry. He reminded that on his arrival: "We pledged the endeavor to maintain the type of service which our people love, and it is for others to judge whether this pledge has been kept." He referred particularly to the church music under the direction of Mr. Willard and Mr. Ender. He noted among other things accomplished that ten young men who had worshipped at St. Paul's had in the past ten years dedicated their lives to the Christian ministry. Two of them had taken their ordination vows in St. Paul's Church—one was Harry Percy Veazie and the other the Rector's own son, Arthur Lee. Dr. Kinsolving estimated that during the twenty years of his incumbency a little under 14,000 services had been held in the church. He announced that the endowment fund, begun in 1888 had now reached $240,000, almost two and one half times the goal originally set. He concluded his sermon with the inspiring challenge: "This parish has had a great past. Let us endeavor by God's help to lay the foundation for a still greater future."

The Doctor prided himself on keeping in good physical condition. Golf and walking were his favorite forms of exercise. How he stayed fit in his advancing years was demonstrated late one night at the Rectory when Mrs. Kinsolving heard someone at the front door. The Doctor had had a hard day and, not wishing to disturb him, she went downstairs and encountered a man whom she took to be a burgular. A call for help brought the Doctor to her side and he gave the intruder a right to the jaw that knocked him out. It also broke three knuckles on the Doctor's hand. When the intruder came to he explained that he was not a burglar but only a "drunk." Distressed at what he had done the Doctor apologized to his victim, sat down in his pajamas beside him on the Rectory steps and urged him to repent and mend his ways.

Through those twenty years the Kinsolving children were growing up, as children have a way of doing. With five beautiful and charming daughters in the old Rectory and beaux constantly in waiting it was a busy and romantic place indeed. In due course all were married. Bruce, the eldest, became Mrs. MacGill James; Eleanor, Mrs. Beverly Ober; Anne, Mrs. John Nicholas Brown; Sally, Mrs. Milton Gundersheimer, and Lucinda Lee, Mrs. Egbert Leigh.

The Rectory, too, attracted many people from the literary and academic world. Mrs. Kinsolving was president of the local poetry society and many poets were entertained there. Among them were Robert Frost, William Butler Yeats, Edna St. Vincent Millay, Carl Sandburg, and Amy Lowell. Mrs. Kinsolving, as a perfect hostess, supplied Miss Lowell with the cigar which was known to be the lady's favorite smoke.

Dr. Kinsolving's greatest gift was that of a pastor. His son Arthur recalls: "It was not unusual for him to make a round of seventeen calls and come in very late for dinner. Not all the visits had been serious—he probably chaffed some of his parishioners and ended up by having a toddy with some congenial ones just before dinner. He was a familiar figure in the hospitals and he quickly identified himself with the trials and fears and suffering of the patients he visited. He rejoiced with them that rejoiced and wept with those that wept. I have known him to go out and buy coal for an old maid he thought was living in too cold a flat and to get Mother to send soup or other food by him to another whom he felt was too poor to be adequately nourished."

When making his rounds, often on foot, Dr. Kinsolving was a familiar figure on the streets. There was a solemnity about his stride that tempted Mrs. Kinsolving to paste up in the nursery a quotation from one of North Carolina's folk poets: "I seen Pa comin' steppin' high, which was of his walk the way." It was captioned in her hand: "Here's ABK to the life."

In spite of his many duties as Rector, the Doctor, too, found time for writing. He contributed many articles to the Historical Magazine of the Episcopal Church, was the author of a "Short History of St. Paul's Parish," a "History of St. Paul's School," a pamphlet on the history of the Diocese of

Maryland, and biographies of his two brothers who were bishops.

Dr. Kinsolving was conspicuous in church legislation. He attended eleven General Conventions as a delegate from the Maryland Diocese and served as chairman of the Committee on Christian Education. He was always a leader at the Diocesan Conventions, being one of an inner group which guided their deliberations. In fact this control was so tight that some of the younger clergy grew restive under it and at one convention tried to break its power. Everybody was aware of the revolt except apparently the veteran leaders against whom it was directed. These gentlemen continued to go about their business as though they enjoyed the loyal support of the entire body. That they knew full well what was going on finally was revealed when Dr. Kinsolving, speaking in behalf of a certain Diocesan charity which was suffering from neglect and was in fact on its last legs, suddenly faced the leaders of the revolt and with a look of scorn declared: "Now there is a challenge for those impatient young men who are trying to drive the elder statesmen from their places!" That ended the revolt; the elder statesmen continued to rule the Convention.

The evening of December 5, 1926, marked a new milestone in the history of the Parish. It was the occasion of the first of five special musical services, and for the first time a St. Paul's service was broadcast by radio. This was to become a regular custom in the case of special services; and, in the course of years with the advance in electronics, televised services would be brought from the church to homes throughout the city and state. That St. Paul's, in spite of its location, was continuing to draw people to its doors was manifested in the Lenten season of 1927, when the midday services with visiting preachers were well attended and the Holy Season, culminated in the Three-hour Service on Good

Friday and several services on Easter Day, attracted an estimated 4000 persons.

November 15, 1927, marked the twenty-fifth anniversary of Mr. Staples as Vicar of the Chapel and Guild House. Present to congratulate him on his achievements were Dr. Kinsolving, Bishop Coadjutor Helfenstein, and Mr. Jeffrey Brackett, the first president of the Guild House Association. Mr. John M. Glenn had come down from New York especially to attend, and also in the company was Miss Lizzie Gilman, another of the pioneers in the program. In the course of the celebration mention was made of thirty organizations that were meeting in the building, while the register showed that, during the twenty years from 1906 to 1926, 1,455 children had been baptized in the Chapel and 947 persons confirmed there.

Meanwhile the Girls' School had been running into difficulties. Enrollment had declined and there had been disciplinary problems. As a consequence, when the trustees met in January, 1927, along with the managers of the Benevolent Society, which still supported the School, it was resolved to shut down at the end of the school year. A committee was appointed to sell the property at 2411 North Charles Street and to consider what was to be done in the future. Pursuant to these discussions the sale was made, bringing the corpus of the Benevolent Society to $335,000. While this was going on it came to the attention of the trustees that Mr. and Mrs. William H. Buckler, who spent much of their time in England, would be willing to rent to the school their Baltimore residence on west North Avenue known as "Evergreen." This considerably changed the complexion of things and encouraged a continuation. A committee consisting of Mrs. Maurice C. Pincoffs, as chairman, Miss Rebecca Penniman and Mrs. George S. Jackson, all of whom had been actively interested in the school's administration, were directed to find a suitable head for a reorganized institution. They found the right person in Miss Emma London, a South Carolinian. In the course of the negotiations the Bucklers very generously offered to sell "Evergreen" at a price far below that which they had asked on the open market. Their offer was accepted, the purchase made, and the name of the school building changed to Evergreen Hall. The property was ideal for this new use, consisting of a spacious manor house with outbuildings set in a large lot. The School reopened in September, 1929, with Miss London as head, Miss Frances Early assistant and athletic director, and Mrs. George Rogers as housekeeper. The enrollment consisted of only eight girls but it was soon to reach its capacity of twenty-four. Another change in the character of the institution was that the education of the girls was passed on to a public school in the neighborhood, Evergreen Hall confining itself to providing a home and such informal training as went with it.

That same year saw the death, at 84 years, of Walter de Curzon Poultney. Mr. Poultney was a bachelor whose fastidious clothes made him a conspicious figure in Baltimore and earned him the title of "Sir Walter." He had long been a trustee and generous patron of the Boys' School and in his will he left it a handsome bequest. Another loss sustained by St. Paul's was the death on November 13, 1930, of Dr. Robert W. Johnson who, prior to his retirement in 1925 had served on the Vestry for 25 years. He headed a family, many members of which have labored industriously for St. Paul's. He was succeeded on the Vestry by his son, Dr. Robert W. Johnson, Jr., an active member from 1925 to 1954, at which time he was elected Vestryman Emeritus. His grandson, Robert W. Johnson, III, followed as vestryman from 1952 to 1964. An elder son, William Fell Johnson, also served briefly on the Vestry. Two daughters, Mrs. Robert Garrett and Mrs. James Mauran Rhodes, have been active

workers in the church, and the family tradition is being
carried on by Harrison Garrett and Mrs. William L. Reed,
other grandchildren of the first Doctor Johnson.

Two other progenitors, whose services, and those of their
descendants and connections by marriage, have spanned several generations are George W. Dobbin and Frederick W.
Brune, Jr. Judge Dobbin served on the Vestry from 1856
to 1891. His grandson, George Dobbin Penniman, was a
vestryman from 1908 to 1943, and his great grandson, Nicholas G. Penniman III followed on the Vestry from 1943 to
1949. Mr. Brune was a vestryman and Register from 1845
to 1878. His son, Herbert M. Brune, in the course of 47
years, from 1901 to 1948, held the offices of vestryman, Register, Junior Warden and Senior Warden. Frederick Brune's
son-in-law, Blanchard Randall, also served as Senior Warden,
and the third generation was represented by two granddaughters, Mrs. Maurice Pincoffs (Katharine Brune Randall), who for a number of critical years was chairman of
the committee on the Girls' School, and Mrs. Edward M.
Hanrahan (Evelyn Barton Randall) a volunteer worker at
the School. Dr. Harry R. Slack, husband of a third granddaughter (Elizabeth Blanchard Randall) was a vestryman.
Mrs. Pincoffs, incidentally, was succeeded as chairman of the
Girls' School committee by Mrs. J. A. Dushane Penniman
(Christine Brown), wife of a great grandson of Judge Dobbin. Also representative of the Dobbin-Penniman family and
ardent churchwomen were Mrs. George Dobbin Penniman
(Harriet Wilson Dushane) and Miss Rebecca Penniman.

Yet another family is that of Mr. and Mrs. W. Graham
Bowdoin. Mr. Bowdoin was a vestryman for 23 years and
was succeeded by his son, W. Graham Bowdoin, Jr., who
served a like term of years. Both Mrs. Bowdoin, Sr. and
Mrs. Bowdoin, Jr., were active in church affairs. So, too,

were the daughters of the senior Bowdoins, Mrs. J. H. Mason Knox and Mrs. John Staige Davis.

In the years following World War I the economy of the country entered a boom period. Common stocks reached unheard-of-heights, bonds bearing generous coupons were issued in profusion. There were heard a few voices of gloom warning that what goes up must come down and that the rate at which things were going could not last forever, but reassurances were had from many of the nation's financiers and publicists, who talked glibly of "the New Economic Era."

The St. Paul's congregation evidently shared in this spirit of optimism, for in the spring of 1929 a meeting was called to discuss starting a campaign to raise funds for completing the tower on the northwest corner of the church. Inquiry of Mr. Hobart Upjohn, son of Richard Upjohn who designed the church built after the fire in 1854, reported that the original plans for the tower were in his father's papers and available for use. That apparently was as far as the project got, for on October 29 the New York Stock Market crashed, leading to "the Great Depression."

The people of St. Paul's like others in Baltimore and throughout the country were hard hit. Things went from bad to worse until a climax was reached in March, 1933, with the closing of the banks. All hope of completing the tower vanished; the question was how the members of the Parish, whose incomes had been sorely cut, could meet running expenses. Pledges upon which the Parish depended for support fell off at an alarming rate; so much so that the Diocese had to call for a recanvass of potential givers.

Even harder hit were the members of St. Paul's Chapel and Guild House. The factories in which most of the men worked had shut down with no prospect of being reopened. The nation's industry was at a standstill. The Guild House at least offered a place where unemployed young men could find diversion. Hitherto it had been available for recreation only in the evening, now it was opened for the whole day. After spending the forenoon looking for work which seldom was found, many of the unemployed went to the Guild House in the afternoon to play checkers, billiards and volley ball. Mr. Staples reported: "The experiment of opening the House in the daytime for these fellows cannot be overestimated. Constantly they express their appreciation by telling the Vicar what it means to have a properly conducted place in which to spend their time."

Then in the very midst of this useful program disaster struck. On the night of November 29 the Chapel was destroyed by fire and the Guild House seriously damaged. Church services and the Church School were moved to the Columbia Theater nearby. For the time being there was an end to recreation in the Guild House. The people of the neighborhood rallied nobly to repair the damage, and were assisted by the Mother Church. Fortunately the property was well insured. The $61,800 obtained from that source was enough to wipe out the mortgage that stood at $14,000; and, thanks to the low cost of building that resulted from the depression, there was almost enough money left to rebuild the Chapel and repair the Guild House. Within a few months both were back in service.

The inauguration of Franklin D. Roosevelt in March, 1933, and the launching of the "New Deal" brought from Dr. Kinsolving a comment in "Parish Notes": "Every serious Christian must hope and pray that out of the anxious days of bank closing and financial anxiety through which we are living there may emerge a saner judgment and attitude on the relative value of material things . . . . After an orgy of gambling and spending, shocking revelations of the breakdown of character in certain responsible places were made. But more serious than this even has been the general fastening of the minds of the people upon money and the comfortable pleasures it brings us."

Even with the "priming of the pump" accomplished by the New Deal, recovery was slow. As late as January, 1935, Mr. Staples reported that unemployment was still high in the Guild House area. Then as the nation's economy was gradually being restored, disturbing reports began to come from Western Europe where Adolf Hitler and his fellow Nazis had seized power in Germany and were threatening their neighbors. In October, 1939, what everybody had feared happened—Hitler invaded Poland and World War II was on. Again Dr. Kinsolving used "Parish Notes" to express his reactions and those of most people in this country. He closed with an appeal for courage: "But to yield to counsels of despair when the Church of God is the one hope of our race, would be a cowardly thing. The very breakdown of human society by reasons of the methods of brutal savagery forced upon even unwilling participants, is a challenge to the church herself and to every member of the Church. Our Lord's words: 'Nation shall rise against nation, and kingdom against kingdom' are being sadly fulfilled. But the Church of God has lived through many crises in the past, and her sacred ministries were never more needed than now."

In the ensuing years the people of St. Paul's watched the fall of nation after nation to the apparently invincible Nazi arms and were reminded of what had happened in 1914–1918. They could only await the outcome while they went about their ordinary daily duties.

On April 7, 1940, Mr. Leigh Bonsal died after having served the Parish as treasurer for 37 years. Only a few days before he had been succeeded in office by Frank L. La Motte, who already had been active as a trustee of the Boys' School as well as pew register and vestryman. February 20, 1941, was a gala day when the congregation rallied to celebrate Dr. Kinsolving's 80th birthday. The church was filled at the morning service and after it the crowd repaired to the Rectory for a reception. Then in the afternoon more than 400 persons attended a reception at the School in Mount Washington and the cutting of the birthday cake. A delegation of alumnae and pupils from the Girls' School also was on hand. This same year Miss Gilman made a gift to the Parish of $3,000 to repair the organ.

In view of his advancing years Dr. Kinsolving had for some time contemplated retiring, and at a meeting of the Vestry on May 19, 1941, he offered his resignation to take effect in October of the same year. This was accepted by the Vestry which also bestowed on him the title of Rector Emeritus accompanied by a modest pension.

Then on December 7, 1941, came Pearl Harbor!

CHAPTER XIII

DR. DOLL'S MINISTRY

IN reviewing the history of St. Paul's Parish through its 275 years, one is painfully struck by the number and frequency of wars which have shattered the tranquillity of its people and taken a toll of suffering and sacrifice. The American Revolution, the War of 1812, the Civil War and World War I called St. Paul's men to the field of battle and St. Paul's women to the performance of auxiliary services. Now those unhappy experiences were to be repeated in World War II.

During the last days of Dr. Kinsolving's tenure as Rector and before a successor had been found, young men of the Parish, of the Chapel and Guild House, faculty and alumni of the Boys' School were being inducted into the armed forces, while hundreds more from The Guild House community labored in local war industries turning out munitions and other military supplies and equipment.

Reminiscent of the services performed by the women in World War I, the Army and Navy Commission of the Episcopal Church in Maryland organized the Service Men's Club, which opened its doors at Emmanuel Church on May 2, 1942. In July it was moved from Emmanuel to St. Paul's House to take advantage of a more central location. The

[183]

Club, as in World War I, offered a place where service men on weekend leave could relax, get snacks and soft drinks, write letters home or have letters written for them, join in singing around the piano and in many instances find invitations to meals in private families. Unlike World War I, however, this service was not provided by St. Paul's alone, but was shared with some 26 other Episcopal churches, each volunteering to act as host on two weekends a year. The St. Paul's women did their share of work under the chairmanship of Mrs. J. Clark Matthai. The Club proved popular with service men and continued operations for the duration of the war. From its move to St. Paul's House in July, 1942, to its closing in December, 1945, it was estimated to have entertained 47,500 service men and written 14,000 letters to their families.

In the course of the year the Vestry was able to announce that it had found a successor to Dr. Kinsolving in the person of the Rev. Harry Lee Doll. Born in Martinsburg, West Virginia, in 1903, Mr. Doll received his college education at the University of West Virginia and William and Mary College, Virginia, after which he entered Virginia Theological Seminary, from which he graduated. Ordained to the priesthood, he served as Assistant Minister of the Church of the Epiphany, Washington; as Rector of historic Christ Church, Alexandria, and of Trinity Church, Houston, Texas, from which he was called to St. Paul's. Following his ordination he was married to Delia Francis Gould, of Birmingham, Ala. In the years ahead he was to mention many times his debt to her for wise and sympathetic counsel. Mrs. Doll was to participate both in Parish and Diocesan activities.

September 1, 1942, the new Rector assumed his duties. He and Mrs. Doll had taken up residence in the Rectory along with two little daughters, Millicent and Chotard. Rebecca shortly was to be born in Baltimore. Within a few years

[184]

Mr. Doll was awarded an honorary D.D. degree. His gift for getting things done was quickly recognized by the Diocese. In 1945 he was elected to the Standing Committee and two years later to the Diocesan Executive Council. In keeping with the St. Paul tradition of close relationship with the Church Home and Hospital, he was made a trustee and vice-president of the board of that institution. In 1949 he was chosen as chairman of the important Department of Christian Education of the Diocese.

A parishioner commenting on Dr. Doll's ministry stressed his unusual ability for making the person to whom he was talking feel his keen interest in that individual. This characteristic was especially valuable in his new assignment. Because St. Paul's was a downtown church far removed from the residential district, the congregation had lost its neighborliness. Although parishioners came together at church services, Dr. Doll found that few of them knew each other. He set to work at once to remedy this situation by using every means available to build up the sense of family in the Parish. At the beginning of each Lent a "Family Packet" was sent to every address on the mailing list. Even an individual who lived alone was considered a family unit and shared with everyone else the unity of daily Family Prayer and the use of the missionary boxes. At Easter the whole congregation came forward with their mite boxes, each family with its own box, and put them under the Cross at the altar rail. In previous years the "Phantom Tea" had proved a popular method of raising funds. Dr. Doll reverted to the real thing. Social gatherings were held at St. Paul's House and the Rectory, and there were picnics at the Boys' School, all designed to make for better acquaintance. To accentuate this communal spirit, at the picnics, instead of each family going off and eating its own food, the practice was introduced of having each bring a particular dish and share it with all the others as is now generally done in the covered-dish supper. Parishioners were constantly reminded to report to Dr. Doll anyone who was ill so that a visit could be made.

Another means of bringing the congregation together was the decorating party at Christmas. In pre-war days a florist had been employed to do the decorating; now the whole Parish was invited to take part. The men hung the garlands and wreaths while the women helped the children set up the crèche. Those who were musically inclined sat in the choir and sang Christmas carols, while the older and less active members fashioned Christmas cards to be sent to the sick and shut-ins. The party closed with a light supper at St. Paul's House.

Dr. Doll kept a sharp eye out for the men and women of the Parish who were serving in the armed forces and growing in number every day. He saw that each of them got a military cross and a Prayer Book. His profound faith in the efficacy of prayer was illustrated by his having introduced in "Parish Notes" what he called "The Prayer Corner" where in each issue was printed a prayer which had particularly struck his fancy. Now, with the war approaching a climax, he introduced a system of praying for each member of the Parish by name at one of the three Sunday services, and likewise for each alumnus of the Boys' School once a month.

St. Paul's became a focal point for comfort, both of the soldiers and their families. Outside her door was set up a little house, manned by the Maryland Council of Churches, where a soldier could find information of all kinds—for overnight hospitality, entertainment, or whatever troubles might need a solution. Inside, in a corner just below the chapel steps, a small altar and prayer desk were set below a scroll bearing the names of the boys from the Parish and the Boys' School who were serving in the armed forces. On the prayer desk was a book in which visitors could write the name of any soldier, and at Intercessions, which were held daily at noon, he was prayed for on that day and for the next three weeks. There was almost always someone in front of this altar.

As reports from the western front in Europe indicated that the landing of the allied forces in France was imminent Dr. Doll obeyed Bishop Powell's injunction that special prayers be said for success on D-Day. When that Day, June 6, 1944, arrived, without any announcement or previous planning, services of prayer were held every half hour, beginning with the first word of the invasion and continuing all through the day. People poured into the Church in a constant stream, and there have probably been few days in her long lifetime that St. Paul's ministered to more anguished hearts than she did on this day.

Almost a year was to pass before V-E Day led to the unconditional surrender of Germany on May 7, 1945 and the end of the war in Europe. Three more months of fighting in the Pacific theater followed before V-J Day and the formal surrender of the Japanese. After that, the nation found itself involved in the small but costly Korean War. Peace at last restored, St. Paul's Parish paused to count its cost. The Mother Church, out of a relatively small congregation, had sent into the service some 115 of its young men and women, of whom six had given their lives. Sunday, December 8, 1946, following Morning Prayer, a solemn ceremony was held to mark the "Dedication of the Lights." These were the lights in the nave, vestibules and porch of the church which had been installed as a Memorial to the six young men who had died in the service and as a thank offering for the safe return of the others. The memorial bears the names of:

[187]

John Cougnet
Richard Dabney Cruikshank
John W. Garrett II
Howard May
Alexander Randall
William Watkins

Of these young men, two were members of families for generations associated with St. Paul's. John Garrett was the grandson of Dr. Robert W. Johnson; Alexander Randall a grandson of Blanchard Randall, a senior warden, and a great grandson of Frederick W. Brune, Jr., and Bernard Carter, both vestrymen for many years.

Approximately 250 names of alumni of the Boys' School appear on its Roll of Honor. In the School Chapel are two plaques, one bearing the names of alumni killed in World War I; the other the names of those who lost their lives in World War II and the Korean War. On the World War I plaque are:

Robert Brinton Hill
Maurice McKnight Hill
James Geoffrey Strugnell

On the World War II and Korean War plaque:

William Nelson Beale
Hunter Cole
Richard Dabney Cruikshank
Richard Donahue
Ralph Upshur Hooper
Donald Hopkins
John Pohlman
Louis Robertson

Dabney Cruikshank was both a communicant of the Church and an alumnus of the School. The Chapel and Guild House Roll of Honor for World War II contains 364 names. Some of them gave their lives, but, unfortunately, in the course of years the list has been lost.

The inevitable working of time witnessed the disappearance of old familiar faces and their replacement by new ones. The Doll ministry had hardly begun when, on November 16, 1942, the Mother Church and the Chapel and Guild House joined in paying honor to Mr. Staples on the occasion of his fortieth anniversary as Vicar of the latter. Four hundred persons crowded the Guild House auditorium to congratulate him on a job magnificently done. A year later he was the preacher at the morning service at St. Paul's Church, after which a portrait of him was unveiled. He resigned in 1944 to enjoy a happy retirement of eighteen years until his death in 1962, and was succeeded by the Rev. John R. Cooper who resigned within the year to accept a call to another parish. January 1, 1946, the Rev. Willard Marvin Entwisle began a career as Vicar and Rector which, after more than twenty years in office, finds him still going strong. The Chapel is now the independent Church of St. Paul the Apostle. A popular institution throughout the history of the Chapel and Guild House was its choir. Mr. Staples was fortunate in obtaining L. Gatewood Segar as organist and choirmaster. Mr. Segar retired along with Mr. Staples, but, because of his long experience with the Chapel, Mr. Entwisle found it well nigh impossible to replace him and prevailed upon him to return. He now supports Mr. Entwisle as capably as he did Mr. Staples.

About this time the Church lost two stalwart members in the deaths of Clarendon I. T. Gould and Phillips Lee Goldsborough. Mr. Gould, who combined the professions of law and banking, was also a police commissioner of Baltimore City. He was a vestryman for 36 years, during twenty of which he acted as Register. A man of even disposition, he was expert in pouring oil on troubled waters when Vestry discussions grew stormy. Mr. Goldsborough was elected to the Vestry in 1922, several years after he had completed a term as Governor of Maryland. While a vestryman at St. Paul's he was elected to the United States Senate and served capably in that body. During World War I, as chairman of the Liberty Loan Committee, he was responsible for the sale in Maryland of the government bonds through which the war costs were met. He was a vestryman for 24 years.

Another loss was that of Robert Wilson Nicolls, senior member of the choir of which he had been a member for 47 years. When he joined it, Dr. Hodges was Rector and Miles Farrow organist and choirmaster. His fine bass voice was in great demand and, in addition to his work at St. Paul's, he sang in a quartet directed by Alfred Willard and in the Bach Choir conducted by Harold Randolph, director of the Peabody Conservatory.

Nineteen forty-six was the year which witnessed a change as revolutionary and as fraught with dynamite as had been the vesting of the choir by Dr. Hodges. This was the "divesting" of the exterior of the church of its yellow paint, which from time immemorial had covered its bricks. Fortunately it was accomplished without bloodshed; and, now that some twenty years have passed, even the most extreme of the traditionalists have recovered from the shock and grown so accustomed to seeing the bricks in their natural state that they would no doubt fight to the death any movement to put the paint back on.

That perennial problem, the St. Paul's graveyard, once more attracted the attention of the Vestry. The inclosure had become a jungle of weeds; and vandals, to whom an old cemetery seems to offer an irresistible challenge, had done great damage to the tombs and those monuments which had managed to survive the ravages of time. On a number of occasions Boy Scout troops and boys from St. Paul's School volunteered to clean the place up, but that was not enough. The Vestry estimated that it would cost from $3500 to $4000 a year to keep it in shape and that $120,000 would have to be added to the existing $16,000 Graveyard Endowment Fund to assure the necessary income. A committee under the chairmanship of W. Graham Bowdoin, Jr. set to work to raise the money; alas, it fell far short of the goal. Some years later the Vestry and congregation voted to give the property to the City, along with the endowment fund, on the understanding that the City would take over its care. Negotiations, however, were interrupted because of the uncertainty over the location of the contemplated East-West Expressway which might pass through it. And there the matter continues to rest. The existing income from endowment does no more than keep the weeds down and support a rearguard action against the vandals.

Following his resignation Dr. Kinsolving continued to enjoy excellent health and to take a keen interest in the world around him. He remained a regular attendant at the services, and on special occasions helped to conduct them. It will be recalled that his eightieth birthday had been enthusiastically celebrated by the congregation in 1941. On February 20, ten years later, friends joined in celebrating his ninetieth! In response to congratulations he remarked: "I never expected to attain the freezing altitude of the nineties." Yet his end was not far away. The following summer, while at Fisher's Island, he died quietly, having preserved his faculties to the last. October 11 a memorial service was held in St. Paul's at which Bishop Powell, Dr. Doll, the Rev. S. Hilton Orrick and the Rev. Philip Jensen, Rector of the daughter parish of St. Thomas' officiated. As

[191]

he surely would have wished, the procession into the church was led by the choirboys of the School, to whose development Dr. Kinsolving had given so much time and thought, singing "Jerusalem, the Golden."

Some years later Alfred Shriver left a provision in his will that a hall for public meetings be erected at Johns Hopkins University and that one of the walls of the foyer be decorated with a mural depicting ten Baltimore "philanthropists," a term popularly associated with men of wealth. And, sure enough, among the ten selected were George Peabody, Enoch Pratt and Johns Hopkins. Mr. Shriver, however, did not limit himself to that narrow definition; instead he chose his subjects according to the literal meaning of the word—one who loves his fellow man. It is not surprising that he included Arthur Barksdale Kinsolving.

In the 275 years of its history there have been so many assistant ministers at St. Paul's that it would be well nigh impossible to do justice to their contributions to the Parish. One of them, Dr. Wyatt, eventually became the Rector. Several moved on to other fields and crowned their careers as bishops. There were two, however, who merit more than passing mention. Mr. Staples already has been noted for his exceptional accomplishment as Vicar of St. Paul's Chapel and Guild House.

Next in length of service, whose labors were centered on St. Paul's Church, was the Rev. Smith Hilton Orrick. Mr. Orrick assumed the duties of Assistant Minister in 1921 during the ministry of Dr. Kinsolving. He continued in that post until ill health made necessary his retirement in 1953 after an unbroken service of thirty-two years. It was on the occasion of his twenty-fifth anniversary at a celebration in St. Paul's House that his virtues were extolled. Dr. Kinsolving then said of him: "Among all assistant ministers I have known no more beautiful Christian character." Dr.

Doll echoed those sentiments: "I know no other man who asks so little for himself and asks so much the chance to serve the Lord." To these encomiums an anonymous layman added: "A true gentleman, embodying the Christian regard for the sanctity of each human life, tolerant, kind and patient in all things, trusting, untiring in the pursuit of his duties and in whose code no thought of his own welfare could come before the needs of his fellows."

Another notable instance of long association with St. Paul's involved a layman, Robert Tucker. He was present at the 11 A.M. service on March 20, 1949, which was his 101st birthday. Mr. Tucker had been a member of St. Paul's throughout his long life. He lived to be 102.

In November, 1951, the old church was put to a novel use as a theater for the performance of Christopher Fry's allegorical play "A Sleep of Prisoners," having to do with the observations on life made by a group of young men imprisoned in a church in Europe in World War II. Choir stalls, the lectern and the pulpit all were occupied by the actors during the delivery of their lines. The solemnity of the occasion quickly dissipated any feeling of irreverence; for in fact Fry was preaching a sermon, albeit one whose profundity left its meaning obscure to many in the audience. On the following Sunday, however, Dr. Doll preached on the play, opening up the theology in it to the delight of those who had been puzzled. It became necessary to have the sermon printed, so great was the interest in it and the play. It had been feared that many people might resent this return to the Church of its ancient role as the setting for morality plays, etc., but with very few exceptions they took great joy in bringing this to Baltimore, and entertained the young English actors lavishly during their week's engagement.

When Mr. Doll accepted the call to St. Paul's he did so

with the understanding that the Vestry would allow him to dispense with the ancient system of rented pews whenever he saw fit to do so. After studying the number of pew-holders, which was comparatively small, and noting that in most cases the pewholders were people of advanced age, he decided that with a little time and patience it could be accomplished without the drastic and painful measures insisted upon earlier. A compromise measure was adopted under which a pew was opened to anybody if the holder did not appear to occupy it within a designated time before or after the opening of the service, and no more pews were offered for rent. After the death of a few of the people to whom the old system was dear, the Rector wrote a personal appeal to those few left with such pews, asking them if they would be willing voluntarily to give up their pews and add the amount of rental to their giving. They responded nobly, and thus on February 1, 1954, St. Paul's became a "free church," easily and without disturbing the Parish.

Several other innovations appeared in the early years of Dr. Doll's tenure. One was the institution of the Order of St. Paul at the Boys' School. Boys over 14 years old were invited to join and serve as crucifers, flagbearers and acolytes. Another was the reorganization of the Woman's Auxiliary in keeping with a nationwide plan. Members were divided into four chapters bearing the names of men prominent in the history of the Parish and the Diocese; namely Chase, Claggett, Glenn and Kemp. It was at this time also that Dr. Doll, with the help of W. Edgar Rhodes, organized a choir of business men to sing at the Lenten midday services, a custom which still continues. The Christmas Eve service in 1948 marked another milestone in communication, for it was the first service in St. Paul's to be televised.

Those responsible for the finances of a parish constantly try to impress other members with the importance of making regular contributions through the envelop system, the only means a vestry has of knowing in advance what money will be available, and consequently enabling them to draw up a reliable budget. Distributing envelopes and crediting the holders with their weekly gifts calls for no little painstaking labor. For many years at St. Paul's that was the particular responsibility of Thomas R. Herring who carried it out with unflagging zeal. At the time of his death in 1951 he held the office of Senior Warden. When a memorial to him was proposed it was altogether appropriate that it should take the form of six alms basons.

In January, 1953, after thirty-two fruitful years as organist and choirmaster, Mr. Ender submitted his resignation, to take effect the following September. The resignation was accepted, and in appreciation for the fine service he had performed, the Vestry bestowed on him the honorary title of Organist Emeritus. He was succeeded by Robert Donald McDorman. The choice was a happy one, for Mr. McDorman's association with the music of St. Paul's had been exceptional. He was educated at St. Paul's School and was a choirboy from 1926 to 1931, a pupil of Mr. Ender, a soloist; and, in 1929, winner of the Choir Medal. He then attended Johns Hopkins University from which he was graduated in 1940. After that he won an organ scholarship at the Peabody Conservatory of Music and continued with Virgil Fox and Charles Courbain the study which he had begun with Mr. Ender. He is completing his fourteenth year in office.

By January 1955 Dr. Doll had been Rector of St. Paul's for twelve happy years and this arrangement, satisfactory both to rector and congregation, seemed all set to continue until it would rival in length the tenures of Wyatt, Hodges and Kinsolving. But it was not to be. Dr. Doll's qualities of leadership and his dedication to his calling had been perceived by clergy and laymen throughout the Diocese; on

January 19, 1955, he was elected suffragan to Bishop Powell. His elevation, of course, meant the end of his ministry at St. Paul's. Sunday, May 15, was the last day on which he officiated as its Rector. His consecration was set for Tuesday, May 24. To Dr. Doll a distressing circumstance of the ceremony was that, because of the limited space, he could not have present all the members of his congregation. Though the consecration was to take place in St. Paul's, it was in fact a Diocesan function. That meant that provision must be made for the officials of the Diocese, all the clergy of the Diocese, out-of-town bishops and clergy, representatives of the State of Maryland and the City of Baltimore and of other Christian communions. That left only 400 seats to be distributed among 150 parishes and missions. As a result, members of St. Paul's who received tickets had of necessity to be limited to the Vestry and Wardens, the Executive Council of the Woman's Auxiliary, officers of the Brotherhood of St. Andrew, trustees of the Boys' School and of the Benevolent Society and teachers of the Sunday School. It was inevitable that some feelings would be hurt. One consolation was that most of the ceremony was to be televised and this enabled Dr. Doll to place a TV set in the Rectory and invite members of the congregation to view it from there.

On the day appointed Dr. Doll was duly consecrated in the historic Mother Church. Consecrator was the Right Rev. Henry Knox Sherrill, D.D., Presiding Bishop, and the co-consecrators were Bishop Powell and the Right Rev. Frederick D. Goodwin, D.D., of Virginia. The presenting bishops were the Right Rev. Oliver J. Hart, D.D. of Pennsylvania, and the Right Rev. Thomas H. Wright of East Carolina; the preacher, the Right Rev. Charles Clingman (Retired) of Kentucky; and litanist, the Right Rev. Richard D. Baker, D.D., coadjutor of North Carolina. Attending presbyters

[196]

were the Rev. Bland F. Tucker, D.D. of Savannah, Ga. and the Rev. Willard M. Entwisle, Vicar of St. Paul's Chapel and Guild House.

Three days after his consecration Bishop Doll addressed a letter to "My Beloved Family of St. Paul's" in which he thanked them for the gift of a pectoral cross and a replica of it in silver on a marble base for Mrs. Doll's prayer corner; an antique candelabra, and a purse to help furnish the Suffragan Bishop's residence. Though Dr. Doll had ended his term as rector he remained in charge throughout the summer while a search was being made for a successor.

Ever since Dr. Kinsolving's death much thought had been given to selecting a suitable memorial to him. The Vestry had granted his family's request to erect a tablet in the church similar to those erected in memory of Bishop Kemp and the Rev. Thomas Chase. Various proposals were considered before they accepted the Memorial Committee's final suggestion that it take the form of glass doors at the entrance of the church to make it possible for people passing by to see the interior. The doors were designed by William F. Stone, Jr., an architect and for more than a decade a vestryman of St. Paul's. The memorial when installed bore the inscription: "To him through whom so many saw shining the light of Christ and through whom so many passed to knowledge and love of the Lord, a grateful and affectionate congregation dedicate these doors that make the sanctuary of God visible to all who pass by."

Another new and delightful feature of the Parish introduced during Dr. Doll's ministry was the Garden. It occupies the space to the south of the church; and its wrought iron gates, which are closed only at night, face Charles Street. The idea was conceived by Mr. and Mrs. John M. Tucker and met with the hearty indorsement of Dr. Doll and the Vestry. Mrs. Tucker, an artist, applied her professional skill to making an over-all design. Since the area is shut in by surrounding buildings there were problems of light and air to be overcome as well as maintaining fertile soil. Experiments had to be made with various growing things before those best adapted to the site were found.

It turned out that ivy did well and the garden now boasts some grown from cuttings from Canterbury Cathedral, England and the National Cathedral in Washington. There was success as well in growing begonias, sultanas, and a few hydrangeas and azaleas. In laying out the garden the Tuckers were helped by, among others, Mr. and Mrs. Marshall McCosh and John B. Mahool. The Garden Committee has since grown to 35 members. During the day the spot is always open to the public, and anyone who wishes to bring a lunch and eat it there may do so. Once a week in June the women of the Parish serve lunches. During the Christmas season a Nativity scene is set up and illuminated with spotlights at night.

The Garden Committee has its Standing Rules and By-Laws stating its object and the measures for carrying it out. The spirit of the place is well expressed in a prayer, written by Bishop Doll: "Almighty God whose blessed Son didst oft resort with his disciples to the cool and quiet of the Garden, there to commune with Thee, grant that all who come within this Garden and see the beauty of Thy handiwork may be led to Thee and go forth refreshed by Thy presence, through the same, Thy Son, Jesus Christ, our Lord. Amen."

CHAPTER XIV

THE BOYS' SCHOOL TODAY

THE move of the Boys' School from East Franklin Street to Mount Washington in 1923 was in the right direction, but it did not immediately solve a chronic problem: namely, finding and holding a headmaster. From 1910 to 1930 there were no fewer than thirteen headmasters or acting headmasters, most of them serving little more than a year or two. An exception was the Rev. William T. Elmer who was with the School from 1910 to 1917. He was remembered by his pupils as a strict disciplinarian and a classical scholar who gave them a thorough grounding in Virgil and Cicero. His successor, a man of great promise, Thomas DeCourcy Ruth had received his Ph.D. from Johns Hopkins where he had studied under the classicist Basil Gildersleeve. He combined with this a gift for music and sang in the St. Paul's choir. He had been in office only a few months, however, when the United States entered World War I and he resigned to join the Army.

It was not until 1932 that stability was at last achieved through the appointment of George S. Hamilton. Mr. Hamilton was a native Virginian who had been graduated from Randolph-Macon College in 1925 and elected to Phi Beta Kappa. From Randolph-Macon he went to the faculty of

the Episcopal High School at Alexandria, where he remained
for five years before moving to New York to engage in business. He was highly endorsed by the heads of two church
schools—Mr. A. R. Hoxton of Episcopal High and the Rev.
Albert Lucas of St. Alban's, Washington. His first session
opened with 60 boys, of whom 36 were boarders and 24 day
scholars.

While the School was still on Franklin Street and shortly
before it moved to Mount Washington three brothers from
Virginia, cousins of Dr. Kinsolving, entered as pupils. They
were John R. Mead, W. Carroll Mead and Frank D. Mead.
On graduation John, or "Jack," left Baltimore to make his
home elsewhere. Carroll and Frank, after completing their
college education, returned to pursue careers as investment
bankers in the city and to continue their support of St. Paul's
Parish both as vestrymen and trustees of the School. Furthermore, before entering banking, Frank had a few years on the
School faculty.

Another pair of brothers who were pupils when the move
to Mount Washington was made were Aubrey and Seeber K.
Bodine. Aubrey made pictorial photography his profession,
and for many years his pictures of the local scene have been
featured in the *Sunpapers*. His work has won both national
and international awards, and some of his pictures are on
permanent display at the Smithsonian Institution. He also
has published four volumes of his pictures taken in the
Chesapeake Bay country, and other parts of Maryland and
Virginia.

Mr. Hamilton quickly showed his ability to get along both
with the boys and the teachers. The latter were composed
of enthusiastic young men who gave him unstinted support.
Among them, in addition to Frank Mead, were Louis D.
Clark, Beverly Randolph Rhett, Donald Pierpont, Lewis L.
Tignor, Whiting Farinholt, Howard Myers, James Boyer,

Robert Kinnaird and Marshall Turner. Some of these men were with the School before Mr. Hamilton took over and had weathered some difficult periods; others joined the faculty later. While it still provided material for the choir which performed admirably under Mr. Ender, the School was rapidly taking shape as one of the leading private schools of the community.

Increasing enrollment called for increased space. The School had been at Mount Washington only three years when the Trustees approved the expenditure of $20,000 to enlarge the main building to accommodate additional boys. Again, in Mr. Hamilton's first year, further extension was made to provide for a choir room and more dormitory space. Soon after that, the purchase of additional land and buildings made possible a Lower School apart from the main school and also an enlargement of the playing field. For many years the School was handicapped by the lack of an adequate gymnasium. In 1937 this was rectified when a committee was formed with Mr. Hamilton at its head to raise building funds. Trustees on the committee were Frank L. LaMotte, William Fell Johnson, W. Carroll Mead, Thomas G. Young and John Baylor. The campaign was successful and the building was completed and put to use in the 1938–1939 session.

As late as 1934 the Parish was contributing $5,000 annually toward the budget; but as the enrollment grew and tuition fees were increased, the School became less and less dependent on the Parish. The Vestry had long since adopted the policy that enrollment should not be confined to boys of limited means. On the other hand, to insure that such boys should not be excluded, the granting of scholarships was continued.

In January, 1944, Mr. Hamilton presented his resignation in order to return to business. After mature consideration the Trustees accepted it, and at the same time adopted a resolution expressing the School's appreciation of his contribution during the twelve years he had served. In that time the enrollment had steadily grown, and now there was a waiting list. Not the least of Mr. Hamilton's achievements was the establishment of an honor system which has worked well over the years.

It had been agreed that Mr. Hamilton's resignation would take effect at the close of the school year, so the Trustees lost no time looking for a successor. Their choice fell on S. Atherton Middleton, who accepted. He was then on the staff of Episcopal Academy, Philadelphia, and simultaneously was coaching the University of Pennsylvania lacrosse team. He had attended Marston's School in Baltimore and also Johns Hopkins University. While at Hopkins he had been president of his class, president of the Athletic Association, and a member of the Student Council. There, too, he had played on the football and lacrosse teams. Further, he had a sentimental attachment to St. Paul's Parish where his grandfather, Alexander H. Robertson, had been in his day a devoted communicant. From his mother, Mary Robertson Middleton, he inherited a gift for teaching. For years she headed Gunston, a girls' school on the Eastern Shore, where Atherton also conducted a summer camp. Immediately upon his graduation from Hopkins he taught for six years at Marston's, serving as assistant head before moving on to Episcopal Academy. In the course of that time he married Catherine Carter Redwood, daughter of Mr. and Mrs. John Redwood, of Ruxton.

During the administration of Mr. Hamilton, the normal progress of the School had been disrupted by the United States entry into World War II. While the boys were not called for military service until after graduation, the faculty was immediately hard hit, and it was only through the Herculean labors of Mr. Hamilton that enough teachers were marshalled to carry the School along. On the return of peace and the removal of the major obstacles with which Mr. Hamilton had had to contend, it was clear that the time was appropriate for raising scholastic standards. Mr. Middleton made this his first objective, and in striving for it he had the support of the majority of the Trustees and also of Dr. Doll who had succeeded Dr. Kinsolving; and who, according to the School's charter, held the office of President of the Board of Trustees.

This objective was pursued so determinedly that, in the surprisingly short time of a year of preparation, St. Paul's was evaluated by a visiting committee of the Middle States Association of Colleges and Secondary Schools and put on the list of accredited institutions. With an end to improving the faculty Mr. Middleton insisted on a pension plan for the teachers and staff and a raise in teachers' salaries. Other moves in the same direction were the cataloguing of the library on an accepted system, the broadening of the curriculum and the instituting of a regular testing program for both old and new students with the aid of several experts in that field. Now that the School was filled to capacity it was possible to exercise greater selectivity in appointments to the faculty and in the acceptance of new pupils; though, as might have been anticipated, there were occasional failures in both groups.

The long-range result of raising the academic standard has been that St. Paul's today has graduates in many different types of colleges with a large geographical spread, including the "Ivy League." Recent graduates are currently doing well in Harvard, Yale, Princeton, Cornell, Brown, Massachusetts Institute of Technology, Williams, Amherst, Trinity, U.S. Naval Academy, University of Virginia, Johns Hopkins and Duke.

As St. Paul's found itself in competition with the large and well established boys' schools, it was not surprising that the pupils of these older institutions adopted a patronizing attitude toward the newcomer. Nor was it any more surprising that the St. Paul's boys reacted by showing an intense loyalty to their own struggling little school. This spirit was in due course to earn for them the name of "Crusaders." It was on the athletic field that the School presented its first serious challenge, and its success and the speed with which it was achieved was astonishing. The magic word was "Lacrosse."

When Frank Mead joined the faculty in 1931, he was fresh from the University of Virginia where he had starred in football and basketball. At St. Paul's he coached these sports and also baseball. In the spring of 1934, appointed athletic director by Mr. Hamilton, he was all set to field another baseball team when he found he was being pressured by some of the better athletes to organize instead a lacrosse team. Prominent among these agitators were Bob Maccubbin, Donald McDorman, Harry Hastings and Oscar Moritz. People who play lacrosse, or think they want to play it, are a stubborn breed. Frank knew when he was beaten and surrendered gracefully. The first practical difficulty—and it was a big one—was that nobody at the School knew very much about the game. Volunteers from outside, however, offered their services and Willie Pugh, an experienced player, was engaged to coach two afternoons a week.

A windfall came in the late summer of 1933 when Donaldson, another Episcopal Church school, in Howard County, closed its doors. Hamilton and Mead learned that quite a lot of athletic equipment was there waiting for disposal. So they made a trip to the school and found the Donaldson treasurer anxious to get the goods off his hands. He gladly accepted the $200 which was all the St. Paul's agents

[204]

could afford to offer for what they estimated to be worth $3000. That was not all that Donaldson's closing provided. Several good athletes transferred to St. Paul's, which now had both equipment and a nucleus of experienced players and was ready to set out on the long climb that would eventually bring it to the summit.

In 1935 Mead resigned from the faculty and recommended as his successor for the post of athletic director Howard Myers, another Baltimorean and athlete whom he had met at the University of Virginia. In the ensuing years St. Paul's did well in football and basketball, but it was in lacrosse that it achieved its remarkable record. Oddly enough Myers, like Mead, had never played the game. Under his regime the seasons from 1936 to 1939 were spent in gradually building toward perfection. In 1940 St. Paul's won its first interscholastic championship which it held for the next six years. During that time it won 58 games and lost only one. For four straight years it defeated the Maryland Scholastic All Stars, a team composed of the best players from all the school teams, with the exception of St. Paul's. It also won victories over college teams—the Princeton Varsity twice and the freshman teams of Hopkins, Navy and the University of Maryland.

The Crusaders won their first two championships when American youths of military age in college, or just graduating from school, were being summoned to a grimmer game in defense of the nation. Once the war was over, many of the old lacrosse players took advantage of the G.I. Bill of Rights to complete their interrupted education at college. Wherever they went they took their lacrosse sticks with them. To St. Paul's large credit is due for introducing the game in many colleges where it had never been played. At home the School continues to win its fair share of scholastic championships—eight or more since the end of the Myers era.

While all these events were taking place at Mount Washington, a crisis had arisen in the St. Paul's Girls' School leading to a radical change in the purposes of the Benevolent Society which had sponsored it for a century and a half. It will be recalled that when the girls moved from North Charles Street to "Evergreen" the School was fortunate in engaging as its head Miss Emma London. For twenty years she had conducted it with marked success and now the time had come for her retirement. The Trustees of the Society and the Lady Managers who shared responsibility for the running of the institution realized that there would be great difficulty in replacing her; nor was the income of the Society really adequate for the School's operation. During the "Evergreen" period the girls had been educated not by the School, but by a public school nearby, and a change in the character of the neighborhood threatened this arrangement. Further, a survey made by the Council of Social Agencies confirmed the opinion that there no longer was public need for an institution of this character which, after all, accommodated no more than about 25 girls.

So it was that at a meeting on March 6, 1950, the Trustees, with the general approval of the Lady Managers, sacrificed sentiment to reason and voted to sell "Evergreen" and close the School for a few years, with the possibility of opening it again at a new location. Shortly thereafter a purchaser was found, at a price of approximately $100,000. Thus came to an end the era of the Benevolent Society during which for 150 years it had followed literally the declared aims of its founders. The growth of its assets in the course of that time is interesting. At its inception the Society was controlled by "contributors," who were limited in number and whose individual gifts were not large. So far as existing records show there was only one other occasion in its long history when an appeal for money was made. The gradual increase in the corpus resulted almost entirely from the profitable sale of real estate and wise investment of the proceeds. So, in addition to its useful contribution to the charitable work of the community, it had after the sale of "Evergreen" assets whose market value was estimated at over $400,000. This was important to the development of the educational program of the Parish already well under way at Mount Washington and on the threshold of entering a new phase.

The question of the next step the Boys' School should take, always of course in the minds of the Trustees and others responsible for its development, was suddenly brought to a head in 1952 when a parent of one of the boys made a gift to it of $10,000. This led to a study of its most pressing needs. A committee representing faculty, trustees and parents was organized to make recommendation, and proposed that the small and inadequate science laboratory in the main building be enlarged. An architect and a contractor were called into consultation. They came back with the dismal report that the main building was "a tired building" and that any money spent on it would be wasted. This quite changed the situation, and by now all parties were restive and receptive to bold ideas. Another committee was appointed to look into the possibilities of moving to an entirely new location. While this committee was considering possible sites a parent brought word that the Emerson property known as "Brooklandwood" was available and urged that it be considered. "Brooklandwood" was originally the country estate of Richard Caton, son-in-law of Charles Carroll of Carrollton, Maryland signer of the Declaration of Independence and one of the wealthiest and most prominent leaders of his day. The property, off the Falls Road in Baltimore county, lies on the rolling hillside which constitutes the northern shoulder of the Green Spring Valley. The community of which it is a part bears the name Brooklandville. The mansion house, considerably altered as

ownership passed through a number of hands, enjoys a commanding view looking south toward Baltimore city. There
were as well dependencies, the most attractive of which was
a commodious brick stable covering three sides of a square,
its central portion capped with a graceful cupola. The
Trustees responded to the tip by sending some of their
members to look over the estate. They were captivated by
its beauty and its desirability as the site of a country day
school. But where was the money to buy it?

During the incumbency of Mr. Middleton, the Trustees
had taken advantage of an opportunity to buy twenty additional acres at Mount Washington. Now the wisdom of that
purchase was realized, for the enlarged property attracted
the University of Baltimore, which needed a playing field
and other facilities on the outskirts of the city. A sale at
a comfortable profit was arranged. The Benevolent Society
having disposed of "Evergreen" had funds available for investment and agreed to take a mortgage on the Brooklandville property for $120,000. With this encouragement the
Trustees went through with the purchase, the owners agree-
ing to the School taking possession June 1, 1952.

That was a hectic summer for the Headmaster and the
volunteers who offered to help with the move. Radical alterations had to be made in the new property. The stable's
stalls, tack room, hay loft and other facilities designed to
accommodate horses, harness, carriages and grooms, had to
be transformed into classrooms, laboratories and a library.
Other buildings on the property had to be converted into
dormitories, offices, infirmary, kitchen and dining rooms.
The work was completed in the time allowed and the School
opened in its new quarters on schedule. It was an experience which those involved will never forget and hope never
to repeat.

While the School was still at Mount Washington Mrs.

[208]

Helen Aleta Linthicum, widow of Congressman J. Charles Linthicum, died, and in her will provided that her jewelry collection be sold and the proceeds used for the building of a chapel for the School. The Chapel was not immediately built, but the jewels were sold and the money from the sale invested. Now it was decided to build the Chapel at Brooklandville. In the eight years since Mrs. Linthicum's death the fund had more than doubled. This was the largest bequest the School had received since that of Miss Asenath Harwood. The Chapel, of modest design, faces the entrance to what was once the stable. It is in daily use and is the center of the School's religious program.

Another innovation which took place after the move to Brooklandville was the change in the character of the Lower School, comprising the first four grades. Here again the Benevolent Society offered its cooperation. It agreed to contribute $75,000 for the construction and equipping of a building to accommodate 136 pupils on condition that the School accept not more than 68 small girls. In addition the Society would give $4500 a year toward the Lower School's operation, as well as provide scholarships for the girls who needed them. The $4500 annual contribution was later discontinued. The School on its part promised to provide "religious training according to the Holy Scriptures and the Book of Common Prayer," and to admit to its board four women members chosen by the Society. It was agreed further that if either party became dissatisfied with the arrangement, it could be terminated by the School repaying the Society the $75,000 it had advanced for the building, less depreciation.

Mr. Middleton, like Mr. Hamilton, enjoyed the loyal support of his faculty. Beverly Rhett and Louis Clark, who already have been mentioned for their services under Mr. Hamilton, stayed on to perform as efficiently under Mr. Middleton. Others who deserve mention are Howard Wooden, Roger Walke, Jr., James Ratcliffe and Paul Long.

At the close of the academic year 1964–65 the School sustained a loss through the resignation of the Rev. James E. Cantler, who had been Chaplain for more than a decade. His connection with the Parish and School went back much farther than that; in fact, as he expressed it on his retirement, it covered more than three-fourths of his life. He was a boy of the School and a member of the choir; he received his first Communion at St. Paul's; and, when he entered the ministry, he was ordained there. He left to accept a call to another St. Paul's Parish, at Centreville on the Eastern Shore. Like the one he left, it is a parish steeped in tradition—a tradition in comparison with which "Old St. Paul's" in Baltimore seems young. For St. Paul's, Centreville, traces its founding back to 1640, when services of the Church of England were being held there, more than half a century before the Establishment.

During these momentous changes the School was fortunate in continuing to attract the interest and talent of business and professional men for service on its board, as it had done throughout its long history. The rule had been to pick them from communicants of the Parish. As the School grew it became increasingly evident that this requirement excluded valuable prospects from among alumni and parents. So the traditional practice was discarded and for fifteen years or more trustees have been elected from this broader field with gratifying results. The Rector of St. Paul's and trustee communicants, however, constitute a majority.

For nearly forty years as a member of the Vestry and Treasurer of the Parish, Mr. Leigh Bonsal was of necessity intimately concerned with the affairs of the School of which he was also a trustee. On his resignation in 1940 he was replaced by Frank L. LaMotte, who for the next ten years applied his skill as a businessman to the many problems that arose while the School was at Mount Washington. He, too, was a trustee of the Benevolent Society. Over a long period of years William Fell Johnson was an ardent worker, his interest going back to East Franklin Street days. Thomas G. Young, a member of the Board for some thirty years, had much to do with the sale of the Mount Washington property to the University of Baltimore.

Other names of trustees which stand out are those of William F. Stone, H. Vernon Stehl, John A. Johnston, Herbert L. Kinsolving, younger son of Dr. Kinsolving; John Baylor, Dr. Robert W. Johnson 3rd and Dr. John Walton. For more than fifteen years George O'Connell has been secretary-treasurer of the Board, and still is.

To these might be added as non-members of the Parish R. Wilson Oster, Harry Dundore, William Bergen, J. Hurst Purnell and Louis Horst. Nor should the women sent to the board by the Benevolent Society be overlooked. Prominent among them was Mrs. Dushane Penniman, who for years served as chairman of the committee which directed the destinies of the Girls' School while it was at "Evergreen." She was also one of the prime movers in the agreement made between the Society and the Boys' School. Others active were Mrs. John T. Howard, Mrs. John A. Johnston, Miss Rebecca Penniman, Mrs. J. William Townsend III, Mrs. Horatio Whitridge and Mrs. Robert S. Hoyt. Mrs. William L. Marbury, as a member of the Board of the Society, was instrumental in putting through the agreement, though she did not serve on the Board of the Boys' School.

After a fruitful administration of twenty-two years which left on the School the indelible impression of his Christian character and high ideals, Mr. Middleton ended his labors to enjoy a well deserved retirement on the Eastern Shore. He was succeeded by John Talbot Ordeman. Born in 1930

[211]

at Huntington, Long Island, New York, Mr. Ordeman attended Phillips Academy, Andover, then took a Bachelor of Arts degree at Williams College and a Master's at Columbia University. He began his teaching career at the Episcopal High School, Virginia, and was on the faculty there for ten years as teacher, athletic coach and Assistant Headmaster. In 1958 he was married to Mary Duthie of Kent, England. The Ordemans brought with them Jennifer, Lee and Elizabeth to swell the ranks of the St. Paul's Parish junior brigade. In addition to his other qualifications Mr. Ordeman is a link between the School which was Dr. Kinsolving's *alma mater* and the School patterned after it which the Doctor hoped St. Paul's in Baltimore would some time be.

The School in the first year of Mr. Ordeman's administration had a student body of 575, of whom thirty were boarders. The faculty had grown to fifty and was expected to be increased by about five in the session beginning in the fall of 1967. Its objective has been stated to be scholastic standards formulated to prepare its graduates to meet the entrance requirements of the nation's most demanding colleges and universities, and bring out in each boy the best that is in him morally, mentally and spiritually.

As it has always done since its founding, the School includes in its curriculum the teaching of the Christian faith, with worship according to the Book of Common Prayer of the Protestant Episcopal Church. The religious program is under the general direction of the Chaplain. Mr. Cantler was succeeded in this office by the Rev. Herman A. di Brandi, who holds degrees from the University of Maryland and General Theological Seminary; and who has studied at Balliol College, Oxford, Catholic University of R.G.S., Brazil, and the William Allanson White Institute of Psychiatry.

In addition to introductory Sacred Studies in the lower

THE BOYS' SCHOOL OF ST. PAUL'S PARISH
Aerial View

"Brooklandwood House"   *Photo by A. Aubrey Bodine*

Campus, St. Paul's School for Girls

forms, the curriculum includes in the junior and senior years courses with credits in Theology and Ethics. One of the School organizations is a Student Vestry similar to that of any parish. It is their responsibility to prepare the program for the Chapel and to work in cooperation with the Chaplain. The vestrymen are licensed as lay readers by the Bishop of Maryland.

Quite a number of old St. Paul's boys have entered the ministry. The list of alumni in Holy Orders, probably incomplete, includes: Hugh Powers '90, Robert Lee Bull '23, Harris Findlay '32, William C. R. Sheridan '35, Morton H. Smith '41, Rockwell M. Smith '43, James E. Cantler '43, James C. Fenhagen, Jr. '47, David LaMotte '48, William Dols '51, Uly Gooch '52, Edward C. Lecarpentier '53, E. James Lewis '54, and David M. Barney '58.

Music, under the direction of Donald McDorman, continues to be emphasized. The program is, of course, vastly different from what it was when the School's chief purpose was to provide boys' voices for St. Paul's choir. Today with emphasis on college preparatory studies, music has assumed the nature of an extracurricular activity. It has to contend also with a variety of "clubs" centered on such attractions as chess, golf, philosophy, photography, radio, science and skiing; yet it manages to hold its own. There are a Contemporary Music Club, a Music Appreciation Club and a Glee Club. Forty boys, on choir scholarships, sing in the choir of St. Paul's and thus maintain the tradition of close to a century. Once a week the men of the choir journey out to Brooklandville to attend a rehearsal in preparation for the Sunday church service.

Under modern conditions it is no longer practicable to perform the elaborate musical programs which attracted crowds to St. Paul's in the days of Dr. Hodges and Miles

Farrow. Nevertheless the choirboys, with and without the men, are in demand for concerts in various parts of the State. There are programs as well in which the Glee Club of the Boys' School joins with that of the Girls' School. In addition to the late Channing Lefebvre and Donald McDorman, a number of alumni who began their musical training in the choir, have made music their career. William H. Welsh, a soloist when he was a boy, now is on the faculty of Davidson College, North Carolina, specializing in organ and composition; William Atwill, another boy soloist, is a church and concert soloist in Hawaii; Otis Clements, a composer, is also appearing in radio and television; John Mann directs the Johnny Mann Singers, engaged in recording and television with headquarters in Hollywood; and Glenn Yarborough, for some time a soloist with "the Limelighters," a folk music group, is now on his own making personal appearances and giving concerts.

It has been said that bricks and mortar do not make an educational institution, but adequate facilities do help tremendously, especially in these days when science laboratories are greatly needed, and when students in school are required to spend a good deal of time in the library. Very recently the Boys' School has had two valuable additions in the Science Building completed in 1964, and the Grover M. Hermann Library, completed in 1966. Other expansion to take care of growing needs is in the planning stage.

The growth and development of the Boys' School from its humble rowhouse dwellings on Franklin Street, to its more spacious home in Mount Washington, and finally to its historic setting on the broad, rolling acres at Brooklandville, has been spectacular. But the educational program of St. Paul's Parish was still only partly done. After all, girls have to be educated beyond the fourth grade at which time, under the prevailing agreement between the Society and the Boys' School, they were turned out on a cold world. Something had to be done about it. The Benevolent Society having terminated its Girls' School, was in need of a new project. One was soon to be found.

CHAPTER XV

AND NOW THE GIRLS' SCHOOL

DR. Doll was succeeded as Rector of St. Paul's on June 1, 1956, by the Rev. Frederick Ward Kates, who came to the Parish from the Cathedral of St. John the Evangelist, Spokane, Washington. There he held the office of Dean. Born in Rochester, N.Y., Mr. Kates received his Bachelor's degree from Amherst, his Master's from Harvard and his B.D. from the Virginia Theological Seminary. Ordained a priest in 1936, he served churches in Missouri, Connecticut, New York and Massachusetts as well as in Washington State.

Mr. Kates found time also to pursue a literary career. He was the author of nine books published between 1931 and 1957, wrote pamphlets for Forward Movement Publications, and many articles for Episcopal Church magazines. He was also editor of the literary remains of Bishop Charles Henry Brent, and for a number of years conducted a religious column for a newspaper in New York State. A contribution to the history of St. Paul's Parish was his small volume entitled "Bridge Across Four Centuries," which in precise language gives an account of the ministries of the Rectors who had preceded him, from the Rev. William Tibbs on down.

On arrival in Baltimore Mr. Kates, with Mrs. Kates and

their children, took up residence in the rectory on Saratoga Street. Soon thereafter, at his request, the Vestry purchased for a rectory the dwelling at 3802 Greenway, in Guilford, and to this the Kates moved, leaving the old Rectory free for needed office space.

The new Rector had been in residence little more than a month when, at the Vestry meeting of October 8, Dr. Johnson reported for a special St. Paul's Chapel Committee that the congregation of the Chapel wished to take over its affairs. Their request was approved. Then, pursuant to the ancient rule recognizing St. Paul's as "the Mother Church," a committee of the Advisory Board of the Chapel asked permission of the Rector of St. Paul's Parish to erect a separate congregation within the metes and bounds of the aforesaid Parish. Permission was granted and on November 12 the Chapel became the Church of St. Paul the Apostle. Thus was brought to a close a missionary endeavor whose history went back a century or more, testifying to the Mother Church's concern over the community of which she is a part.

The outstanding event in Mr. Kates's ministry was the founding of the new St. Paul's School for Girls at "Brooklandville." After lending a helping hand to the Boys' School, which included additional loans for development and construction of the Lower School building, the Benevolent Society still had substantial funds left over. The trustees were united in the belief that this money should be put to some good use, and the minutes of their meetings frequently referred to discussions on how it might be applied. While negotiations over the move of the Boys' School to Brooklandville were still going on the Society lost its Secretary, John A. Johnston. Mr. Johnston had long served the Parish as vestryman. He also was at one time treasurer of the Society and proved most useful in several financial crises. A resolution adopted on June 20, 1952, praised him for "his sterling character, fidelity to duty, and loyalty and love to family, friends and St. Paul's Church." He was replaced as secretary by Thomas F. Cadwalader, Jr. at the earnest solicitation of Dr. Doll. Thomas F. Cadwalader, Sr. had long been active as a vestryman and trustee of the Society.

The Vestry, too, was concerned over the Society's plans. It will be recalled that when the Girls' School closed at "Evergreen" mention was made of the possibility of its eventually being opened at some other site. That still was in the minds not only of the Trustees of the Society but of the Vestry as well. However, five years passed without action being taken. Then on April 23, 1957, a momentous meeting of the Society's Trustees was held at which a definite proposal was made. H. Vernon Stehl, a vestryman and also vice-president of the Board of Trustees of the Boys' School, was introduced, and he presented facts and figures to show how a girls' school could be operated at Brooklandville in conjunction with the Boys' School.

Mr. Stehl's arguments were so convincing that a motion was made and passed to appoint a committee of the Society to meet with one from the Boys' School for the purpose of working out an agreement for the purchase of more land and the erection of a building. The Society chose as its representatives Mrs. Penniman and Mr. Cadwalader, Sr. At this point the Church, the Boys' School and the Society met with a signal loss by the resignation of Mr. LaMotte as vice-president and treasurer of the Society and from the Vestry to take up residence on the Eastern Shore. At the next meeting Mr. Cadwalader, Sr. was elected Vice-President, and Richard R. Harwood, Jr. a member of the Board and Treasurer.

The discussions of the land committees of the Society and the Boys' School proved eminently successful. At the meeting of the Society's Trustees on May 28 a resolution was passed to buy 36 acres on the Falls Road from Brooklandwood, Inc. on condition that the Boys' School buy 17 acres adjoining. This purchase added to the 35 acres originally bought would bring the entire tract of land owned by the Society and the Boys' School to 88 acres. That would allow 36 acres for the site of a girls' school, while at the same time giving 17 extra acres to the Boys' School and providing for an extra playing field. To enable the Society to make the purchase the Boys' School repaid the $120,000 mortgage held by the Society. In turn, the Vestry took out a $160,000 mortgage on the Boys' School.

Though this new purchase of land was not consummated until the following September, the prospects were sufficiently encouraging to justify a motion to engage Mr. Stone, the vestryman who had designed the glass doors of the Church in memory of Dr. Kinsolving, to draw up plans for a girls' school. At this juncture two veteran trustees, Miss Rebecca Penniman and Mr. William W. Cloud resigned and were at once elected Trustees Emeriti. In their places were chosen Dr. Janet Howell Clark and William L. Reed. The appearance of Dr. Clark at this juncture was most important. A scholar of distinction from a family of scholars and a former headmistress of The Bryn Mawr School for Girls, she was highly qualified to give expert professional advice on the project. Mr. Reed, an associate vestryman and a business-man, was equally well qualified to deal with the practical problems of operation.

All of this was rather like putting the cart before the horse. It is true that land had been purchased as the site of a school, and plans had been authorized; but as yet there had been no formal decision to establish a school. However, Mr. Reed and Mr. Harwood had been appointed as a committee to report on the "Feasibility of Establishing a School for Girls." By March 7, 1958, they had completed a progress report which testified to their energetic labors from the time of their appointment. The report was highly optimistic. The Committee had consulted quite a number of professional people—among them Mr. Middleton, head of the Boys' School; Henry H. Callard, headmaster of Gilman School; and Miss Anne Healy, headmistress of the Roland Park School for Girls. They had found among these educators general agreement that there was room in the community for another private school for girls of the kind contemplated. In respect to the financing they reported that $300,000 of the funds of the Society could be made available for building a school on the land owned by it at Brooklandville. They estimated the total cost of construction at $260,000 and recommended that $150,000 of this be paid in cash and $110,000 raised through a mortgage on the property. That would leave the Society with $150,000, the income from which would be sufficient to pay the minimum of $4500 annually committed to the Boys' School and minor expenses of the Society. That substantially was the plan of financing carried out.

The committee assumed that the Boys' School would continue to receive girls in the first four grades of the lower school. They therefore recommended that the proposed girls' school should eventually include grades five through twelve. It would begin the first year with grades five to nine, then add a grade in each of the next three years.

With this report before them the Trustees were ready to make their momentous decision. On the afternoon of March 13, 1958, a meeting was held at the historic old Rectory on Saratoga Street. Incidentally, in all their discussions they had been most fortunate to have the legal advice of the Board's Vice-president, Mr. Cadwalader. In the absence of the Rector, Mr. Kates, he presided at this meeting. Others present were Mrs. Penniman, Mrs. Marbury, Mrs. John T. Howard, Dr. Clark, Mr. Harwood and Mr. Reed; and Mr. Stone of the

Vestry. The Secretary, Thomas F. Cadwalader, Jr., was there to keep the minutes.

The interim report was the main topic of discussion. Mr. Cadwalader, Sr. spoke on the legal aspects, expressing the belief that there would be no trouble in getting authority from the courts to go ahead, provided the institution remained non-profit.

At last Mr. Reed brought the matter to a head by asking the question: "Is it the intent of this Board to start a girls' school? If it is, action to have the Charter changed, and to get a headmistress, and other necessary actions can be initiated." There followed further discussion of the report during which Mr. Cadwalader stated that on further reflection he was inclined to believe that no change in the charter would be necessary.

Then in reply to Mr. Reed's question, a motion was made by Mrs. Penniman and seconded by Mrs. Marbury, and passed that: "It is the intention of this Society to erect a building on the Society's property at Brooklandville to carry on the education of girls beyond the fourth grade."

Thus the die was cast.

Now the road was clear to proceed with plans for the School. By-laws were passed under which administration was to be under the School's own Board of Trustees. This would be made up of the Rector of St. Paul's Church, who is also President of the Benevolent Society, as chairman ex officio; the eight remaining trustees of the Benevolent Society, and eight trustees chosen at large by the Benevolent Society from among outstanding citizens of the community on a rotating basis.

Subsequently these provisions were embodied in a formal agreement between the Trustees of the Girls' School, which by then had been incorporated, and the Benevolent Society. In this agreement allusion was made to the fact that, during the 160 years since the granting of its charter, the Society had pursued its declared purpose of maintaining and educating poor female children. It had been the practice in the early days, said the agreement, to "bind out" girls for domestic employment, but that had long since been abandoned in the community, while the free education of poor children today was generally supplied by the state and municipal bodies. Hence there was no present need for the service originally performed by the Society, but on the other hand there was need for schools for the education of girls, and especially schools where Christian teaching was the background, since this was forbidden in public schools. Therefore the Society had resolved to create and help maintain "a Christian school for girls to be known as St. Paul's School for Girls."

The purpose thus set forth, the agreement then provided that the Society rent the building and the site of approximately 36 acres at Brooklandville to the Girls' School, on condition that it operate a school of the nature described. The School also promised not to change the method of electing trustees as provided in the by-laws, and it was privileged to buy the property leased, subject to payment of the amount expended by the Society.

Shortly after the meeting of March 13, the decision was made to set September, 1959, as the date for opening the School. Mr. Stone was authorized to go ahead with the drawing up of the plans in cooperation with a building committee consisting of Dr. Clark, Mr. Reed and Mr. Harwood. A committee composed of Dr. Clark, Mr. Kates, Mrs. Penniman and Mrs. Marbury, directed to outline a philosophy of the school, reported in general terms that it should be a country day school. It was determined further to institute the office of Episcopal Visitor which Bishop Doll would fill.

The matter of most vital concern, however, was the selection of a headmistress to steer the institution on its initial and uncertain course. This major responsibility had been given to a committee composed of Mrs. Penniman as chairman, Mr. Kates and Dr. Clark. For several months it was busily at work inquiring into prospects and weighing the respective merits of those proposed. A name which kept appearing in the discussions was that of Rosalind Robinson Levering (Mrs. Wilson K. Levering, Jr.). Finally, at a meeting of the Trustees of the Society on September 16, 1958, a motion was made that Mrs. Levering be offered the position of Headmistress. It was passed unanimously; Mrs. Levering was notified of the action and accepted. The choice could not have been more fortunate. A graduate of Wellesley, she had had practical experience as assistant head of Bryn Mawr School in charge of its middle school. She had combined this with domestic duties as the mother of two girls and a boy.

Thanks to the labors of the various committees, the new head, the architect and the builders, the School was ready for opening at the time set. It was realized that until tuition fees were sufficient to carry running expenses the School would have to continue to look to the Benevolent Society for help. To ease this situation the Boys' School graciously consented to forego the $4500 contributed annually to it by the Society. To cement relations between the two schools, Mr. Middleton, head of the Boys' School, was invited to sit in at the meetings of the Trustees of the Girls' School.

Sunday, October 11, 1959, was a great day in the history of the School, for it was then that the dedication exercises were held in the new auditorium. Presiding was Mr. Cadwalader, President of the Board. On the platform with him were the Right Reverend Harry Lee Doll, then Bishop Coadjutor of Maryland and Episcopal Visitor to the School; the Reverend Alfred Noble Redding, Chaplain; Mrs. Levering and the twelve members of the faculty. The Reverend Mr. Kates, Rector of St. Paul's and ex-officio chairman of the Board, was absent on a preaching mission to the U.S. Air Force in Europe.

Seated in the auditorium, which was filled to capacity, were Trustees, pupils, parents and friends. On the School's first Board, in addition to Mr. Cadwalader, many of whom had labored hard in founding the institution, were: C. Keating Bowie and William L. Reed, vice-presidents, Miss Barbara Johnson, secretary, Richard R. Harwood, Jr., treasurer; Thomas F. Cadwalader, Jr., Henry H. Callard, Dr. Janet H. Clark, Frederick W. Doolittle, Jr., Mrs. Arthur U. Hooper, Mrs. John Tilden Howard, Mrs. William L. Marbury, James McHenry, Mrs. J. A. Dushane Penniman, and H. Graham Wood.

After the invocation by Mr. Redding and the singing of a hymn, Mr. Cadwalader gave a brief history of the Benevolent Society beginning with its founding in 1799, and details of the task recently completed in establishing the new school. He was followed by Mrs. Levering who introduced the members of the faculty, expressed her appreciation for the opportunity to "help build here in this surpassingly lovely and peaceful setting, a school dedicated to independent Christian education in a democracy." She concluded: "I know that I speak for all of us when I say that we want to make this a school that is not only sound and balanced in learning, but more than that, one that gives encouragement and help to each student to grow in character as well as in mind."

After the singing of another hymn Bishop Doll led the congregation in the Dedication Service and Prayers; and then, one by one, dedicated the class rooms, the library, the office, the auditorium and the science laboratory.

The school opened with 86 students. Its curriculum included English, history, science, mathematics, Latin, French, art, music and dancing. The open country in which it was located afforded ample opportunity for an athletic program which included field hockey, lacrosse and tennis. Within a few years this was rounded out when, with money loaned by the Benevolent Society, the School erected a $75,000 gymnasium.

While the School was in the process of organizing, a committee was appointed to frame the School's philosophy. Its informal statement served until 1965 when, in anticipation of evaluation for accreditation, a revised and much more comprehensive statement of policy was issued. This had been prepared by the faculty and the administration, with the approval of the Board. It set forth that it was to be a personal, intimate school which sought to develop a program and school life based upon Christian principles and one which emphasized the fullest possible growth in personality and character. Its curriculum was not to be vocational and it was recognized that its budget, which was not extensive, would restrict its activities. On the other hand, it had the advantages of being small and, as a private church school, free to include a religious program.

While the school would undertake to prepare girls for college it was not to be confined to this group, but would include girls with a "wide variety of endowments and gifts, whether hoping to go to college or take some other preparation for adult life." It was realized, too, that most of the pupils would come from prosperous middle class families characteristic of American suburban life today. Consequently, one of the purposes stated was "to arouse in a group of sheltered girls a sense of involvement in and response to the needs of society in a rapidly changing world." The ideal sought, therefore would be "to build a character so strong, mind and heart so tempered during the youthful period of natural idealism that the student can emerge from the school world into the larger world eager to commit herself to the Christian principles for which the School stands."

The School's relationship to the Episcopal Church was described as that of an associated church school, since under its charter the majority of the trustees were members of St. Paul's Parish.

Then there was the question of the relationship between the Girls' School and its near neighbor, the Boys' School. The latter continued to admit girls to its lower school, thus relieving the Girls' School of responsibility for the first four grades. Otherwise joint activity was to be confined to singing in combined glee clubs, the staging of plays, and bus transportation. The last was an arrangement that has caused not a few headaches, not all of which have been confined to the drivers of the buses.

The School has enjoyed another advantage in that it is free from the stereotyped qualifications required of public school teachers. In a community like that of Baltimore there are many women with exceptional educational backgrounds who have married and devoted themselves to the making of homes instead of pursuing careers in teaching for which they are eminently fitted. When their children grow older and no longer need intensive care, these mothers frequently find free time to resume their academic interests. St. Paul's Girls' School has used this rich source of material for the strengthening of its administration and faculty, to the great benefit of the School and the satisfaction of these domesticated scholars.

Mrs. Levering was greatly assisted by the faculty in getting the School on its feet. Miss Claris Crane, who had retired from the Bryn Mawr School faculty, returned to active duty to set up the English department and help organize the library. Carol Ober (Mrs. Richard Ober) was a mainstay in developing the athletic program and assisting in administration. Barbara Boyce (Mrs. John Boyce) and Libby Schultheis (Mrs. Carl Schultheis) concentrated on mathematics, and Jane White Mason (Mrs. Robert Mason) on science. Thanks to their efforts the academic standards went up rapidly, and in 1966 the School won accreditation from the Middle States Association of Colleges and Secondary Schools. Although it has been only five years since the first class was graduated St. Paul's alumnae have been accepted by some sixty colleges and junior colleges.

Having led the School in this auspicious beginning, Mrs. Levering expressed a wish to retire at the close of the school session in June, 1966. She was succeeded as Headmistress by Mary Frances Wagley, wife of Dr. Philip Wagley. The new Head is an example of the School's policy of making use of the academic talent that is so plentiful in the Baltimore community. Her versatility was early demonstrated in her career when she went from Foxcroft School, popularly associated with Virginia country life and fox hunting, to the stern scientific disciplines of the Massachusetts Institute of Technology. Having graduated from M.I.T., she proceeded to Oxford University, England, where she received the degree of Doctor of Philosophy in physical chemistry. She returned to the United States to teach, first at Smith College and then at Goucher. Her academic career was temporarily suspended while she devoted all her attention to raising a family. She is the mother of two girls and one boy. Her household now firmly established, she has found it possible simultaneously to assume the responsibility of directing a school.

The enrollment of the School during the 1966–1967 school year was in the neighborhood of 230 girls, and there is a waiting list. The Faculty has grown to 30 members, of whom half are full time and half part time.

The historically minded might have noted with mild satisfaction the negotiation of the land deals at Brooklandville and the firm establishment of the two schools there. Through this means St. Paul's Parish has recovered some of the territory generously surrendered when St. Thomas' Parish was created some 250 years ago.

CHAPTER XVI

BATTLE FOR DOWNTOWN

"I N the age of the secular city," says Harvey Cox, theologian, "the questions with which we concern ourselves tend to be mostly functional and operational. We wonder how power can be controlled and used responsibly. We ask how a reasonable international order can be fashioned out of the technological community into which we have been hurried. We worry about how the wizardry of medical science can be applied to the full without creating a world population constantly hovering on the brink of famine. These are pragmatic questions, and we are pragmatic men whose interest in religion is at best peripheral." Cox's secular city is a community undertaking to live without any form of religious faith and worship.

Bishop Stephen F. Bayne, Jr., coining the phrase "optional God," draws attention to the indifference to religion of believers and unbelievers alike; of believers whose faith is only skin deep, and unbelievers who, neither impatient nor angry, regard believers with an amused tolerance. The question is asked "Is God dead?" The whole world, inside and outside the Church, is witnessing the breakdown of old moral standards and the search for new ones better adapted to the present space age; and, as though that were not confusion enough, the flight of population from the city to the suburbs is creating immense economic and sociological changes.

How is Old St. Paul's, the Mother Church, affected by all this? What is she to do; and what, if any, is her future? On her 275th birthday, having attained an age which surely should merit repose, she finds herself in the forefront of the battle, planted in the very center of the sort of secular city Harvey Cox has described.

January 1, 1961, Mr. Kates resigned as Rector to accept a call to a parish in New Jersey. The Vestry took the occasion to express their appreciation for the rebuilding of the undercroft, which had been done under his direction; for his initiation of the midweek preaching services outside of Lent, and for his efforts and enthusiasm in the establishment of the new Girls' School. They accompanied this with a resolution assuring him that their prayers went with him for success in his new assignment. At the same time his assistant, the Rev. Alfred N. Redding, was appointed Priest-in-Charge while search was being made for a new rector.

This period of uncertainty was ended when a call was extended to the Rev. Halsey Moon Cook, who accepted it in July, to take effect the following September 1. Mr. Cook was born in Brooklyn, N.Y., April 26, 1928, the son of William Pierson and Gladys Moon Cook. Educated at McBurney School, he entered Columbia University where he was graduated as a Bachelor of Science in Industrial Engineering. While there his objective was radically altered when he elected to enter the ministry. Upon graduation he attended Edinburgh University, Scotland, seeking a broader education than the engineering school afforded. He graduated from General Theological Seminary in New York City with the degree of Bachelor of Sacred Theology in 1952. In the same year he was ordained Deacon and Priest and was married to Marcia Mary Healy, a native of Iowa and a Phi

Beta Kappa graduate of the University of Iowa, whom he had met as a fellow student at Edinburgh.

Following a curacy at Grace Church, Utica and five years as Rector of Calvary Church, Syracuse, New York, Mr. Cook came to Baltimore in 1958 as Executive Secretary of the Department of Christian Education of the Diocese of Maryland. Simultaneously he held office as a member of the National Council's Advisory Committee on Leadership Training, and of the Special Study Committee on the Total Ministry of the Church. In 1960 he was installed as Honorary Canon of the Cathedral Church of the Incarnation, Baltimore. From 1962 to 1966 he was a member of the Executive Council of the Diocese; and since 1959 he has been an Examining Chaplain. In his thirty-fourth year, Mr. Cook was at the right age to approach his new responsibilities with youthful vigor and enthusiasm.

His training as an engineer was not lost. It has enabled him to approach the problems of the Church with what might be described as a "slide rule approach," taking a careful measure of their dimensions before proceeding to the business of solution.

Another asset, especially in taking up the task of guiding the destinies of a parish the age of St. Paul's, was his sense of historical values. That is not to say he cherished a mere sentimental attachment to the past. Unlike so many members of his congregation, he had no background connected with St. Paul's. He soon was to acquaint himself with events both great and small in the long life of the Parish. These he used as history should be used, applying a knowledge of the past to plotting a course for the future.

There was, however, one way in which Mr. Cook fitted into St. Paul's tradition; that, oddly enough, was because he was a New Yorker. For it was from New York State that his predecessors Dr. Bend, Dr. Wyatt, Dr. Mahan, Dr.

Hodges and Mr. Kates had come. Even Dr. Kinsolving, Virginian though he was, arrived at St. Paul's by way of Mr. Cook's Brooklyn. Incidentally, Dr. Hodges, like Mr. Cook, received his ministerial education at General Theological, and Dr. Mahan once filled a chair on its faculty.

By the time Mr. and Mrs. Cook reached Baltimore they already had the beginnings of a sizable family. This included three girls and a boy—Cynthia Mary, William Pierson, Heather Elizabeth, and Kathleen Healy, respectively 8, 6, 5, and 2 years old. In September they moved into the rectory in Guilford which had been vacated by the Kates family eight months before.

One of Mr. Cook's first official acts was the appointment of some half dozen committees having to do with such routine matters as property supervision, finance, Christian education, ushering, memorials and the ever present problem of the graveyard. There was another committee somewhat out of the usual line, whose importance was soon to be felt. It bore the name Strategy Planning. Its chairman was Dr. John Walton, Professor of Education at Johns Hopkins University, a member of St. Paul's Vestry who had definite constructive ideas on a future program. The other members were Lloyd H. Denton, Miss Helen Garvin, Mrs. James A. Hamilton, Richard R. Harwood, Jr., Samuel Hopkins, William L. Marbury, Marshall K. McCosh, H. Vernon Stehl, Charles Stokes and Mrs. J. William Townsend III. They brought to it a fund of talent and experience.

In anticipation of the expanded program Mr. Cook had in mind he at once instituted what he called "an adult seminar" which he conducted himself, and which was designed to enlighten its members on the true mission of the Church in general and St. Paul's in particular. Further, he asked for and was granted by the Vestry a second assistant minister. Choice fell upon the Rev. George P. Donnelly, then

[234]

Associate Rector of St. Bartholomew's Church, Baltimore, who had worked with Mr. Cook in the Maryland Diocesan Department of Christian Education. A native of Clinton, Mass. he had been graduated from Trinity College, Hartford, prior to which he spent seven years in business before deciding to enter the ministry. He received his theological training at the Episcopal Theological School, Cambridge, and after ordination served parishes in Massachusetts before coming to Maryland. He brought with him to St. Paul's his wife, Muriel, and two sons—Gordon Lawrence, aged 7, and Roger Paul, aged 5. A daughter, Karen Louise, was born in 1962.

As another step in extending the ministry of the Church, a program of weekly businessmen's luncheons was planned for the month of January following, to discuss "The Downtown Battle" and the Church's involvement in it. That Old St. Paul's must prepare itself to meet the shock of radical departure from ancient tradition and custom was manifested when, at a Vestry meeting on January 8, Dr. Walton, moved that a request be sent to the Diocesan Convention that women of the Parish be granted the right to vote for members of the Vestry. This privilege hitherto had been jealously reserved for the men. The motion was passed with but one dissenting vote. The request was granted and women voted for the first time at the Annual Parish Meeting April 23. What is more, the Vestry, throwing caution to the winds, then resolved that women be made eligible to serve on the Associate Vestry. The first woman to be so honored was Mrs. James A. Hamilton. And the skies didn't fall; nor have they fallen thus far as a result of the belated official recognition of the immense contribution that women have made to the Church's work.

In April Mr. Marbury was elected Chancellor of the Diocese. His distinction as a leader of the Maryland bar and his mature judgment already had been recognized far beyond the bounds of the Parish. In May the congregation was distressed at news of the death of Edward D. Martin, who had served for thirteen years as associate vestryman and vestryman, and for the last ten years as Register. Only a month before he had resigned his office and been elected Vestryman Emeritus. In a resolution of that body he was honored as "an able and diligent lawyer, a devoted member of this parish, a sincere and loyal Christian."

With the coming of summer, and the vacation period of both clergy and laity, the activities of the Parish were considerably curtailed. For the convenience of members of the Parish who lived in the suburbs a morning service was scheduled for each Sunday in the Boys' School Chapel at Brooklandville, where the use of the school grounds for picnicking, including the privilege of the swimming pool, were thrown in as extra inducements.

It was apparent that Mr. Cook's mind had been occupied with thoughts about the Parish while he was vacationing, for upon his return he presented to the Strategy Planning Committee what he described as "The Rector's Working Paper for Strategy Planning." He had written it, he said, with two purposes in mind. The first was to provide him with the discipline of ordering random thoughts about the future of St. Paul's and to share them with the committee. It was not, he explained, a finished essay or even a presentation of definite proposals, but rather a draft, a working paper, which the committee might care to discuss. He had purposely taken the discouraging, but he believed accurate, side of things in order to provoke discussion and realistic planning.

The situation as he viewed it was that St. Paul's was a congregation whose average age was going up and whose contributions were going down. While the endowment fund had increased, he saw a limited number of men and women of "top leadership." He found the response to liturgical services limited. He noted that in St. Paul's Parish as in other parts of the world profound and sociological changes were taking place. It was characterized by a "Post-Christian secularist culture in which God is considered optional and the Church irrelevent to overwhelming segments of the population." He blamed this on the ineffective witness and stewardship of the Church.

The problem in his opinion was that few people knew why the Church is here, that it is generally regarded merely as a soothing balm in a crisis and a source of social respectability. He said that dedication in depth was lacking, and that there was little or no discussion among church people about the Church historically or where it is going; that the Church on its part was saying little that was relevant to individuals or to society generally.

Having outlined the situation he turned next to what should be the goal. That of St. Paul's he thought was no different from that of the Church as a whole. This goal he divided into what he called "Intensive Ministry" and "Extensive Ministry." The former had to do with members of the congregation; it involved corporate worship, pastoral ministry of the clergy to the people, educational programs and organizational activity. "Extensive Ministry" covered St. Paul's responsibility to the downtown community in which it was situated. This included opportunity for weekday worship, an imaginative adult educational program, pastoral counselling for those who wanted it, concern with and meeting the social and cultural needs of the area in such fields as housing, fair employment practices and the like, and finally, the training of lay leaders and clergy.

The strategy to be employed in reaching this goal as he saw it was, in the case of the Intensive Ministry, to foster religious education as to the nature and purpose of the

Church, to recruit more persons to help share in the leadership and to increase the financial support.

For the Extensive Ministry he proposed the establishment of what he called an "Academy," which would begin informally and gradually develop as an institution in the downtown area. It would eventually employ a full-time director working under a strategy and policy-making board to prepare programs for midweek services, counselling, public relations, and the future use of St. Paul's House, which then provided living quarters for some 18 residents. The implementation of these proposals he regarded as a task for the Vestry's Strategy Planning Committee.

Mr. Cook closed his paper with the basic declaration that, first, "God is Supreme (Creator) and intimately and presently concerned with the welfare of men, and indeed of creation"; secondly, "our task is derivative from God's unique action in history of becoming Incarnate in the person of Jesus. The Church's obedience is to its Lord. Its concern is for men and that they be brought to Him. The Church is important only because it is God's instrument in the world for bringing men to Him. The Church's business is not its own survival but rather obedience."

After studying the Rector's paper the steering committee of the Strategy Planning Committee came back with a report of its own to the Vestry which was in essence an acceptance of the Rector's conclusions and program. It stressed the need for the Parish Church regaining strength by increased membership and individual giving, and enlarging the Sunday School. It saw opportunity for improvement in pastoral care. The one feature which came in for praise was the "superb liturgical program." It repeated the Rector's recommendations for improving the Extensive Ministry and in addition alluded to the opportunity provided by the increasing leisure among the general public. It also reminded that any thinking on the activities of the Parish should include the two schools at Brooklandville.

One of the immediate steps taken to broaden St. Paul's mission in the downtown was the inauguration of a program of daily noontime services which provided for an Organ Recital by Mr. McDorman on Monday, Prayers and sermon on Tuesday, Holy Communion on Wednesday, Bible readings on Thursday and a Healing Service on Friday. The businessmen's weekly luncheons in January were continued for a second year, discussions being led by Dr. Walton and the Rev. Ian Wilson, then pastor of Franklin Street Presbyterian Church. The traditional relationship between St. Paul's Parish and her eldest daughter was revived when members of St. Thomas' engaged in business and the professions in the downtown area, joined the luncheons and discussions, an historic connection which eventually was to bear fruit. The revival of still another Parish tradition, this one symbolical of St. Paul's origin in the days of the colonies, was the observance in April of the Feast of St. George, when members of the St. George's Society attended services in a body. On that occasion it was recalled that the first Chaplain of the Society had been the Rev. Dr. Milo Mahan, then Rector of St. Paul's.

The program of Extensive Ministry entered a new and broader phase in the fall of 1963 when the four Episcopal churches in the downtown area, through their rectors, joined in a public "Statement of Mutual Responsibility." The manifesto pointed out that in the context of a changing urban culture the churches located in or near the center of a large metropolitan area were presented with a new and unique opportunity. Past methods, it said, were "irrelevent and obsolete." It held that the central truth of their faith was a mission in response to the living God and a unity in Christ, and that the time had come for this unity to find a new level of expression and corporate obedience. Therefore the rectors proposed to their congregations the establishment of a Metropolitan Mission, an associated enterprise of St. Paul's Parish, Christ Church, Emmanuel Church and Grace and St. Peter's. There would be a Metropolitan Mission Council composed of the rectors of the four churches and three laymen from each church. Its function would be to study the opportunity and resources for the mission, to determine priorities, and to refer specific recommendations to the respective vestries. The Statement was signed by Mr. Cook of St. Paul's; the Rev. Alfred B. Starratt of Emmanuel, the Rev. Warren C. Skipp, then Rector of Christ Church, and the Rev. Rex B. Wilkes of Grace and St. Peter's.

This proposal won the enthusiastic indorsement of the four vestries involved. At a meeting of the Vestry of St. Paul's the four representatives elected to the Council were Mr. Cook, Mrs. Walter R. Richardson, Mr. Marbury and Mr. Harwood. In a sermon to the congregation Mr. Cook explained the plan, the purpose of which he said, was "To make Jesus Christ and His saving power known within the secular urban culture of Baltimore." These four churches, he said, had joined together because of their proximity, similar history and similar attitudes. The launching of the mission was symbolized by a special "Service of Witness" in November at which Bishop Doll was the Celebrant, and the sermon was delivered by the Rev. Dr. Joseph G. Moore, Executive Secretary of the Presiding Bishop's Strategic Advisory Committee. As auspicious as was the creation of the Metropolitan Mission Council, it turned out to be only an interim measure on the way to an even wider and more ambitious program.

In the same month Dr. Walton presented to the Vestry a full report of the Strategy Planning Committee which was in fact a blue-print for the implementation of a downtown ministry. Its fundamental recommendation was that

St. Paul's continue to operate on its present site. Among the reasons given were that such a decision would witness to its being "the Mother Church," that the prospects were for an increasing population in the downtown area, that St. Paul's geographical position would be unique for such a mission, and that the involvement of the congregation would help the Parish itself to develop into a serving, witnessing, worshipping community. It recognized that so ambitious a program was not to be realized in a day and therefore divided it into several phases. It proposed that the study theme for 1964 be "The City and the Church." It called for a more thorough soliciting of pledges and an intensive calling by the clergy on members of the Parish and prospective members to define active membership more accurately, and it recommended the engagement of another assistant to the Rector who would devote half his time to the downtown mission. The report also gave a recapitulation of what already had been accomplished, including the organization of the Metropolitan Mission Council, the January luncheons of the men of St. Paul's and St. Thomas', and the program of weekday services.

Meanwhile, in the last few days of the year, an unexpected and somewhat dramatic incident served to emphasize the sincerity of St. Paul's participation in a downtown mission. It will be recalled that during the ministry of Mr. Kates a new rectory had been purchased in Guilford and the old one on Saratoga Street converted into administrative offices. Now, at the December meeting of the Vestry Mr. Cook suggested that, to demonstrate the willingness of the Vestry and the Rector to integrate the Parish's property into a revitalized downtown and to indicate their faith in the civic program of urban renewal, he and his family move back to the old Rectory. This was a bold proposal for a man with a wife and five children and the prospect of the imminent arrival of a sixth. Halsey Moon, Jr. had been born November 13, 1962, and Jenifer Reynolds would arrive July 8, 1964. Mr. Cook said he realized there would be practical difficulties, but he had studied the matter carefully and was confident they could be overcome. The first one that must have occurred at once to all married vestrymen present was what Mrs. Cook thought of the plan. Mr. Cook put their minds at rest on that score, reporting that before sounding out the Vestry he had consulted Mrs. Cook and had won her complete support. Not only that, but the older children had set down the "pros" and "cons" in two columns, found that the "pros" out-weighed the "cons," and indorsed the move.

The proposal thus forcefully presented, it was a foregone conclusion that the Vestry would go along—and so they did. Since extensive alterations were needed to make the old Rectory livable, a date for the move was set for June of 1964, the Cooks preferring to undertake that laborious task before, rather than after, their summer vacation.

When the news of the decision got around, it was received with enthusiasm on all sides. A letter of praise came from Mayor Theodore Roosevelt McKeldin and another from the Greater Baltimore Committee, while many parishioners by word or letter expressed their hearty approval. So once more the charming old mansion came alive; once more were heard within its walls the voices of children, which had echoed there from the days Dr. Bend and his family first occupied it in 1791 through the ministries of Kemp, Wyatt, Mahan, Hodges, Kinsolving, Doll and Kates.

Apart from sentimental and symbolical reasons for the return, there were very practical ones in view of the program in which Mr. Cook and the Vestry were engaged. In a sermon Mr. Cook pointed out that by living downtown and so close to the Church he would enjoy greater accessibility to members of the congregation. Further, he saw that it would make for better relationships with persons outside the Parish, particularly in the matter of counselling which he hoped to make one of the vital services in the Extensive Ministry.

One of the major tactical goals set by the Committee on Strategy Planning had been increasing the income from pledges. When the Treasurer made his report in the first week of the new year, 1964, he could announce that within two years they had jumped from $42,000 to $62,000, a gratifying response to the appeal to the congregation for a more hearty participation in the expanded Parish program. An equally auspicious factor was that 131 parishioners volunteered to work for it.

Simultaneously a drastic departure from ancient custom was made when, at the meeting on March 10, the Vestry voted to abolish the so-called Associate Vestry and to create in its stead a rotating Vestry. The proposal called for four year terms, two vestrymen being rotated off each year and ineligible for re-election for a year. In order to start it the eight vestrymen drew lots to determine the "Classes," or the years, in which two of them would be ineligible for re-election. It so happened that Bishop Powell was in the Rectory where the meeting was being held. The Rector, spying the Bishop's old felt hat (he was not wearing his mitre that day), put the lots in it, and it was from this that they were drawn.

In 1964 the Parish lost by death H. Vernon Stehl. Mr. Stehl had a long record on the Associate Vestry and the Vestry. He also was for many years vice-president of the Board of Trustees of the Boys' School and played an active part in the move from Mt. Washington to Brooklandville. His appearance before the trustees of the Benevolent Society to argue the feasibility of establishing the Girls' School on the adjoining property has already been mentioned. His talents also were recognized by the Diocese on whose Executive Council he served. This year also saw several changes in the staff. In March, Mr. Redding resigned as Assistant Rector to accept a call to be Rector of St. Mark's Church, Aikin, in the Diocese of Easton. Simultaneously, Mr. Cook announced the retirement of Oscar Swenson, for many years Sexton, praising him as one of the unsung heroes of the staff. Mr. Swenson's ties with St. Paul's were not completely severed, however, since he continued to serve part time as Verger. A valuable acquisition to the staff was Miss Betty Whaley, who joined it as Parish Secretary. Miss Lillian H. Dushane, who for eight years had nobly borne the double burden of Secretary and Assistant Treasurer, became Secretary to the Rector.

In June, pursuant to a recommendation of the Strategy Planning Committee, announcement was made of the appointment of the Rev. Alan H. Gee as Assistant Minister, who would assume his duties in September. A native of Massachusetts, Mr. Gee received his A.B. degree from Gettysburg College in 1950. After spending seven years in the insurance business he felt a call to the ministry and entered the Episcopal Theological School, Cambridge, from which he was graduated. His particular interest was the urban mission of the Church and it was in this field that he was to devote the major part of his attention. He also was appointed Chaplain of the Girls' School. Mr. Gee brought with him his wife, Joan Therese, and three children—Lincoln Alan, 7, Brian Andrew, 3, and Maria Therese, 2 months. With the three Donnelly children, the Gees and the five Cooks, to say nothing of the announcement of the imminent arrival of a sixth Cook, the official St. Paul's family assumed a refreshingly youthful aspect.

September 13, the 150th anniversary of the writing of "The Star Spangled Banner" was celebrated with a special service of commemoration, reminding of Francis Scott Key's association with the Parish through his friendship with Bishop

Kemp, through his daughter who was a communicant, and through the adaptation of his poem to music by Thomas Carr, the organist. The lesson was read by Mayor McKeldin, the National Anthem was sung, and also Hymn 454 which Key wrote in 1819.

Soon thereafter, another approaching anniversary began to absorb the attention of the Vestry. They recalled that St. Paul's Parish would have its 275th birthday in 1967, which would coincide with the completion of the major part of the redevelopment plan for downtown under the name "Charles Center." Discussion led to the conclusion that an observance simultaneous with this radical change in the complexion of St. Paul's environment would be more appropriate than waiting a quarter of a century to celebrate the round figure of three centuries. It might, in fact, serve as a stepping stone to this. Before decisive action was taken, however, the proposal was turned over to an "exploratory committee." Following the summer recess of 1965, the committee presented a report endorsing an observance in 1967 and suggesting that it lay emphasis on St. Paul's continuing ministry to the Baltimore community.

The year 1965 will be remembered for a narrow escape from disaster, when on Decoration Day a fire broke out in the Rectory. Fortunately, prompt action by the Baltimore Fire Department brought it under control. The damage, covered by insurance, was soon repaired.

The Vestry meeting of October 12 was eventful in that the Committee on the 275th anniversary presented a detailed report on a program. It included the development of architectural plans designed to cover the needs of the Parish for the next 25 years, a $275,000 capital funds drive and development of the theme "Christianity in the City." Other features proposed were a Symposium to attract scholars and leaders of the Church, a liturgical art exhibit, special anniversary services, and a Parish history. This met with general approval.

Another significant feature of this meeting was the Rector's announcement of the formation of an interdenominational group, composed of churches of the inner city. This organization was to be known as "The Central Churches of Baltimore." It stated as its purpose a co-operative study and action to develop a more effective ministry for the physical, mental, moral and social welfare of the residents of the area and the business community. The area covered would be that bounded on the south and north by Pratt Street and Mount Royal Avenue, and on the east and west by the Fallsway and Eutaw Street.

The plan envisioned sharing responsibility for specialized areas of work such as that among youth, students, young adults, the aged and others with special needs: combined staff work, united action on social and civic issues, making the churches more aware of the needs and problems of the downtown area, and enlisting laymen in programs of personal service and action. There was a co-ordinating committee, and under it committees on civic and political interests; social service, guidance and counseling; moral issues; special age groups and the business community.

The churches participating in the program were the Basilica of the Assumption (Roman Catholic), Christ Church (Episcopal), Emmanuel Church (Episcopal), First Presbyterian, Franklin Street Presbyterian, Grace and St. Peter's Church (Episcopal), Greek Orthodox Church of the Annunciation, Mt. Vernon Place Methodist, St. Ignatius' Church (Roman Catholic), St. Paul's Parish (Episcopal) and Zion Lutheran. Heading the Co-ordinating Committee was a rotating Chairman, and the first to hold the office was Mr. Cook, assisted by Mr. Donnelly as Secretary. Since the purposes of the Central Churches of Baltimore were identical

[246]

with those of the Metropolitan Mission in which the four downtown Episcopal Churches were associated, it was understood that the former would replace the latter, the Mission Council being limited to special meetings.

In furtherance of the Parish's expanded program the ministerial staff received an addition. To carry on work with students in the downtown area the Diocese established the office of Diocesan Downtown College Worker who would, for practical purposes, be affiliated with St. Paul's. The first appointee was the Rev. James J. McNamee III who shortly received and accepted an overseas call, and was replaced by the Rev. David H. Poist.

Meanwhile plans for the 275th Anniversary celebration had been approved and the immediate need was for a General Chairman. There was no doubt that the first choice for this exacting task was Harrison Garrett, for years identified with the Parish as Vestryman and in various other capacities. He also had been active in Diocesan matters as member of the Executive Council and of the Standing Committee, and as Lay Deputy representing Maryland at General Convention; on the National Council (now the Executive Council of the National Church), serving as chairman of the Finance Department; and Trustee of the Church Pension Fund. Outside the Church and his business directorships he was a Trustee of The Evergreen House Foundation; the Robert Garrett Fund for the Surgical Treatment of Children; the Johns Hopkins Hospital; the Children's Hospital; the Hospital for Consumptives; Princeton University, St. Timothy's School and Calvert School. The only question was his availability. In spite of his commitments in so many fields, Mr. Garrett cheerfully consented to shoulder the burden.

Meanwhile the Rector and Dr. Walton had been meeting together to discuss the Symposium, scheduled to be held early in November, 1967, and to solicit the participation of leading theologians and scholars as speakers and respondents. They decided that the theme would be the "Theological Prospects for Man in a Rational Society." This subject would be treated from a theological rather than sociological point of view. It was forseen that because of the distinction of the persons taking part, the Symposium would make a valuable and original contribution to the discussion of the problems raised by our changing culture; and would attract nation-wide attention when the papers delivered were published.

A project stemming from the Central Churches of Baltimore, and so-to-speak still on the drawing board was the proposed establishment of a Business Community Institute. For a year and a half a sub-committee of the Central Churches, composed of clergy and businessmen, beginning with the assumption that man's economic life and his religious life have always been related, had been evaluating traditional approaches to standard problems and attempting to develop programs designed to meet contemporary needs. They came to the conclusion that the old parochial institutions are inadequate to relate creatively to the entire business community; that, except as places of worship, the institutional churches, designed to serve an agrarian culture, have been outdistanced by the complexities and challenges of modern economic life. They concluded further that an approach by any one denomination is inadequate in our pluralistic society, and that if service is to be rendered, the business community must be "economically structured across denominational and faith lines."

The subcommittee therefore recommended the establishment of an independent, incorporated Business Community Institute, designed to serve the needs of the business, professional and industrial communities in traditional and experimental ways, as a logical and practical means by which religion could be related to economic life.

[248]

The Institute would function in three major areas of concern. The first would be Chaplaincy to the business, professional and industrial community, making the traditional Jewish and Christian ministries of worship and counselling available in specialized ways. The second would be Educational, providing opportunities for creative conversation and improved communication by means of seminars and consultations. The third would be Research and Development directed toward determining long range goals and immediate objectives of the Institute. It was recognized that in its infancy, and until its objectives were more clearly defined, its structures should be flexible and minimal. At the outset there would be only an Executive Committee and an Executive Secretary on a part time basis. If, after a reasonable trial, it was found that the work of the Institute was ineffective or illusionary, it could be abandoned.

St. Paul's primary role in the program would be to get it started. To accomplish this it called for and received help from its daughter, St. Thomas'. The vestries of the two parishes adopted the proposal and agreed to underwrite some of the budget requirements. St. Paul's is to provide physical facilities and a portion of Mr. Gee's time as Executive Director. Mr. Cook, the Rev. George E. Sinkinson, Jr., Rector of St. Thomas', together with the Rev. Norman W. Clemens, Minister of Mt. Vernon Place Methodist Church and Chairman of the Committee on the Business Community of the Central Churches of Baltimore, Rabbi Abraham D. Shaw of Oheb Shalom Congregation and the Rev. Thomas Simmons, Rector of the Basilica of the Assumption selected representatives of their congregations to meet as a steering committee. This group is presently meeting to expedite the proposal.

There is special significance in this proposal. One of the factors held responsible for the existence of the secular city is the flight of the well-to-do and more representative elements of the community to the suburbs, leaving the urban problems behind them. St. Thomas' involvement in a downtown program is a new departure which, adopted by other suburban congregations in Greater Baltimore and in metropolitan areas throughout the country, presents unlimited possibilities.

Churchgoers at the 11 A.M. service at St. Paul's on Sunday, January 15, who had not been forewarned, no doubt were startled at being greeted by ushers in cavalier dress and to see the Rector, the Rev. Mr. Gee and the Rev. Mr. Poist in the chancel, bewigged and clothed in vestments patterned after those worn by the clergy at the close of the seventeenth century. The Communion service and the accompanying music were arranged to resemble as closely as possible what our ancestors would have known when St. Paul's Parish was established in 1692. Even the prayer for the heads of state referred to William and Mary.

This was the first of a series of monthly services in observance of the 275th Anniversary, designed to acquaint the congregation with different Anglican Church rites. Among those following were services according to the Scottish Communion office of 1764, a new format to be proposed to the next General Convention, a folk mass composed by Ian Mitchell featuring guitar music, the rite used by Coventry Cathedral, England, that used by the Church of Canada and a liturgy proposed for churches of the Anglican Communion in Africa.

Another Sunday service was devoted to compositions by persons associated with the long and eventful history of music at St. Paul's, including those by Dr. Hodges, those by former organists, choirmasters and choristers—Christopher Meineke, Channing Lefebvre, Madeley Richardson, Wilmer Welsh and Edmund S. Ender, Organist Emeritus, and one by Mr. Ender's daughter, Elizabeth. The service opened with an organ recital by Mr. Ender, who had journeyed to Baltimore from his home in Florida especially for the occasion.

An equally ambitious musical program a few weeks later was the presentation of Josef Haydn's "Lord Nelson" Mass. Taking part were the St. Paul's Choir, the Glee Clubs of St. Paul's School for Girls and the Boy's School of St. Paul's Parish under the direction of Mr. McDorman, and members of the Peabody Orchestra. Norman Johnson of the Peabody was the conductor. This was the first time an orchestra of the Peabody had taken part in a program at St. Paul's since the Christmas Communion Service in 1873, arranged by Dr. Hodges and the Peabody's Hamerik. The Mass was splendidly performed and the young people from the schools could not have failed to be impressed with the musical tradition to which they are heirs, and which they, in their turn, were so admirably sustaining.

Not a part of the anniversary celebration, but an annual event also testifying to the relationship between the Schools and the Parish is the joint Baccalaureate Service each June which the students of both schools and their parents and friends attend. It is heartening to reflect that these members of the younger generation may catch some of the spirit of veneration for the old Mother Church which has made her a force in the community in the past and on which the future depends.

THE REVEREND HALSEY M. COOK, B.S., S.T.B.
Present Rector

CHAPTER XVII

"FROM GENERATION TO GENERATION"

HE time comes to bring this history to a close. But there can be no last chapter. For the history of St. Paul's Parish continues to be made from day to day by the hundreds of people young and old, in the Congregation and in the Schools. Between the time the last word is written and the book comes from the printer, enough will have happened to fill a new chapter. All that can be done by way of conclusion is to reflect on the past and conjecture the future.

The structure of the Parish today is uncomplicated; it has been stripped of nonessentials. Administration is headed by the Rector and Vestry. Its distaff side is in the capable hands of the Episcopal Church Women, divided into three chapters of good working size bearing the names Claggett, Kemp and Kinsolving. The Altar Society, whose history covers more than a century, continues to perform its sacred duty. Supporting the Altar Society are the Acolytes. There are *ad hoc* committees on ushering, the Garden and the 275th Anniversary. So much for the "Organizations."

Then there are the "Institutions"—The Boys' School of St. Paul's Parish, the St. Paul's School for Girls, and the Benevolent Society of the City and County of Baltimore, which 167 years after its founding, is ready to offer a helping hand where needed.

In the Battle for Downtown, St. Paul's Parish does not stand alone. It is recognized today that no single church or single denomination can provide the spiritual sustenance needed in the area. So St. Paul's is affiliated with the Central Churches of Baltimore, and actively engaged in its program. The reconstruction of the undercroft of the church building, into which a large part of the proceeds of the Capital Funds Campaign will go, is designed specifically with the use in mind of St. Paul's as a center of the joint downtown ministry.

The great and fundamental truth that the history of St. Paul's reveals is that, from the day when Baltimore Town was laid out and the first of those churches built where the present one now is, its people have recognized their responsibility to the community and lived up to it.

What of the future? Let successive rectors speak for the Parish. In a sermon preached in 1878, when St. Paul's was first beginning to suffer from the move of its parishioners to churches farther from the center of town, Dr. Hodges declared: "Here is the place for the Church, to stand from generation to generation . . . . Here should the rich and poor alike feel that they can come to the Father's House, and be fed continually with the meat which endureth until everlasting life." And St. Paul's stayed on.

Nearly half a century later Doctor Kinsolving, on the occasion of his twentieth anniversary as Rector in 1926, gave further assurance: "This parish has had a great past. Let us endeavor by God's help to lay the foundations of a still greater future."

A quarter of a century after that Dr. Doll, then Rector, had this to say: "One of the factors that brought your present Rector to accept the call of the Vestry was the deep conviction that St. Paul's must live and bear witness for our Lord in downtown Baltimore."

In the light of the conviction of these three of his predecessors on the permanence of St. Paul's, so abundantly fulfilled, the statement of the present Rector, Mr. Cook, made in an address before the annual meeting of the congregation in 1962, is pertinent: "The uniqueness of this parish has to do with the central values of churchmanship it has consistently maintained and represented through succeeding generations in Baltimore. There is a stability and an honor and a rootedness and an integrity about the Mother Parish . . . . One of the high privileges you and I have is to see to it that this Parish remains in the love of our Lord and its witness to His Lordship."

This short history may well be closed with the conclusion of Mr. Cook's address: "God has Purpose in raising up a strong parish in the heart of this city. I believe that purpose is to preach Jesus Christ as Lord—Lord of life, Lord of history and Lord of all the affairs and relationships of men. If we are to do this powerfully we are called upon to dedicate ourselves anew to the task that is before us. Now, and in the future, we will be called upon to make great sacrifices to keep the Mother Parish strong."

ACKNOWLEDGMENTS

Requests for information and other help in writing this history met with a generous response from everybody connected with St. Paul's Parish and its affiliated schools.

Mr. Cook, the Rector, was never too busy to bring out official records, make constructive suggestions and supply material from his fund of knowledge about St. Paul's past. His sympathetic understanding was a constant source of encouragement.

I am grateful to Mr. Harrison Garrett, Mr. Lloyd H. Denton, Dr. John Walton, and my wife, Rosamond Randall Beirne, for their critical reading of the manuscript. To Mr. Henry Haller credit is due for performing the exacting task of compiling lists of the Rectors, Assistant Rectors and the Vestrymen of St. Paul's Parish of whom there is record from 1692 to the present day. The list of Vestrymen is believed to be complete from 1888. In addition, he has prepared the Index and read proofs. In the latter undertaking he was ably assisted by Mrs. Cook and the Rev. George P. Donnelly. Appreciation is due Mrs. John Arnold Johnston and Miss Helen Garvin for guidance in reporting on the contribution of the women of the Parish. Miss Garvin also drew up the list of presidents of the Women's Auxiliary, now known as the Episcopal Church Women. Mrs. John Tucker provided information on the Garden, in whose planning and maintenance she has been a moving spirit.

For information for the chapter on the Boys' School I am indebted to Mr. S. Atherton Middleton, retired Headmaster, and Mr. John T. Ordeman, the present Headmaster. Mr. R. Donald McDorman, Organist and Choirmaster, supplied details of the School's musical program and the choir as they are today; Mrs. McDorman, Alumni Secretary, brought from her files data on the careers of some of the St. Paul's boys following graduation. Help was given also by Mr. Frank L. LaMotte, Mr. Frank D. Mead and Mr. W. Carroll Mead, who have been associated with the School in various capacities and saw it through many crises. Mr. S. Page Nelson and the late Channing Lefebvre, boys of the School when it was on Franklin Street, contributed lively reminiscences of that period. To Aubrey Bodine, another old St. Paul's boy, our thanks for permission to use selected photographs with which his name is now popularly associated.

Mrs. Wilson K. Levering, Jr., first Headmistress of the Girls' School, furnished a comprehensive briefing on its founding and early years; and Mrs. Philip Wagley, the present Head, brought the narrative up to date.

Thanks are due the Rev. Willard N. Entwisle for answers to questions having to do with the former St. Paul's Chapel and Guild House, now the Church of St. Paul the Apostle; and to Mr. L. Gatewood Segar for a conducted tour of the buildings.

A biographical sketch of Dr. Kinsolving, written by Mrs. Kinsolving shortly after his death, provided intimate details of his life. Mrs. John Nicholas Brown and the Rev. Dr. Arthur Lee Kinsolving, responded generously to an appeal for recollections of their childhood in the Rectory.

For the chapter dealing with his ministry, Bishop Doll contributed notes which added much to an understanding of the aims so well achieved.

The chief source for the history of the early years of the Parish was the "Historical Sketches of St. Paul's Parish in Baltimore County, Maryland," by the Rev. Ethan Allen, sometime Archivist of the Diocese of Maryland. This work was completed in 1855 but never published. The manuscript, in Mr. Allen's fine handwriting, is preserved in the

Rector's study; an enlarged mimeographed copy in two volumes is in the library of the Maryland Historical Society. Supplementing the Allen manuscript is a mass of correspondence, most of which passed among the Maryland clergy going back to the days of Bishop Claggett. These letters, running into the thousands, are being filed and indexed by Mr. F. Garner Ranney, present Archivist. For years in the keeping of the Peabody Library, they are finding a permanent home with the Maryland Historical Society. Mr. Ranney was most helpful in explaining the use of the index and vertical files and in calling attention to letters of special interest.

In the collection of material, the staffs of the Maryland Historical Society, the Maryland Room of the Pratt Library and the Peabody Branch of the Pratt provided their customarily generous assistance, as did also Mr. Wilbur T. Hunter, Director of the Peale Museum.

Other sources of material were "Parish Notes," the files of Baltimore newspapers, and recent Minutes of the Vestry and the Benevolent Society. Unfortunately, the Vestry Minutes covering the crucial Civil War period are missing. The account of the ministry of the Rev. Thomas Chase is based on an article by Mrs. Beirne which appeared in the Maryland Historical Society magazine. I am indebted to Mr. Denton for his research into the setting of "The Star-Spangled Banner" to music by Thomas Carr, St. Paul's organist; to Lieutenant-Commander Martin C. Bourdillon, British Royal Navy, for biographical data on his ancestor, the Rev. Benedict Bourdillon; and to Charles Scribner's Sons for Sidney Lanier's letter describing the Christmas Communion service in 1873, which was first published in "Scribner's Magazine" for May, 1899.

The story of St. Paul's Parish is primarily the story of generations of people who have worshipped and served there.

Special effort has been made to mention in the narrative as many as possible of those members whose names have appeared conspicuously in the records. Obviously in a chronicle covering two and three-quarter centuries, many people who contributed generously will have been missed. To those whose forebears or who themselves may have been overlooked, the author offers his humble apologies and asks that they treat his shortcomings with that Christian charity that one has come to expect of members of the St. Paul's family.

FRANCIS F. BEIRNE

Ruxton, Maryland
September, 1967

THE LAY LEADERSHIP
of ST. PAUL'S PARISH

Vestrymen, Wardens and Officers
of the Parish

This is of necessity an incomplete listing. All records from 1696 to 1721 have been lost.

Between August 26, 1776 and June 7, 1779, the Vestry met only once, on August 5, 1777 (during the period of transition from the Church of England to the Protestant Episcopal Church in the United States of America.)

No vestry records from 1818 through 1888 have been found. Names of Delegates from St. Paul's Parish to the Diocesan Conventions, and of some other lay leaders of the Parish, are taken from the Journals of the Diocese of Maryland during that period.

SYMBOLS

c—clerk

D—delegate to Diocesan Convention,
    presumed to be Vestryman or Warden

E—emeritus

PR—pew register

R—registrar or register

T—treasurer

AT—assistant treasurer

ET—envelope treasurer

V—vestryman

AV—associate vestryman

W—warden

JW—junior warden

SW—senior warden

Mr. Robert Adair	w 1764–1765	1768–1769
Mr. William Aisquith	w 1764–1765	v 1767–1770
		1773–1774
Mr. James Alcock		v 1783–1784
Mr. Robert Alexander	w 1762–1763	v 1768–1771
Mr. Thomas S. Alexander		D 1845
Mr. Owen Allen		v 1772–1775
Justice George Ashman		v 1692–1695
Mr. George Ashman		v 1739–1742
Mr. John Bailey	w 1742–1743	
Mr. Thomas Bailey	w 1794–1796	
Mr. Benjamin Baker		v 1799–1802
Mr. Howard D. Baker, Sr.	JW 1948–1953	AT 1950–1952
Mr. Joseph Bankson		v 1753–1754
Mr. William Barney	w 1726–1728	
	1735–1736	
Mr. Solomon Belts	w 1816–1817	v 1815–1820
Mr. William Bradford Bend	R 1811–1812	v 1811–1812
Mr. Thomas Biddeson		v 1721–1722
Mr. David Bien		AV 1947–1949
Mr. Edward Wyatt Blanchard		v 1870–1877
Dr. William J. A. Bliss		v 1910–1938
Mr. G. Herbert Boehm	JW 1899–1900	
	sw 1901–1902	
Justice John Boering		v 1723–1726
Mr. Leigh Bonsal	T 1903–1940	v 1901–1940
Mr. Thomas Boone		v 1751–1752
Mr. Charles B. Bosley		AV 1956–1959
Mr. W. Graham Bowdoin		v 1881–1904
Mr. W. Graham Bowdoin, Jr.		AV 1935–1936
	R 1944–1949	v 1936–1953
		VE 1953–1958
Mr. Benjamin Bowen	w 1732–1733	v 1729–1731
Mr. Edward Bowen		v 1757–1759
Mr. John Bowen		v 1727–1730
Mr. Daniel Bowley		v 1775–1776
		1779–1781
		1784–1785
Mr. William Branson	w 1798–1799	
Judge Nicholas Brice		v 1817–1818
		1819–1820
Mr. D. S. Briscoe		D 1881–1893
		1896–1897
Mr. Dixon Brown		v 1795–1799
Mr. Frederick William Brune		v 1845–1878
	R 1845–1878	
Mr. Herbert M. Brune	JW 1901–1902	
	sw 1902–1903	v 1904–1924
	R 1906–1924	1926–1948

[262]

Mr. George Buchanan	w 1734–1735	v 1731–1734
	1749–1750	1737–1740
		1745–1748
Mr. William Buchanan of George		v 1786–1788
		1790–1793
Mr. Andrew Buchanan	w 1759–1760	v 1762–1765
		1767–1770
Dr. George Buchanan		v 1798–1799
Mr. William Buckner		v 1725–1729
Mr. Henry Butler		v 1723–1726
Mr. Thomas F. Cadwalader		AV 1935–1938
		v 1938–1965
Mr. Archibald Campbell		v 1794–1797
Mr. John Carman	w 1754–1755	v 1760–1767
Mr. Christopher Carnan	w 1757–1758	
Mr. Charles R. Carroll		D 1861–1869
Judge James Carroll		v 1803–1813
Barrister Charles Carroll of Mount Clare		v 1779–1782
Richard Carson, Jr.		v 1797–1800
Mr. Bernard Carter		v 1903–1912
Mr. James Cary	w 1752–1753	
Mr. James W. Chapman, III		AV 1961–1964
Mr. Richard Chase		v 1753–1755
The Hon. Samuel Chase		D 1794, 1801
Mr. Hezekiah Clagett		v 1799–1800
		1813–1815
Mr. (?) Clapham		v 1815–1820
Mr. James Clark	w 1776–1777	
Colonel William Clemon	w 1795–1796	
Mr. Edward I. Coale	w 1804–1807	
Dr. Samuel Stringer Coale	w 1779–1780	v 1780–1781
Mr. John Cockey		v 1722–1723
		1733–1736
Mr. John Cole	R 1816–1817	v 1816–1817
Mr. Samuel Cole	R 1803–1811	v 1802–1811
Mr. William Cole		v 1798–1799
Mr. Cornelius Comigys	w 1812–1813	v 1810–1815
Mr. William H. Conkling, III		AV 1959–1962
Mr. Edward Cooke	c 1723–1726	
Mr. William Cooke		v 1800–1803
Mr. Nicholas Corban		v 1692–1696
Mr. James Corrie	w 1800–1802	
Mr. Hercules Courtenay		v 1781–1786
Mr. Robert Courtenay	w 1792–1793	
Mr. Joseph Cromwell		v 1739–1742
		1748–1751
		1758–1761
Mr. Richard Cromwell		v 1692–1698

Mr. Charles Crookshanks		v 1789–1790
		1794–1795
Mr. Charles Croxall		v 1757–1758
Mr. James Davidson	w 1796–1798	
Mr. Alexander W. Davis	w 1786–1787	
Mr. Daniel Delozier		v 1810–1814
Mr. Lloyd H. Denton		AV 1962–1965
		v 1965–
The Hon. George W. Dobbin		v 1856–1891
Mr. Samuel J. Donaldson		D 1816
		1819–1848
Mr. Thomas Donellan	w 1780–1783	v 1779–1780
		1783–1784
Dr. Mones Dorling	w 1784–1792	v 1782–1783
Mr. John Dorsey	w 1779–1780	
Mr. Robert Dorsey		v 1787–1788
Colonel John Dorsey of Edward		v 1721–1722
Miss Lillian H. Dushane	AT 1956–	
Mr. John Eager		v 1721–1722
Mr. Abraham Eaglestone		v 1748–1751
		1754–1757
Mr. John Eaglestone	w 1722–1729	
	1731–1732	
Mr. James Edwards		v 1776–1778
Mr. John Edwards	w 1737–1738	
Mr. Lewis M. Elphinstone	JW 1946–1948	
Mr. Thomas L. Emory		D 1821
Mr. A. S. Ennals	w 1772–1773	
Mr. Andrew S. Ennals		v 1788–1794
Mr. John Ensor	w 1736–1737	
Mr. John Ensor, Jr.		v 1759–1762
Mr. Thomas Ensor, Jr.	w 1754–1755	
Mr. Hugh Davey Evans		v 1828–1862
Mr. Job Evans	w 1743–1744	
Mr. Gilbert H. Eyre	JW 1954–1966	
	sw 1966–	
Mr. William Fell		v 1733–1736
		1740–1743
Mr. John Forney		v 1695–1698
Mr. Edward Fotteral		v 1741–1742
Captain Thomas Franklin		v 1747–1748
Mr. John Frazier		v 1754–1755
Mr. Frank Frick, Jr.	sw 1902–1903	
Mr. George Arnold Frick		D 1923, 1934
Mr. Richard Frisby	w 1813–1814	v 1814–1820
Captain Alexander Furnival	w 1798–1790	
Dr. Thomas B. Futcher		v 1924–1932
Mr. James Gardner	c 1741–1750	v 1741–1750

Mr. Harrison Garrett		AV 1946–1947
	T 1950–1966	V 1947–1965
		1966–
Major Thomas Gates		V 1780–1784
Mr. John Gay	C 1692	
Mr. N. Ruxton Gay	W 1758–1759	V 1752–1755
		1762–1765
Mr. John Gibson	T–1813	D 1813, 1821,
		1825
Mr. John Gibson, Jr.		D 1843
Mr. William Gibson		V 1783–1785
		1791–1794
Mr. John Gill	W 1739–1740	
Mr. Christopher Gist	V 1737–1740	V 1742–1748
Mr. Nathaniel Gist	W 1741–1742	
Justice Richard Gist	W 1731–1732	V 1726–1729
	1738–1739	1734–1737
	R 1739–1740	1739–1741
Mr. John M. Glenn	T 1901–1903	V 1896–1903
Mr. John M. Glenn, Jr.		V 1904–1907
The Hon. Phillips Lee Goldsborough		V 1922–1946
Mr. Lyde Goodwin	W 1745	
Dr. Lyle Goodwin	W 1745–1746	
	1752–1753	
Mr. William Goodwin		V 1774–1776
Mr. Harry Dorsey Gough		V 1772–1774
Mr. Clarendon I. T. Gould		V 1912–1948
	R 1924–1944	
Mr. Robert Green		V 1748–1751
Mr. William Green	W 1747–1748	
Mr. George Grundy	W 1788–1789	V 1789–1793
Mr. Nicholas Haile		V 1735–1738
Mr. J. M. Dryden Hall, Sr.		AV 1962–1965
Mr. George S. Hamilton		AV 1943–1946
Mrs. James A. Hamilton		AV 1962–1966
Colonel William Hamilton		V 1723–1724
		1732–1735
Mr. C. Willis Hammond	JW 1966–	
Mr. John Hammond	W 1784–1785	V 1787–1790
Colonel William Hammond		V 1730–1732
Mr. Edward Hanson	W 1770–1771	V 1775–1776
		1778–1779
Mr. Jonathan Hanson	W 1740–1741	V 1747–1750
Mr. George Harriman		V 1748–1751
Mr. Lloyd Harris	W 1736–1737	V 1729–1732
Mr. Hall Harrison	W 1816	V 1815–1820
Mr. Thomas Harrison	W 1745	
Mr. Robert S. Hart	JW 1944	AV 1935–1944
Mr. James Harwood		D 1837

Mr. James Kemp Harwood		v 1878–1895
Mr. Richard R. Harwood, Jr.		av 1954–1957
		1960–1962
		v 1964
Mr. Govert Haskins	w 1804–1810	
Mr. John Hayes		v 1695–1698
Mr. Richard K. Heath	w 1811–1813	v 1810–1811
		1816–1817
Mr. John Hedden	c 1738–1740	v 1738–1740
Mr. Mayberry Helm	w 1744–1745	v 1748–1750
	1750–1751	1751–1754
Mr. Mayberry Helm	w 1757–1758	v 1754–1755
	1760–1761	1772–1775
	r 1754–1755	1777–1782
Mr. Thomas R. Herring	sw 1942–1951	
	et 1943–1951	
Mrs. Thomas R. Herring	at 1952–1953	
Mr. Hugh K. Higgins		av 1951–1954
		1955–1958
Mr. Solomon Hillen		v 1743–1746
Mr. Francis Hinckley	c 1734–1738	v 1734–1738
Mr. Thomas Hines		v 1722–1723
		1728–1731
Mr. Benjamin M. Hodges, Jr.		d 1861–1862
		1868–1870
		1874–1880
Mr. John S. B. Hodges		av 1958–1961
Mr. George Hoffman	w 1801–1802	v 1805–1820
Mr. J. Latimer Hoffman	jw 1870–1899	
Mr. John Hoffman		d 1821
Mr. Peter Hoffman		d 1824, 1827
Mr. Thomas Hollingworth, Jr.		v 1797–1816
Mr. Samuel Hopkins		av 1958–1962
	at 1966–	v 1964–
Mr. George Howard		v 1765–1766
The Hon. John Eager Howard		v 1785–1789
		1792–1795
		1803–1806
		1809–1813
Dr. John Tilden Howard		av 1945–1948
		1963–1966
Mr. Daniel Hughes	w 1774–1776	
	1781–1782	
Mr. John Israel		v 1722–1723
Mr. George S. Jackson		v 1911–1922
Mr. William Jacob	r 1782–1785	v 1782–1785
Mr. Edward Johnson		v 1785–1788
The Hon. Reverdy Johnson		v 1885
Dr. Robert W. Johnson		v 1900–1925

Dr. Robert W. Johnson, Jr.		v	1925–1954
		ve	1954–
Dr. Robert W. Johnson, III		av	1952–1954
		v	1954–1964
		v	1967–
Mr. Samuel Johnson		v	1785–1794
Justice Thomas Johnson		v	1757–1761
			1792–1796
Mr. William Fell Johnson, Jr.		d	1911
Mr. John A. Johnston		av	1944–1947
	r 1949–1952	v	1948–1952
Mr. Nicholas Jones		v	1770–1771
Mr. Philip Jones		v	1724–1727
			1732–1735
Captain Philip Jones		v	1748–1751
Judge Thomas Jones		v	1762–1764
Judge Edward D. Kemp		d	1840, 1843
			1849
			1859–1861
			1863–1865
			1867
Mr. Charles V. B. LaMotte		av	1953–1956
Mr. Frank L. LaMotte	pr 1936–1939	av	1939–1940
	t 1940–1950	v	1940–1955
Mr. Alexander Lawson	w 1737–1738	v	1746–1749
Mr. Alexander Lawson	w 1755–1760	v	1763–1764
Mr. James Lawson		v	1773–1775
Mr. Richard Lawson		v	1794–1800
Mr. J. Harry Lee	jw 1906–1911		
Mr. Richard Lenox		v	1726–1728
Mr. Edward Lewis, Jr.	r 1756–1759	v	1756–1759
Mr. George Lindenberger	w 1800–1801	v	1802–1803
Mr. G. Easby Lindsay		v	1955–1961
		av	1951–1955
Mr. John Long		v	1751–1753
Mr. William Lorman	w 1794–1795	v	1797–1805
Captain Darby Lux	w 1743–1744	v	1744–1747
	1749–1750		1750–1751
Mr. Darby Lux	w 1768–1769	v	1753–1754
	r 1753–1754		
Mr. George Lux		v	1779–1782
Mr. William Lux	w 1762–1763	v	1752–1755
	1772–1773		1759–1762
Mr. Patrick Lynch	w 1748–1749		
Mr. William Lynch		v	1747–1751
			1754–1757
			1766–1767
			1772–1773
Dr. William Lyon		v	1753–1756

Mr. William Mackubin		v 1749–1752
Mr. Zechariah Mackubin		v 1755–1758
		1759–1760
Mr. William Maclean	r 1751–1752	
Dr. Kemp Malone		av 1943–1945
		1947–1950
Mr. William L. Marbury		av 1948–1951
		v 1953–
Mr. Edward D. Martin		av 1949–1952
		v 1952–1962
	r 1952–1962	ve 1962
Mr. John C. Matthai, Jr.		av 1956–1958
Mr. Joseph F. Matthai, Jr.		1961–1962
Mr. Howard May		av 1935–1941
Mr. Charles F. Mayer	r 1903–1904	v 1875–1904
Mr. Marshall McCosh	sw 1951–1966	
The Hon. William McCreary	w 1785–1786	v 1791–1792
Mr. Isaac (?) McKim		v 1812–1814
Mr. Allan McLane	r 1904–1906	v 1899–1910
Mr. George E. McIlheiny	r 1817–1818	v 1817–1818
Mr. Frank D. Mead		av 1947–1948
		v 1948–1957
Mr. W. Carroll Mead		av 1945–1948
Mr. Gilmor Meredith		v 1882–1901
Mr. John Merryman		v 1723–1726
Mr. John Merryman	w 1739–1740	
	1741–1742	
Mr. John Merryman		v 1785–1790
	t 1790	1791–1792
Mr. John Merryman		v 1800–1810
Mr. John Merryman, Jr.	w 1748–1749	v 1743–1746
Mr. John Merryman, Jr.	w 1763–1764	v 1765–1769
Mr. John Merryman, Sr.	w 1742–1743	
	1746–1747	
Mr. Nicholas Merryman of Sand.	w 1755–1756	
Mr. Samuel Merryman		v 1726–1729
Mr. Samuel Merryman	w 1756–1757	
Mr. S. Atherton Middleton		av 1948–1951
Mr. Peter Mieler	w 1798–1799	
Dr. Mitchell Miller		av 1950–1953
Dr. Robert T. Miller, Jr.		v 1932–1936
Mr. John Moale		v 1730–1733
Mr. John Moale	w 1753–1754	v 1761–1763
	1758–1759	1770–1773
	1765–1766	1782–1784
	1767–1768	1786–1789
Mr. John Moale, Jr.	w 1758–1759	
Mr. Richard Moale	w 1761–1762	v 1763–1766
Mr. William A. Moale, Jr.		d 1877

Mr. James Moore	c 1726–1734	
The Hon. Nicholas Ruxton Moore		v 1780–1816
Mr. James Mose		v 1721–1722
Mr. Joseph Murray		v 1723–1724
Mr. Josephus Murray, Jr.	w 1740–1741	
Mr. Henry Nicols		v 1795–1798
		1800–1803
		1815–1819
Mr. George Sommerville Norris	sw 1870–1901	
Captain Robert North	w 1735–1736	v 1738–1741
Mr. Edward Norwood	c 1721–1723	
Mr. John Orrick		v 1721–1723
Mr. John Orrick		v 1760–1762
Mr. William Otty	w 1761–1762	
Mr. Richard H. Owen	w 1818–1819	
Mr. Richard Owings		v 1722–1723
Mr. Samuel Owings		v 1735–1738
		1744–1745
Mr. Buckler Patridge		v 1728–1731
Mr. George Dobbin Penniman		v 1908–1943
Mr. Nicholas G. Penniman, III		av 1942–1945
		1947–1949
Mr. Brian Philpott	w 1759–1760	v 1754–1755
	1763–1764	
Mr. John Philpotts	w 1774–1775	
Mr. J. Hall Pleasants		v 1865–1899
Mr. Edgar Allan Poe		v 1920–1925
Mr. John P. Poe		d 1877, 1881
Mr. James Powell		v 1724–1726
Mr. George Presstman		v 1776–1777
Mr. Mark Pringle		v 1801–1810
Mr. Blanchard Randall	jw 1932–1936	
	sw 1936–1942	
Mr. Christopher Randall	w 1722–1724	v 1724–1727
		1741–1744
Mr. Abraham Raven	w 1744–1745	
Mr. William L. Reed		av 1954–1957
Mr. Charles Reimer		d 1913–1918
Mr. Walter A. Richardson	at 1961–1966	av 1960–1961
	t 1966–	v 1961–
Mr. James Rider	w 1726–1727	
Captain Charles Ridgely	w 1745–1746	v 1750–1753
	1765–1766	1767–1768
Mr. Charles Ridgely of John	w 1775–1776	
Major Charles Ridgely	w 1732–1733	v 1728–1731
	1735–1736	1736–1739
Mr. John Ridgely	w 1747–1748	v 1752–1754
		1758–1761

[269]

Judge Richard Ridgely		v 1779–1783
		1784–1785
Mr. Matthew Ridley	w 1772–1773	
Captain John Risteau	w 1728–1729	v 1742–1745
Mr. James Roberson	w 1729–1730	
Mr. Jonas Roberson	w 1729–1730	
Mr. George Roberts		v 1794–1797
Mr. Walter Roe	w 1782–1783	v 1783–1784
		1788–1789
		1790–1791
Colonel Nicholas Rogers		v 1784–1785
		1795–1798
		1799–1802
Mr. Benjamin Rogers		v 1762–1765
		1771–1773
Mr. Nicholas Rogers	w 1746–1747	
Mr. Philip Rogers	w 1776–1777	
Mr. William Rogers	w 1760–1761	v 1751–1753
		1756–1759
Judge William Russel		v 1773–1776
		1781–1785
Mr. Moses Rutter	w 1751–1752	
Mr. I. L. Salstonsall	r 1794–1795	v 1794–1795
Mr. Richard Sampson		v 1692–1698
Mr. William Donald Schaeffer		v 1967–
Captain Jeremiah Sellott		v 1784–1785
Mr. John E. Semmes		v 1901–1920
Major Thomas Sheredine		v 1722–1725
		1726–1729
		1730–1732
		1734–1737
Dr. Charles C. Shippen		v 1892–1901
Mr. William Singleton	w 1796–1798	
Dr. Harry R. Slack		av 1944–1947
Mr. J. Donnell Smith (Capt.)	sw 1903–1928	
The Hon. Thorowgood Smith		v 1794–1797
		1803–1810
The Hon. William Smith		v 1795–1796
Mr. Basil H. Snowden	jw 1915–1932	
	sw 1932–1935	
Mr. Hithe Sollers		v 1755–1758
Mr. Sabret Sollers		v 1747–1748
Mr. Sabret Sollers		v 1770–1771
Mr. Thomas Sollers	w 1767–1770	v 1781–1782
Mr. Edmund Stansbury		v 1764–1767
Mr. Luke Stansbury		v 1727–1730
Mr. Thomas Stansbury		v 1725–1728
Captain Tobias Stansbury		v 1754–1755
Mr. Tobias Stansbury		v 1722–1723

Mr. Tobias Stansbury		v 1746–1749
Mr. Tobias Stansbury of Tobias		v 1754–1755
Mr. John Stark	w 1793–1794	
	1802–1804	
Mr. H. Vernon Stehl		AV 1952–1957
		v 1957–1961
Captain John Stenchcomb		v 1748–1751
		1754–1757
Mr. Nathaniel Stenchcomb		v 1742–1745
Mr. Edmund Stevenson	w 1734–1735	
Mr. R. King Stevenson		v 1756–1759
Captain Alexander Stewart	w 1768–1769	v 1761–1763
Mr. Charles Morton Stewart	T 1870–1900	v 1860–1900
Dr. James Stewart		v 1818–1820
Mr. Charles Stokes		AV 1948–1950
		v 1961–1966
Mr. William F. Stone, Jr.		AV 1950–1953
		v 1953–1964
Mr. Richardson Stuart (Stewart?)	w 1791–1794	
Mr. Edmund Talbot	C 1751–1753	v 1752–1753
	w 1751–1752	1764–1767
Mr. Thomas Taylor	w 1724–1725	
Mr. Thomas Tennant		v 1802–1816
Captain John Terry		v 1692–1695
Mr. J. Marshall Thomas	JW 1903–1904	v 1904–1906
Mr. Thomas Todd		v 1731–1734
Mr. Thomas Todd		v 1770–1771
Mr. J. William Townsend, III	JW 1953–1954	AV 1953–1956
Mr. Luke Trotter		v 1722–1723
Mr. John M. Tucker		AV 1957–1961
Mr. Alfred Tyler	JW 1936–1946	
Mr. Thomas Usher	w 1773–1774	
Mr. Thomas Usher		v 1793–1796
Mr. Cornelius VanHorst	AT 1953–1956	
Mr. William Van Wyke		v 1793–1795
Mr. Edward Vidler	R 1802–1803	v 1802–1803
Dr. George Walker	w 1730–1731	v 1736–1739
	1735–1736	
Mr. John Walker	C 1749–1752	
Mr. Samuel Walker	w 1802–1804	
Dr. John Walton	R 1962–1965	AV 1957–1960
		1961–1962
		v 1962–1965
Mr. Lemuel Warfield	w 1806–1812	
Dr. Mactier Warfield	JW 1911–1915	
Mr. Francis Watkings, Sr.		v 1692–1695
Mr. John Weatherburn		v 1785–1790
Mr. Charles R. Webber		AV 1940–1945
Mr. Bowen P. Weisheit		v 1965–

Mr. William Wells		v 1754–1757
Mr. Wilmer Welsh		av 1949–1952
Mr. Harrison Weymouth		av 1943–1944
Mr. William Wilkenson		v 1695–1698
Mr. N. Winslow Williams		d 1913
Mr. William H. Wilson, Jr.		av 1962–1965
	r 1965–	v 1965–
Mr. David Winchester		v 1812–1815
Judge William Winchester		v 1790–1791
		1805–1812
Mr. M. Lee Winkel		av 1954–1955
Mr. John Wooden, Jr.		v 1753–1754
Mr. George Woolsey	w 1773–1774	
Mr. Larn Wright		v 1789–1790
	r 1791–1794	1791–1794
Mr. Charles Hanfield Wyatt		v 1870–1904
	r 1880–1903	
Mr. R. Hence Young		av 1957–1960
Mr. Thomas G. Young, Sr.		av 1936–1943
		v 1943–1953

PRESIDENTS
of the
WOMAN'S AUXILIARY
from 1897 to 1967

Mrs. John E. Semmes

Mrs. James L. McLane

Mrs. Nicholas G. Penniman

Mrs. Robert W. Johnson

Miss S. Asenath Harwood

Mrs. Emily P. Cuyler

Miss Elizabeth Gilman

Mrs. George Dobbin Penniman

Mrs. James M. Rhodes

Mrs. William E. Waring

Mrs. C. I. T. Gould

Mrs. Robert Garrett

Mrs. Samuel K. Sanford

Mrs. Beverly Ober

Mrs. Alfred Tyler

Miss Helen Garvin

Mrs. Frank L. LaMotte

Mrs. Howard Hyle

Mrs. Marshall McCosh

Mrs. M. Lewis Townsend

Mrs. James Hamilton

Mrs. Bowen P. Weisheit

RECTORS of ST. PAUL'S PARISH
SINCE ITS ORGANIZATION in 1692

WILLIAM TIBBS   1702–1732

JOSEPH HOOPER   1732–1739

BENEDICT BOURDILLON   1739–1745

THOMAS CHASE   1745–1779

WILLIAM WEST   1779–1791

JOSEPH GROVE JOHN BEND   1791–1812

JAMES KEMP   1812–1827
Suffragan Bishop of Maryland   1814–1816
Second Bishop of Maryland   1816–1827

WILLIAM EDWARD WYATT   1827–1864
Associate Rector   1814–1827

MILO MAHAN   1864–1870

JOHN SEBASTIAN BACH HODGES   1870–1905
Rector Emeritus   1905–1915

ARTHUR BARKSDALE KINSOLVING   1906–1942
Rector Emeritus   1942–1951

HARRY LEE DOLL   1942–1955

FREDERICK WARD KATES   1956–1960

HALSEY MOON COOK   1961–

[274]

Other Clergy who have served St. Paul's Parish

Missionaries of the Bishop of London

The Rev. John Yeo	1675–1686
The Rev. Edward Topp	1698–1702

Assistants to the Rector

The Rev. Thomas Bayle	1713–1718
The Rev. William Cawthorne	1732
The Rev. James Macgill	1732
The Rev. Sutton Morgan	1750
The Rev. William Duke	1792
(Minister to St. Paul's Chapel, Back River)	

Associate Rectors (Priests-in-charge, Christ Church)

The Rev. John Ireland	1796–1801
The Rev. Francis Barclay	1801–1802
(Priest-in-charge, only)	
The Rev. Dr. Elijah D. Rattoone	1802–1805
The Rev. Dr. James Whitehead	1806–1808
The Rev. Dr. Frederick Beasley	1809–1813

Priest-in-charge

The Rev. Henry Moscrop	1812

Associate Rector

The Rev. Dr. William E. Wyatt	1814–1827
(later, Rector of the Parish, 1827–1864)	

Assistants to the Rector

The Rev. James Pilmor	1821–1822
The Rev. Thomas Billopp	1827–1829
The Rev. Thomas J. Wyatt	1839–1842, 1845–1846
The Rev. Matthias L. Forbes	1842
The Rev. John W. Hoffman	1842–1843
The Rev. Samuel R. Gordon	1843–1845
The Rev. Francis Asbury Baker	1845–1851
The Rev. Horace Stringfellow	1852
The Rev. Edward O. Flagg	1853
The Rev. John Marshall Gerron	1854
The Rev. James Stephenson	1855

Associate Rector

The Rev. Dr. James D. McCabe	1855–1857

Assistants to the Rector

The Rev. Horatio Hewitt	1857–1858
The Rev. Charles C. Grafton	1859–1864
(later, the 2nd Bishop of Fond du Lac, 1889–1912)	
The Rev. Julian E. Ingle	1864–1868
Assisting Minister and Chaplain,	
Church Home and Infirmary	1869–1870
The Rev. John S. Miller	1867–1868
Missionary, Wyatt Memorial Chapel	1871–1878
Priest-in-charge, St. Matthew's Chapel	1877
The Rev. Theodore C. Gambrall	1868–1870
Minister, St. Paul's Chapel, Avalon	
(and Rector, Trinity Parish, Howard County)	
The Rev. Thomas D. Pitts, Deacon	1868
The Rev. William F. Lewis, Deacon	1869–1870

Assisting Minister

The Rev. Richard C. Hall	1869–1871

Assistants to the Rector

The Rev. Henry T. Lee	1869–1870
Assisting Minister and Warden,	
Church Home and Infirmary	1870–1871
The Rev. James Chipchase	1871–1879
Missionary, Wyatt Memorial Chapel	
Priest-in-charge, Chapel of St. John Baptist	
The Rev. Edward W. Meany	1871–1872
The Rev. Isaac L. Nicholson, Jr.	1872–1875
Priest-in-charge, St. James' (African) Church	1874–1875
(later, the 5th Bishop of Milwaukee, 1891–1906)	
The Rev. Frank Hallam	1873
The Rev. Pierre DuGué Trapier	1874–1875
The Rev. Henry N. Wayne	1875–1882
Priest-in-charge, Wyatt Memorial Chapel	1875–1877
The Rev. George E. Cranston	1875–1878
The Rev. Charles R. Hale	1877–1885
(later, Bishop of Cairo, Egypt, 1892–1900)	
The Rev. George W. Bowne	1881
The Rev. Alfred Harding	1883–1887
Priest-in-charge, St. Paul's Chapel, Avalon	1884–1885
(later, the 2nd Bishop of Washington, 1909–1923)	
The Rev. M. L. Poffenberger	1886–1887
The Rev. G. U. Graf	1887
The Rev. Edward L. Buckey	1887–1888
The Rev. Thomas H. Gordon	1887–1888
The Rev. G. W. Gates	1888
The Rev. H. Greenfield Schorr	1888–1889
The Rev. M. L. Woolsey	1889–1890

The Rev. T. C. Foote	1889
The Rev. George Calvert Carter	1890–1892
The Rev. Charles A. Jessup	1893–1899
The Rev. Dr. Walter Baker	1894–1897
and Priest-in-charge, St. John Baptist's Chapel	
The Rev. David P. Allison	1897–1899
and Priest-in-charge, St. John Baptist's Chapel	
The Rev. William L. Glenn, Deacon	1897–1899
The Rev. E. deS. Juny	1897–1899
The Rev. Robert S. Wood	1899–1906
and Headmaster, St. Paul's School for Boys	
Assisting Minister only	1899–1900, 1904–1906
The Rev. John C. Gray	1901–1903
The Rev. Frank Hay Staples	1902–1909
Vicar, St. Paul's Chapel	1909–1944
Minister-in-charge, St. Paul's Chapel, Avalon	1930–1934
Vicar, retired	1944–1962
The Rev. E. Briggs Nash	1903–1906
Priest-in-charge	1906
The Rev. William D. Gould	1905–1909
Priest-in-charge, St. John's Chapel, St. Denis	
(and Rector, St. Mark's Church)	
The Rev. William Adams McClenthen	1906
The Rev. Scott Kidder	1906–1907
The Rev. George A. Griffiths, Deacon	1907
The Rev. R. Gould	1907
The Rev. J. Wilson Sutton	1907–1910
The Rev. John L. Jackson	1909–1910
(later, the 6th Bishop of Louisiana, 1940–1948)	
The Rev. Jessee R. Bicknell	1910–1911
Assistant, St. Paul's Chapel	1911–1919
The Rev. William T. Elmer	1910–1917
and Headmaster, St. Paul's School for Boys	
The Rev. Paul F. Hoffman	1910–1914
The Rev. Francis Henry Smith	1914–1918
The Rev. Paul O. Keicher	1918
The Rev. John F. Kirk	1919
The Rev. John Knox Tibbits	1919–1920
The Rev. T. J. M. Van Duyne	1920–1921
Headmaster, St. Paul's School for Boys	
The Rev. Henry H. Marsden	1920–1921
The Rev. S. Hilton Orrick	1921–1953
Assistant, retired	1953–1957
The Rev. Percy F. Coulthurst	1921–1924
and Headmaster, St. Paul's School for Boys	

Assisting Minister

The Rev. Arthur Lee Kinsolving, Deacon	1924

Assistants to the Rector

The Rev. Dr. Wyllys Rede	1927
Headmaster, St. Paul's School for Boys	
The Rev. Janney Hutton	1927–1929
and Headmaster, St. Paul's School for Boys	
The Rev. Arthur J. Blythe	1938
The Rev. John R. Cooper	
Assistant, St. Paul's Chapel	1943–1944
Vicar, St. Paul's Chapel	1944–1945
The Rev. Willard Marvin Entwisle	
Vicar, St. Paul's Chapel	1946–1958
(Rector, independent congregation, 1958–)	
The Rev. John H. Blacklidge	1950–1952
The Rev. Arnold M. Ross	1953–1954
The Rev. James E. Cantler	1953–1957
(Chaplain, St. Paul's School for Boys 1957–1965)	
The Rev. Jon Chapman Crosby, II	1954–1956

Priest-in-charge

The Rev. Edward L. Reed	1955–1956

Assistants to the Rector

The Rev. David Corbin Streett, II	1957–1958
The Rev. Alfred N. Redding	1958–1964
Priest-in-charge, 1961	
The Rev. George P. Donnelly	1961–
The Rev. Alan H. Gee	1964–
The Rev. James J. McNamee, III	1966
and Diocesan College Worker	
The Rev. Herman A. diBrandi	1966–
Chaplain, St. Paul's Schools	
The Rev. David H. Poist	1966–
and Diocesan College Worker	

INDEX